Fun Programming Projects for Kids in C, C++, Python:

4 Books in 1

Table of Contents

Book 1: Coding for Kids in C#

Disclaimer

No part of this book can be transmitted or reproduced in any form including print, electronic, photocopying, scanning, mechanical or recording without prior written permission from the author. While the author has taken utmost efforts to ensure the accuracy of the written content, all readers are advised to follow information mentioned herein at their own risk. The author cannot be held responsible for any personal or commercial damage caused by information. All readers are encouraged to seek professional advice when needed.

Free Gift

We do want you to succeed in coding. To ensure your success, we are giving you a free list of projects that you can work on once you are completed with this book.

https://coding.gr8.com/

Introduction

Programming was a relatively unknown term in the past, as computer programmers were thought of as hardcore geeks who knew the ins and outs of the machine right in front of your eyes every day.

Nowadays, everything has shifted. In fact, Programming is one of the top skills any person can have, and starting out as a teenager is a massive plus, since you have the biggest advantage on your side - time.

Not only does programming help you with practical & everyday situations, it could also help you land the job of your dreams. Most programmers throughout the world have top-paying jobs with excellent benefits - like remote work, flexible hours, and amazing projects.

In this book, we will teach you programming in one of the most popular, practical, and effective programming languages - C# (read as C-sharp). With it, you will learn all of the basics of programming, but also dabble with slightly more difficult topics.

SET UP WORKSPACE

What You Need

- A Laptop/Desktop Computer
- Internet Connection
- Web browser installed (Firefox, Chrome or Internet Explorer)

Download and Install Visual Studio

Download the latest version of an IDE of your choice. I recommend choosing between one of the following:

- Visual Studio
- Tabnine
- SlickEdit
- Elipse aCute

I personally recommend using Visual Studio. You can download the latest version below:

https://visualstudio.microsoft.com/downloads/

How to Start Using Visual Studio

Open Visual Studio from your installation folder or Start Menu.

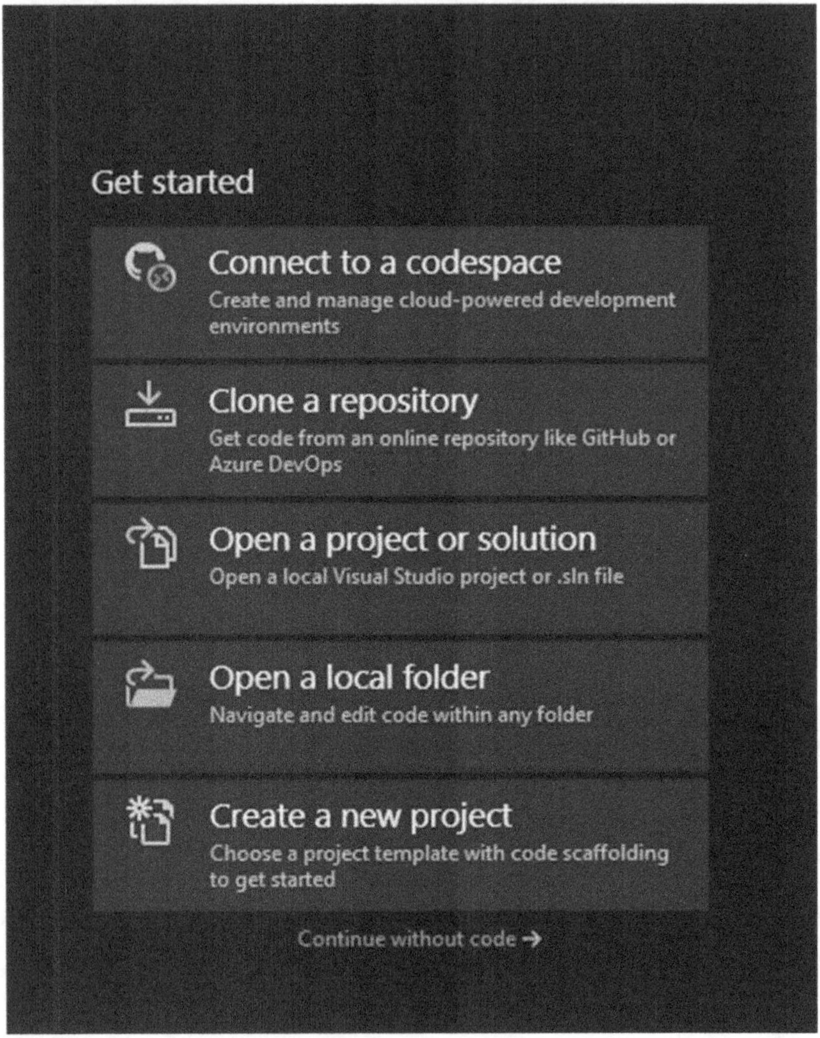

Choose "Create a new project"

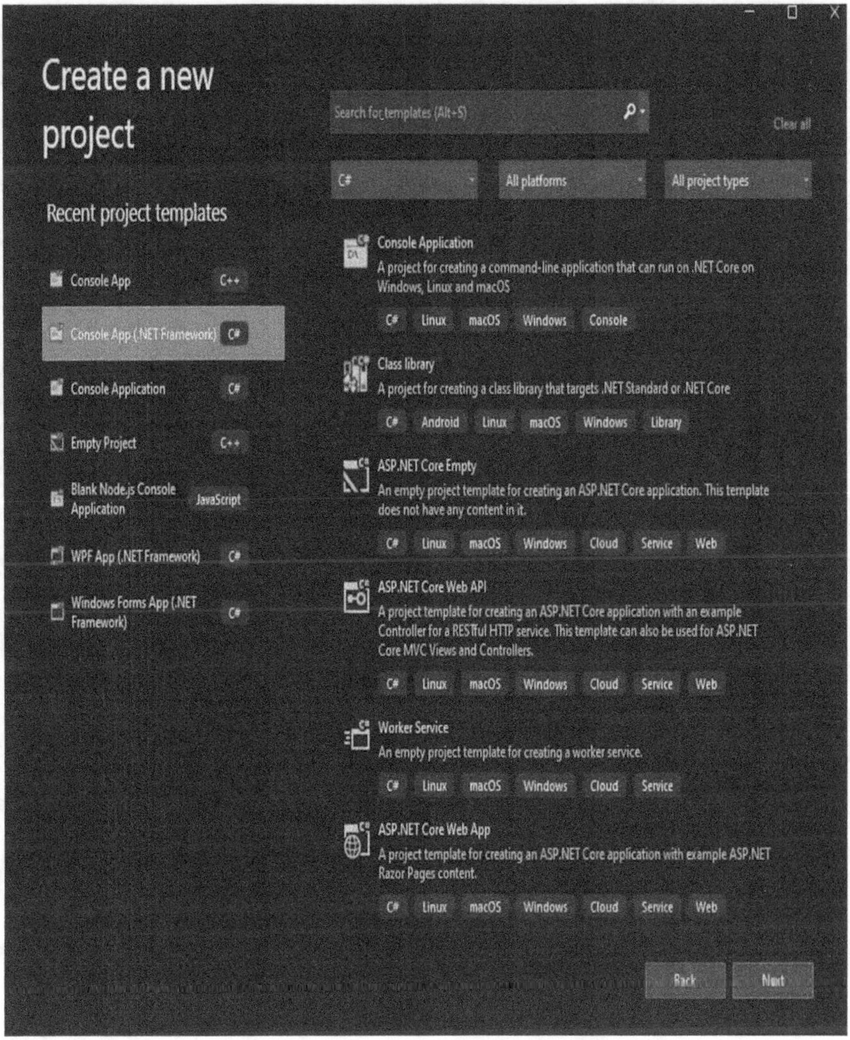

Choose C# and select “Console Application”.

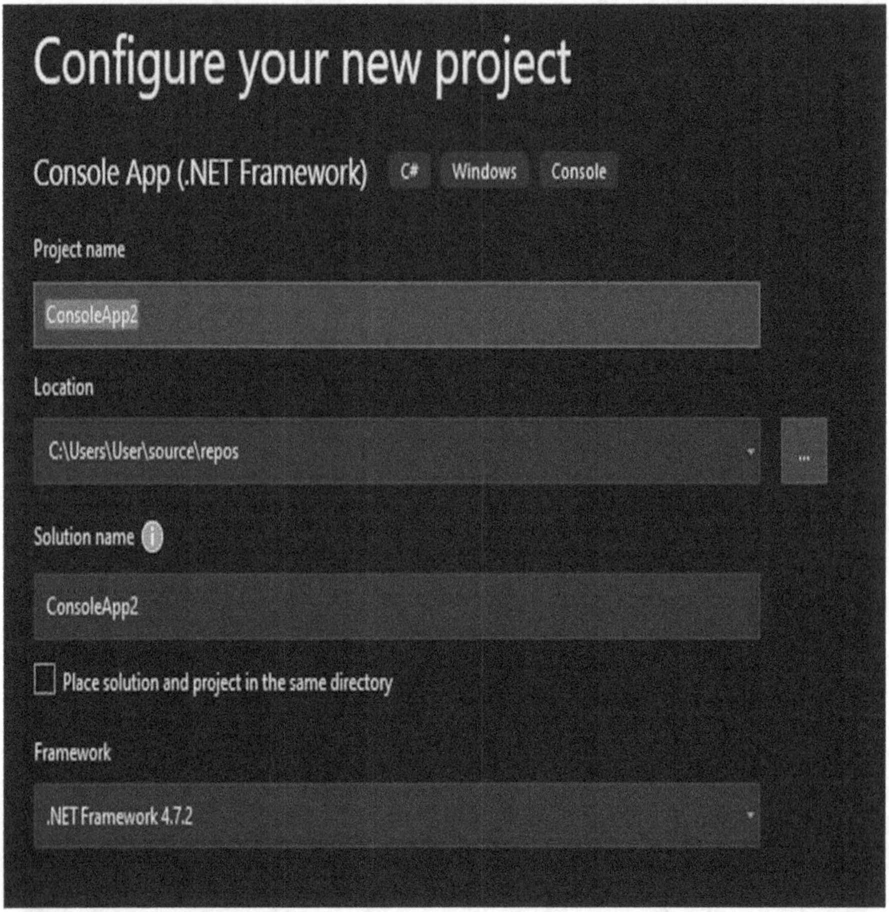

Name your project and set a directory where you want the project to be placed.

Then, your new project will open in a new window

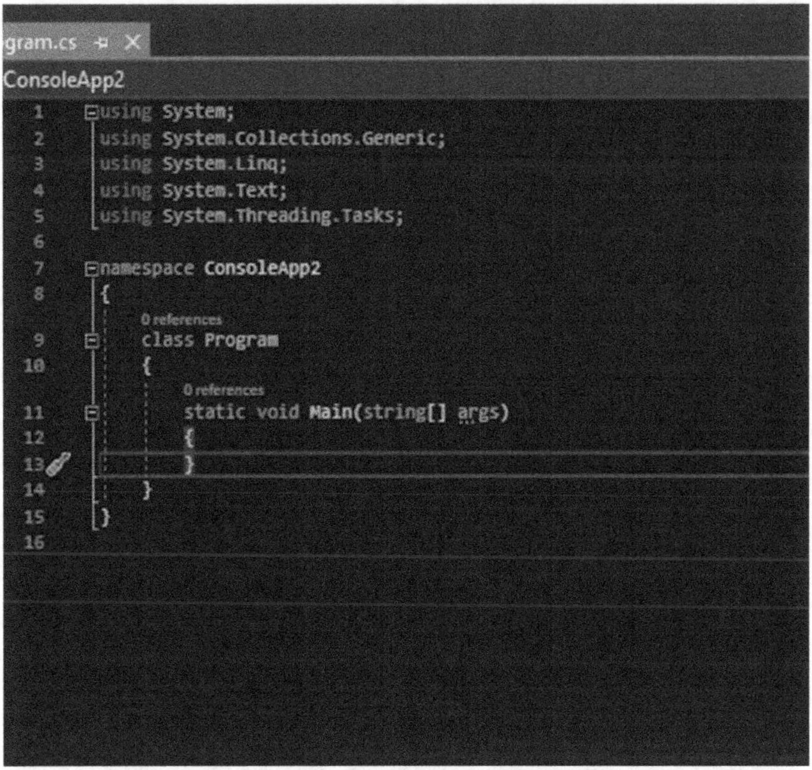

Write your first lines of code, for example:

- Console.WriteLine(“Hello World”);

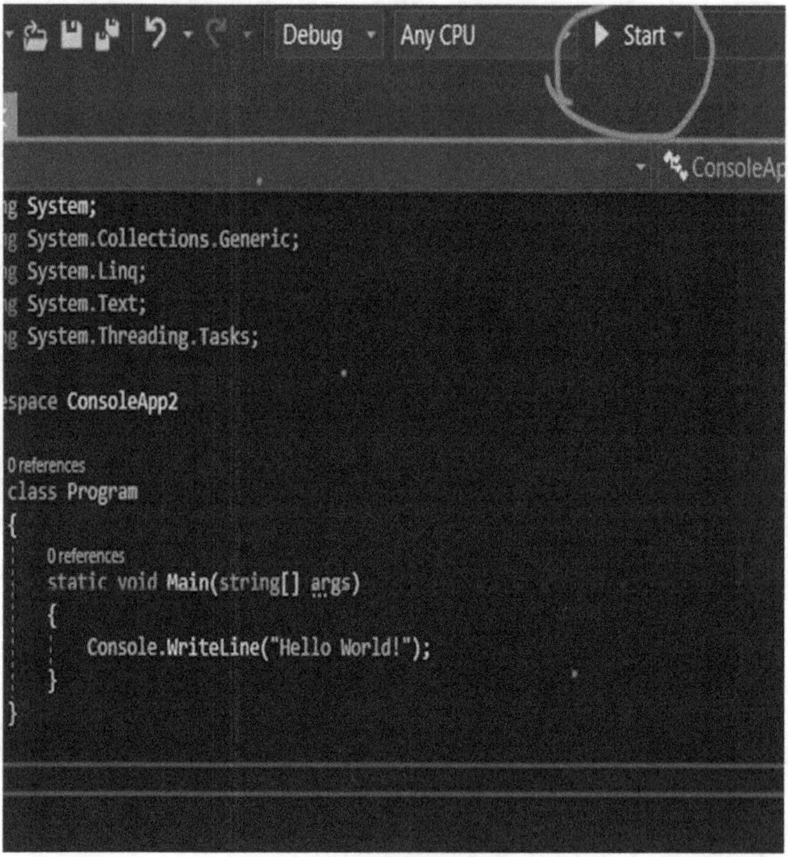

Press the “Start” button in the top menu, and your code will start running.

Intro to C#

C# (pronounced as C-Sharp) is an object-oriented programming language that runs on the .NET Framework. It was made by Microsoft in 2002, and since then, it has had 8 versions.

Where is C# Used?

C# is a general-purpose language, meaning that it has a lot of use cases. It can be used for making:

- Mobile apps
- Desktop apps
- Web apps
- Games
- Virtual reality apps
- Database apps
- Augmented reality simulations
- And much more.

Why Should You Use C#?

C# is one of the most popular programming languages in the world. According to most statistics it's easily in the top 10.

Moreover, the language is not difficult to learn, and has massive community support on multiple forums and websites. This means that there's always a channel to contact in case you have an issue.

The language is also very similar to other programming languages, like C, C++, Java, and Kotlin, so you'll have no trouble learning another one of them once you get the hang of C#.

Example Code in C#

```
using System;

namespace ConsoleApp2
{
    class Program
    {
        static void Main(string[] args)
        {
            Console.WriteLine("Hello World!");
        }
    }
}
```

- Code output:

```
Hello World!
```

Explaining individual components:

using System;

- We're taking all the classes and functions from the **System** class.

namespace ConsoleApp2;

- Namespace refers to the name of the project - it's simply the label of the application (i.e. how you named it).

class Program

- A container for all the methods and the code you'll write. Everything you write in C# must be within a class. We'll talk more about classes in a later chapter.

Simple C# Code Example

Now that we've gotten the basics out of the way and explained what each line of code does, let's take a look at a **slightly** more complicated C# code example:

```
using System;

namespace ConsoleApp2
{
    class Program
    {
        static void Main(string[] args)
        {
            var a = 5 + 5;
            Console.WriteLine(a);
        }
    }
}
```

So, what will be the example output?

- If you answered 10, your answer is correct

This was a really simple arithmetic exercise. We declared a **variable** called **a,** and we assigned a **value** of **5+5** to it (which is 10).

- Code output:

```
10
```

Conditionals

If you’ve learned the basics of mathematical logical conditions, conditionals in C# will probably be incredibly easy for you. Here is an example from classic mathematics:

- **a > b:** a is bigger than b
- **a <= b:** a is bigger than or equal to b
- **a == b:** a is equal to b
- **a != b:** a is not equal to b

Based on these conditions (i.e. whether they are fulfilled or not) you can make your code take a totally different direction. With the help of conditions and **conditional statements,** you can make the code decide for itself and do a specific thing. These are the conditional statements in C#:

- **if(condition):** if the condition inside the parentheses - the symbols “(“and “)” - is true, then the code below the statement will execute
- **else:** the else condition can **only** be written after an **if** condition. If the condition in the **if** statement is not true, then the **else** code block will get executed

- **else if(condition):** you can line up an **else if** only after an **if** and before an **else.** If the first “if” statement doesn’t fulfill the condition, then the condition for the **else if** block will get checked and the code will be executed.
- **switch:** the **switch** conditional statement is used when you have many different cases & a variety of conditions that could be met. You can totally avoid using the **switch** case, though there are specific scenarios where it’s quite useful.

Examples of Conditionals

Now that we've got the theory out of the way, let's get a more practical sense of how conditionals in C# work:

```
int a = 50;
int b = 49;

if(a > b) {
     Console.WriteLine("a is greater than b");
}

else {
     Console.WriteLine("b is greater than a");
}
```

In the example above, we have two variables - **a** and **b** - and one of them is larger (50 is larger than 49). Thus, the code after the **if** statement - the **Console.WriteLine()** - will get executed. Then, it would print out "a is larger than b".

If **b** was larger than **a** (i.e. if **b** was at least 51), then the code in the **else** statement would get executed. It would print out "b is larger than a"

- Code output:

```
a is greater than b
```

Now that you've got a basic idea of how an **if** and **else** statement work, let's take a look at a slightly more complex example:

```
int a = 20;
int b = 5;

if (a > b) {
     Console.WriteLine("a is bigger than b");
}

else if(a == b) {
     Console.WriteLine("the numbers are equal");
}
else {
     Console.WriteLine("b is bigger than a");
}
```

A beginner programmer wouldn't see the need for the **else if** block in this scenario. In the first **if** statement, you're checking if **a** is bigger than **b** - if **a** is NOT bigger than **b**, then it has to be smaller, right?

Absolutely not! **b** could also be equal to **a,** which is why there is an **else if** code block. Even though this is an incredibly simple (and frankly bizarre) example with only 3 possible outcomes, coding doesn't simply narrow down to **true** and **false**. There are many examples where another conditional statement could make the project at hand much easier.

- Code output:

```
a is bigger than b
```

Example 2: A simple program to check one's age and tells he/she is an adult or not. Example code is given below.

```
using System;

namespace MyApplication
{
  class Program
  {
    static void Main(string[] args)
    {
      int age = 15;
      if (age > 18)
      {
        Console.WriteLine("Person is an adult");
      }
      else
      {
        Console.WriteLine("Person is a child");
      }
    }
  }
}
```

In this example code variable **age** is assigned with a value of 15 and under the if else condition it checks whether the age variable is more than 18. Since age is more than 18 and the condition becomes true, the codes inside the if block gets executed. The "Person is an adult" statement gets printed. If anyhow the variable age becomes lower than 18 and the condition becomes false, the code under else block get executed and statement "Person is a child" gets printed.

Output is as follows:

```
Person is a child
```

Example 3: A simple program to check whether one has passed the exam by scoring more than 35 marks from the examination paper.

Sample Code is as follows:

```
using System;

namespace MyApplication
{
  class Program
  {
    static void Main(string[] args)
    {
      int marks = 50;
      if (marks > 35)
      {
        Console.WriteLine("Congratulations. You've passed the exam.!!!");
      }
      else
      {
        Console.WriteLine("Appreciate your efforts. Please try again.");
      }
    }
  }
}
```

In this example code, variable **marks** is assigned with a value of 50 and under the if else condition it checks whether the **marks** variable is more than 35 to check whether the person have passed the exam. Since marks is more than 35 and the condition becomes true, the codes inside the if block gets executed. Then the statement "Congratulations. You've passed the exam.!!!" gets printed.

Output is as follows:

```
Congratulations. You've passed the exam.!!!
```

Example 3: A simple program to initial 2 variables with values of 10, 20 respectively and add 3 to the second value if the sum of 2 numbers are more than 25.

Sample code is as follows:

```
using System;

namespace MyApplication
{
  class Program
  {
    static void Main(string[] args)
    {
      int x = 10;
      int y = 20;
      int total = x+y;
      if (total > 25)
      {
        y=y+3;
        Console.WriteLine("Second Number is " + y);
      }
      else
      {
        Console.WriteLine("Second Number is " + y);
      }
    }
  }
}
```

Here the two variables **x** and **y** are initiated as 10 and 20 respectively. Another variable **total** is assigned with the sum of **x** and **y**. Under the If condition it checks whether the total is greater than 25 or not. Since here sum of x and y variables are 30, the total is higher than 25. So the if condition becomes true and the codes inside the if condition gets executed. There y value gets incremented by 3 and the final value gets printed as 23. Essentially 3 is added to the number if the sum is greater than 30.

Output is as follows:

```
Second Number is 23
```

Switch Examples

The example code shown below takes the number of weekdays to calculate the weekday name:

```
namespace MyApplication
{
  class Program
  {
    static void Main(string[] args)
    {
      int day = 5;
      switch (day)
      {
        case 1:
          Console.WriteLine("Monday");
          break;
        case 2:
          Console.WriteLine("Tuesday");
          break;
        case 3:
          Console.WriteLine("Wednesday");
          break;
        case 4:
          Console.WriteLine("Thursday");
          break;
        case 5:
          Console.WriteLine("Friday");
          break;
        case 6:
          Console.WriteLine("Saturday");
          break;
        case 7:
          Console.WriteLine("Sunday");
          break;
      }
    }
  }
}
```

In this example, integer type variable day is assigned with the value of 5. Under the switch block, different cases are listed out. Case value is equal to the value of the day, which is checked under the switch block gets executed. Since there is a break command at the end of case 5 other cases will not be checked after case 5 and will terminate the program in running under the switch block commands.

This executes the block of code under case 5 and prints "Friday".

The output is as follows:

```
Friday
```

Else if condition Examples

A simple program to get a grade for the examination marks as per the following conditions.

If 0 < marks <= 35, it prints "Lower Pass"

35 < marks <=60, it prints "Good Pass"

60 < marks <= 100, it prints "Excellent Pass"

Sample code is as follows:

```
using System;

namespace MyApplication
{
  class Program
  {
    static void Main(string[] args)
    {
      int marks = 50;
      if (marks > 0 && marks <= 35)
      {
        Console.WriteLine("Lower Pass");
      }
      else if (marks > 35 && marks <= 60)
      {
        Console.WriteLine("Good Pass");
      }
      else if (marks > 60 && marks <= 100)
      {
        Console.WriteLine("Excellent Pass");
      }
      else
      {
        Console.WriteLine("Marks are not valid");
      }
    }
  }
}
```

Here the variable **marks** are assigned with the value 50. There are different conditions to check whether to which range the marks variable belongs to. In the first condition it checks whether the marks is greater than 0 and less than or equal to 35. If that condition satisfies the user has obtained a "lower pass". Similarly, the passes are given to the user after checking with the ranges of marks. Since the **marks** variable has a value of 50, it satisfies the condition of marks greater than 35 and less than or equal to 60. Hence, the final output becomes ‘Good Pass’.

Output is as follows:

```
Good Pass
```

Examples to Practice

1. Write down a long string (preferably, find a quote on the internet). Then, use an if/else code block to check if the number is odd or even. If it's even, print "even", otherwise, print "odd" (hint: use **if (a % 2 == 0)** to check if a number is even).
2. Create a simple C# and assign values to 4 variables (a, b, c, d). Check if a is bigger than b, or if c is bigger than d. If both fail, print out "test failed".

Nested Conditionals

You've now seen the importance of conditionals. If you're frequently around technology, you're probably going through conditionals every day - when opening websites, logging in, registering, playing your favorite video game, and much more.

However, conditionals alone won't do the job in many cases, which is why we use **nested conditionals.** These are the same conditionals we learned about above, but they're **nested** in each other. Let's take a look at a simple example.

```
int a = 20;
int b = 10;
int c = 25;

if(a > b) {
      if(a > c) { // nested conditional
        Console.WriteLine("a is bigger than b and
c");
            }
```

```
        else  { // another nested conditional
            Console.WriteLine("a is bigger than b, but
not bigger than c");
        }
}
```

With the first **if** block, we checked if **a** is bigger than **b**. Then, we did a second check to see the size of **c**, and in this case (**a** is smaller than **c**), we will get the second **WriteLine()** as output → "a is bigger than b, but not bigger than c".

- Code output:

```
a is bigger than b, but not bigger than c
```

Nested Conditionals Examples

- A simple program checking the length of names.

```
string name1 = "Marco";
string name2 = "Johnny";
string name3 = "Sebastian";

if(name3.Length > name2.Length) {
      if(name3.Length > name1.Length) {
            Console.WriteLine("Sebastian is the
longest name");
      else if(name3.Length < name1.Length) {
            Console.WriteLine("Marco is longer than
Sebastian & smaller than Johnny");
}

else {
      Console.WriteLine("Sebastian's name is not
longer than Johnny's name");
}
```

- Code output:

```
Sebastian is the longest name
```

- A slightly more advanced example - checking the values of numbers with nested conditionals.

```
int number = 12;

if (number < 5)
     {
     Console.WriteLine("{0} is less than 5",
number);
      }
else
     {
     Console.WriteLine("{0} is greater than or
equal to 5", number);
}

Console.WriteLine("The program ends here!");
```

- Code output:

```
12 is greater than or equal to 5
The program ends here!
```

Examples to Practice

1. Using nested conditional, make a program that compares the values of 3 variables. With nested if, else if, and else loops, find the highest, the lowest, and the value in between.
2. Make a string long 10 - 20 characters (think of some sentence). If the string has an even number of characters (hint: use **if(a % 2 == 0)** to check if a number is even), then nest another conditional to check if the length is equal to 14, 16, or 18. Print out the adequate result.

A Short message from the Author:

Hey, are you enjoying the book? I'd love to hear your thoughts!

Many readers do not know how hard reviews are to come by, and how much they help an author.

I would be incredibly thankful if you could take just 60 seconds to write a brief review on Amazon, even if it's just a few sentences!

Thank you for taking the time to share your thoughts!

Your review will genuinely make a difference for me and help gain exposure for my work.

Loops

Loops in C# are used when you want to execute some written code multiple times. Programming offers us the power of automation, and loops are the perfect example of how automation makes everything easier. First, we'll take a look at the different types of loop, and how they work, and then we'll look at a practical example.

- **while(condition):** these types of loops (often called **while** loops) will continue executing the code inside of them until the condition is false.
- **for(statement 1, condition, statement 2):** known as **for** loops, these are more popular loops as they have more use cases. They work like this:
    - **statement 1:** a statement that executes before the loop starts
    - **condition:** the loop will continue running the code until the condition is false.
    - **statement 2:** a statement that executes when the loop ends an iteration.

Here is an example of a while loop:

```
int i = 1;
while( i < 5)  { // smaller than or equal to 5
      i++; // the same as i = i + 1, increases i by
1
}
Console.WriteLine(i); // what is the value of i
now?
```

After the loop ends, **i** is equal to 5. Here's the output:

```
5
```

A **for** loop looks slightly more complicated, but it's used in a wider variety of cases:

```
for(int i = 1; i <= 5; i++) {
      Console.WriteLine(i); // will print 1, 2, 3,
4, 5
}
```

With the **for** loop, we declared the value of **i** in the first statement (see above), we defined the condition - **i** is smaller than 5 - and we set the second statement - increase i by one.

If you could define the code above in one simple sentence, it would be:

- Make the number i equal to 1, and increase it until it reaches 5.

As you can already imagine, there are many use cases for loops. We've taken a simple real-world example of code that shows the importance of loops (a simple countdown program).

```
Console.WriteLine("Counting down from 5 to 1: ");
Console.WriteLine("5");
Sleep(1000); // this function tells the program to
make a 1 second pause
Console.WriteLine("4");
Sleep(1000);
Console.WriteLine("3");
Sleep(1000);
Console.WriteLine("2");
Sleep(1000);
Console.WriteLine("1");
```

```
Console.WriteLine("Countdown successful!");
```

A 5 second countdown is hardly a difficult task, but in this case, it required more than 10 lines of code - for a simple countdown! Which is exactly why we need loops.

```
Console.WriteLine("Counting down from 5 to 1: ");
for(int i = 5; i >= 1; i = i - 1) {
     Console.WriteLine(i);
     Thread.Sleep(1000); }
Console.WriteLine("Countdown successful!");
```

We've now successfully cut the code in half (from 11 lines to 5), and made it significantly easier to read.

- Code output

```
Counting down from 5 to 1:
5
4
3
2
1
Countdown successful!
```

Examples For Loops

There are many situations where loops will be useful.

- **Program that calculates anything iteratively.**

Let's say that you want to multiply every second number from 1 to 10 with 5. Without loops, it would be quite a tedious task, but with them, it would look something like this:

```
int finalValue = 0;


for(int i = 1; i <= 10; i = i + 2) {
     finalValue = finalValue + (i * 5);
}
Console.WriteLine(finalValue);
```

- Code output:

```
125
```

There's no need for loops to be used strictly automatically. You can also use them with strings. Let's say you want to print every third letter from some text.

- **C# program that takes every third letter with loops**

```
string text = "Some random text";

for(int i = 0; i < text.Length; i = i +3) {
     Console.WriteLine(text[i]);
}
```

- Code output:

```
S
e
a
o
t
t
```

Loops can be considered as a block of code with an instruction sequence which gets repeated till some defined condition is reached. Loops can help in saving time, reducing errors and making code more readable.

While Loop

While loop runs through the loop till the condition is true.

Example: A simple program to find the even numbers between 0 to 100 in a single line.

```
using System;

namespace MyApplication
{
  class Program
  {
    static void Main(string[] args)
    {
      int i = 1;
      while (i < 50)
      {
        if(i%2==0)
        {
        Console.Write(" " + i);
        }
        i++;
      }
    }
  }
}
```

In this code, variable i is assigned with the value of 1. i value gets incremented by 1 each and every time when the programs runs each and every time which it runs the while loop till variable i value becomes 50. Under the while loop body, i values which are divided by 2 (even numbers) get printed till the value i reaches 50.

Output is as follows:

```
2 4 6 8 10 12 14 16 18 20 22 24 26 28 30 32 34 36 38 40 42 44 46 48
```

Do / While Loop

Do while loop is a variant of While loop where the loop runs once without considering the condition and then runs till the condition is true.

Given below is an example where do/while loop is used. Sample code is as follows:

```
using System;

namespace MyApplication
{
  class Program
  {
    static void Main(string[] args)
    {
      int i = 0;
      do
      {
        Console.WriteLine(i);
        i++;
      }
      while (i < 5);
    }
  }
}
```

This is a simple code where we initialize the integer variable i as 0. Under do block i is written to be printed without checking any conditions. Then i value is incremented by 1. Then it goes to the while loop body where i is checked whether it is less than 5. As soon as i value exceeds 5 it gets terminated from the loop and i will not be printed anymore.

The output is as follows:

```
0
1
2
3
4
```

For Loop

A simple code example where it uses “for” loop is given below.

```
using System;

namespace MyApplication
{
  class Program
  {
    static void Main(string[] args)
    {
      for (int i = 0; i < 5; i++)
      {
        Console.Write(" " + i);
      }
    }
  }
}
```

In this code integer i variable is initialized as 0. Then i is incremented by 1 till i reaches i=5. Till that condition where i < 5 is satisfied, i gets printed on the same line.

The output is as follows:

```
0 1 2 3 4
```

Let's do another example. Let's consider that you need to print the even numbers between 0 to 20. We can use a simple for loop to write that. The sample code is as follows:

```
using System;

namespace MyApplication
{
  class Program
  {
    static void Main(string[] args)
    {
      for (int i = 0; i < 20; i=i+2)
      {
        Console.Write(" " + i);
      }
    }
  }
}
```

In this code, integer i variable is initialized as 0. As the condition i gets incremented by 2 once every time it passes through the loop. Under the for loop there is a condition to check whether i is less than 20. So, till that condition is satisfied i is printed as in the loop body.

The output is as follows:

```
0 2 4 6 8 10 12 14 16 18
```

As another example let's consider that you need to print the numbers in a descending order from 10 to 1. For that we can write a simple code using for loop as follows:

```
using System;
using System.Collections.Generic;

public class Program
{
    public static void Main()
    {
        for(int i = 10; i > 0; i--)
        {
            Console.WriteLine("Value of i: {0}", i);
        }
    }
}
```

Here variable **i** is assigned with value 10 and it gets decremented by 1 each time **(i--).** And the values are printed making the output as follows:

```
Value of i: 10
Value of i: 9
Value of i: 8
Value of i: 7
Value of i: 6
Value of i: 5
Value of i: 4
Value of i: 3
Value of i: 2
Value of i: 1
```

Exercises to Practice

1. Make a **while loop**. Choose any number between 1 and 10 and set **int a** as your number (ex: int a = 5). Then, with the while loop, increase the number **a** to 100, and print its value to check if it's okay.
2. Make a long string with at least 20 characters (maybe think of your favorite quote and write it down). Then, with a **for loop**, go through each character and find the letter "a". If you find the letter "a", print it out. If there's no letter "a" in the string, print out "b" as the output.

Arrays

Understanding Variables and Arrays

So far, you've seen this type of code **int a = 10** many times now, which is a way of declaring a **variable**. The **int** describes that the number is an integer (i.e. a whole number), the letter **a** is its name, and **10** is the value we're assigning it. In C#, there are different types of **variables,** including:

- **int:** integers - whole numbers without decimals, can be positive or negative
- **double:** numbers with decimals, like 20.55, or 3.14
- **char:** characters, usually containing one letter or number, like "g" or "w"
- **string:** strings store text, like "Hello there!"

With how far C# has come, it now has many different variables thanks to all of its frameworks, though the 4 we've mentioned above are enough for a beginner.

Variables are quite useful. A typical example of their usage would be storing grades, writing down names, birth dates, etc.

However, you can't write more than one value in a single variable. If you wanted to store all of your grades, for example, you'd have to manually declare every variable:

```
int historyGrade = 7;
int geographyGrade = 10;
int englishGrade = 8;
```

What if there was a way to store multiple values of the same type in a single variable? This is where **arrays** come in.

Examples of Array Usage

Arrays allow you to store multiple values in a single variable - and they're really simple to understand too. These are some simple examples of arrays:

```
int[] grades = {7, 10, 8};

string[] favoriteNames = {"Barbara", "Laura",
"Ivy", "Annah", "Eva"};

string[] bestCars = {"BMW", "Porsche", "Mercedes",
"Audi"};
```

With **arrays,** you can store many values in a single variable, which will be incredibly useful when you will be programming bigger projects.

Your programs will become much more powerful if you combine **arrays** with **loops,** which we already learned about in the previous chapter. Let's imagine a situation where you'd like to print out all of your favorite names from the array we wrote above:

```
string[] favoriteNames = {"Barbara", "Laura",
"Ivy", "Annah", "Eva"};
for (int i = 0; i < favoriteNames.Length; i++) {
    Console.WriteLine(favoriteNames[i]);  // will
print the i-th
                                          // name
of the array
}
```

- The code above will print the names in the same order we've written them → Barbara, Laura, Ivy…
- Code output:

```
Barbara
Laura
Ivy
Annah
Eva
```

If you've noticed something unfamiliar, it might be the **favoriteNames.Length** part of the code. This is just a simple line of code that accesses the number of elements we have in the array (in this case it's 5).

Same type of different elements can be stored in one unit by using an array. To declare an array, it is required to define the variable type with square brackets.

string[] fruits;

We now have declared an array in the type of string. Here we can store a large number of values of strings with comma separated.

string[] countries = {“USA”, “UK”, “India”, “Japan” }

In the similar way, arrays can be used to store set of different integers, double, chars etc. in one variable.

int[] myNum = {2, 4, 8, 10, 12}

char[] letters = {‘a’, ‘b’, ‘c’, ‘d’, ‘e’}

double[] values = {10.5, 12.56, 11.78, 15.9}

There is a specific way of accessing the elements in an array. Following sample code shows an example of accessing the elements of an array.

```
using System;

namespace MyApplication
{
  class Program
  {
    static void Main(string[] args)
    {
      string[] fruits = {"Mango", "Banana", "Apple", "Grapes" };
      Console.WriteLine(fruits[0]);
    }
  }
}
```

Here the first element in the first array is named as fruits[0] and the second element as fruits[1] and incremented accordingly. In the sample code fruits[0] access the 1st element of the fruits array. So the output of this simple code is as follows:

```
Mango
```

Array elements can also be changed by simply accessing the elements using the index number. Example code is given below.

```
using System;

namespace MyApplication
{
  class Program
  {
    static void Main(string[] args)
    {
      string[] fruits = {"Mango", "Banana", "Apple", "Grapes"};
      fruits[0] = "Oranges";
      Console.WriteLine(fruits[0]);
    }
  }
}
```

Here the first element of the array which is “Mango” (fruits [0]) is replaced with the “Oranges” and then the new element is accessed and get printed.

The output is as follows:

```
Oranges
```

Arrays have a separate special property to find the number of elements inside an array. Given below is a sample code to illustrate that property.

```
using System;

namespace MyApplication
{
  class Program
  {
    static void Main(string[] args)
    {
      string[] fruits = {"Mango", "Banana", "Apple", "Grapes"};
      Console.WriteLine(fruits.Length);
    }
  }
}
```

Length of an array is taken by "*ArrayName*". Length function. In the example, array name is "fruits". By fruits.length function we can get the number of elements in the fruits array which is 4. So, the output is as follows.

```
4
```

There is a special function called **foreach** loop, which is used exclusively to loop through elements in an array:

```
using System;

namespace MyApplication
{
  class Program
  {
    static void Main(string[] args)
    {
      string[] fruits = {"Mango", "Banana", "Apple", "Grapes"};
      foreach (string i in fruits)
      {
        Console.WriteLine(i);
      }
    }
  }
}
```

The example above can be read like this: **for each** string element (called **i** - as in **i**ndex) in **fruits**, print out the value of **i**. So the output will be as follows:

```
Mango
Banana
Apple
Grapes
```

Exercises to Practice

1. Create a basic C# program and run it. Then, make an array of at least 10 elements and print each one of them (you can use loops if you think they'll help you). Change the 3rd element of the array to a different value (if it's 5, make it 7, for example). Print out the entire array.
2. Make an array with your favorite 3 names. Then, check if the 2nd name is shorter in length than the 1st one (hint: use an if statement - nested if needed). Then, do the same for the 2nd and 3rd name. The 1st name should be the shortest, and the 3rd one the longest. The 2nd one should be in the middle.

Strings

In this book so far, you've encountered strings a lot. Now, let's dive deeper into what they are and how they work. In the simplest terms possible, strings are just **variables** used for storing texts - i.e. anything that's more than one character (for single characters, we use **chars**).

It's worth mentioning that strings have their own sets of **methods** that you must use if you intend to operate with them as data. Now that we've got the basics of the theory behind us, let's take a look at some practical examples.

Examples of Strings

Basic C# String Usage

Let's take the simplest usage of a string as our first example:

```
string txt = "abcdefg";
Console.WriteLine("Our string is " + txt);
```

Output:

```
Our string is abcdefg
```

Using String Methods in C#

Strings have many methods that are used in conjunction with them, like **Length, ToUpper(), ToLower(), Concat()**, etc. Take a look at the following example:

```
string firstName = "Mark ";
string lastName = "Donovan";
string name = string.Concat(firstName, lastName);
Console.WriteLine("The name is " + name + " and the
length is:" + name.Length);
```

Output:

```
The name is Mark Donovan and the length is:12
```

Comparing Strings Together

With the method **Equals()**, you can compare the content of two strings and check whether or not they are equal. The **Equals()** returns true or false - true if the strings are identical, false otherwise. Let's take a look at an example:

```
string string1 = "I love C#";
string string2 = "I love C#";
string string3 = "I love C";

Boolean result1 = string1.Equals(string2);
Console.WriteLine("strings string1 and string2 are
identical: " + result1);

Boolean result2 = string1.Equals(string3);
Console.WriteLine("strings string1 and string3 are
identical: " + result2);
```

The output is quite easy to predict. Can you guess it without seeing below?

```
strings string1 and string2 are identical: True
strings string1 and string3 are identical: False
```

Using String Interpolation

If you decide to take a career in programming, you'll probably hear the term interpolation more often. In C#, **string interpolation** refers to using & inserting variables inside of a string. However, to insert a variable inside a string, you must use special symbols, which we will show below:

```
string firstName = "Philipp";
string message = $"Hello {firstName}, welcome"; //
this is string interpolation
Console.WriteLine(message);
```

The output is the following:

```
Hello Philipp, welcome home
```

Example On Using Special Characters in Strings

You've probably noticed already that strings are strictly defined with double quotes (this symbol " "). We need one double quote (") to mark the beginning of the string, and another one to mark the end of the string ("). So, what happens if we have a string with a double quote inside of it?

```
string example = "This is an example of a double
quote " usage";
```

If you try compiling the code above, you will get an error. You can even see by the colors that the compiler automatically detects that something is wrong. So, how can we use a double quote inside a string? With an **escape character**.

In C#, the character is the backslash symbol \. When you use it, it tells the compiler to ignore the next char and not compile it. Now, let's run the same code again with the **WriteLine()** function:

```
string example = "This is an example of a double quote \" usage";
```

Output:

```
This is an example of a double quote " usage
```

Exercises to Practice

1. Think of a sentence you said to a friend or family member today. Write it down in your C# project and print it out. Then, print out its length and see if it's longer than 10 characters.
2. Think of two sentences you said today and write them down as separate strings - **string1** and **string2**. Then, convert all of the characters in the first string to lower letters (hint: see above in the examples) and the second one's characters to upper letters.
3. Write a string with more than one special character inside. Consider using some of the following: *, ", ', ^. If you get an error in your compilation, use **escape characters** to run your code successfully.
4. Create the following string: "Hi there {}, how are you today {}?". Then, create a new string with your favorite name. Use **string interpolation** to fill out the spaces where there are empty brackets → {}. (hint: look at the example for **string interpolation**)
5. Create two strings. One of them should be "Hello there, " and the other one should be "how are you today?". Use the string methods we talked about above to concatenate

them, and create a new string that's composed of both them. Then, print it out.

Math Functions

Programming, as a way to work with a computer, wouldn't exist today without the help of math and mathematicians. So, it's completely expected that the same is true vice-versa, as programming is now used as one of the best tools to improve the field of math as a whole.

This is why you will learn about math functions in C#. Math functions in C# are components of the **Math** class (if this is unclear, reread chapter **classes)**. As we said, a class consists of properties and methods, which we will be using right now in our math functions lesson. Let's go over the basics first.

So, how can you start using the **Math** class? All you have to do is write one line of code - **using System.** The **using System** keyword refers to the namespace *System* where the **Math** class is. Before going through some complex examples, let's take a look at a simple one where you can see how you can start using the **Math** class:

```
using System;
Console.WriteLine(Math.Max(5, 10));
```

Output:

```
10
```

To start using the math class, all we had to write down is **using System.** Then, we used the method Math.Max() which returns the bigger value of the two we give it (using Math.Min() does the opposite). Now, let's dive into some slightly harder examples

Using the *Floor* and the *Square Root* Functions

Almost all programming languages allow for the usage of the **Floor** and **Sqrt** functions. The floor function takes a decimal number (let's say 12.5) and returns its *floor,* i.e. how the number would look without the decimal (in this case, 12).

Square root, on the other hand, is self explanatory, though the function has proven to be *incredibly useful*, simply because there hasn't been found a way to consistently calculate square roots in an accurate manner. Let's take a look at an example:

```
using System;
Console.WriteLine(Math.Floor(500.800));
Console.WriteLine(Math.Sqrt(289));
```

Guessing the output for the first function is pretty easy - but can you do it with the second one? Most people don't know square roots off the top of their heads, but now, there's really no need to know them at all. With the Sqrt() function, we can calculate the square root of the number given to us and return the whole value.

Output:

```
500
17
```

Calculating Cube Roots With C#

Depending on the number of math classes you've taken until now, you might or might not be quite familiar with cube roots. If a square root shows what the number we would receive from multiplying the same number **twice,** a cube root shows the number we'll get if we multiply it **three times.**

As you can already guess, cube roots are a lot harder to calculate than square roots, as they add an entirely new dimension to the picture. Let's take a look at some code:

```
using System;
Console.WriteLine(Math.Cbrt(1000));
Console.WriteLine(Math.Cbrt(4913));
Console.WriteLine(Math.Cbrt(1000000));
```

Can you guess the output? Whether or not you have studied cube roots, it's still quite complicated to do so. No worries though - you've got C# to calculate for you:

```
10
17
100
```

Going Over Other Math Functions

C# has other functions in the **Math** class too, but there's no need to practically show them as most of them are easy to understand.

- Math.Abs() - returns the absolute value of a number

```
Console.WriteLine(Math.Abs(-5));
```

Output:

```
5
```

- Math.Pow() - raises a number to a specific power and returns the value

```
Console.WriteLine(Math.Pow(5, 3));
```

Output:

```
125
```

- Math.Ceiling() - opposite of Math.Floor(), raises the value of the decimal to an **int**

```
Console.WriteLine(Math.Ceiling(5.5));
```

Output:

```
6
```

- Math.Sin() - returns the sine of a number (important for geometry)

```
Console.WriteLine(Math.Sin(90));
```

Output:

```
0,8939966636005579
```

- Math.Cos() - returns the cosine of a number (also important for geometry)

```
Console.WriteLine(Math.Cos(180));
```

Output:

```
-0,5984600690578582
```

Exercises to Practice

1. Write down two integer values and a float - a decimal number. Consider making all of these values double-digit. Regarding the float, use the Math.Ceiling() and Math.Floor() functions and try to calculate the output. Then, calculate the square roots of the integers and try to predict the output.
2. Think of a whole number and write it down as an integer. Then, write the same number in another integer, but with a minus in front of it - i.e. make it negative. Use one of the functions listed above to make the two numbers **equal** (i.e. think of a way to flip the minus to a plus).
3. Use the geometrical mathematical functions we mentioned above (Cos() and Sin()). Experiment with values and try to get them to return the same value.
4. Think of a number from 1 to 10. Then multiply it on paper 3 times over (ex: 5*5*5). Using the Math.Pow() function, check if your answer is correct
5. Write down the number from exercise 4. Then, go through the functions we described above and think of a way to reverse the number and get your original input (if it was 5*5*5, use a function that will return 5 when you input 125).

Pointers

We've got all of the easy subjects out of the way, and now we'll dive right into pointers, which will probably be slightly more challenging than any of the topics we've covered so far. So, let's get some basic theory out of the way first.

Pointers are variables (just like strings, chars, and ints) that hold the **memory address** of a variable. A memory address is the specific place in your computer's memory where the variable in question is stored. So, with pointers, you'll have direct access to your computer's hardware. How cool is that? Let's take a look at some examples.

Examples of Pointers

The following example will consist of everything there is to know about pointers, so make sure you pay close attention:

```
int random = 1234567890;
int* pointer = &random;
Console.WriteLine(pointer); //Shows the address
(where it's stored)
Console.WriteLine(*pointer); //Shows the value of
the address.
```

This is our output:

```
-447224820
1234567890
```

Keep in mind that if you test the same code in your own C# project, you won't get the same result for the first line. Why is that? This is the case because the computer this project is run on is not the same as your computer - therefore, the memory is different also.

The same code might print out at an output of -382213992 (a totally different address) even though you're storing the **exact same value**. This is the power of pointers - being able to directly access the memory address inside of the computer's hardware. Let's take a look at another example:

```
int a = 500;
int b = 1000;
int* pointer1 = &a;
int* pointer2 = &b;
Console.WriteLine((int)pointer1);
Console.WriteLine((int)pointer2);
Console.WriteLine(*pointer1);
Console.WriteLine(*pointer2);
```

Output:

```
1815602604
1815602600
500
1000
```

Similarly, in this example, the first two values of the output (1815602604 and 18150602600) refer to the physical address of the values **a** and **b.** The last two values are just the values of the variables **a** and **b** (notice that we can print out the value of a variable through a pointer).

Given below is another simple example of declaring a pointer variable.

```
using System;

namespace MyApplication
{
  class Program
  {
    static void Main(string[] args)
    {
      unsafe{
        int x = 100;
        int* ptr = &x;
        Console.WriteLine((int)ptr);
        Console.WriteLine(*ptr);

      }
    }
  }
}
```

Here variable x is assigned with 100. A pointer variable (ptr) is declared to get the address of the memory location of x variable. Pointer variable is declared by the following code line.

int* ptr = &x;   here & is used to get the memory address of x and then it is assigned to the pointer ptr.

Then by printing (int)ptr command, we can get the memory address of the x variable. And by *ptr command we can get the value of the memory location pointed here.

The output is as follows:

```
1363370640
100
```

Given below is another example where pointers are used.

```
using System;
using System.Collections.Generic;

public class Program
{
    static unsafe void Main(string[] args) {
     int val = 50;
     int* x = &val;

     Console.WriteLine("Data: {0} ", val);
     Console.WriteLine("Address: {0}", (int)x);
     Console.ReadKey();
    }
}
```

Here **unsafe keyword** is added to the main method. Here **val** variable is declared with the value of 50 and integer type x variable is used to get the address of the x variable. Output of the above code can be obtained as follows:

```
Data: 50
Address: 1350713136
```

Given below is an example where two pointers are used to store memory addresses of two variables.

```
using System;
using System.Collections.Generic;

public class Program
{
    static unsafe void Main(string[] args) {
     int m = 10, n=20;
     int* ptr1 = &m, ptr2 = &n;

     Console.WriteLine("Data:  " +m+ ", " + n);
     Console.WriteLine("Address: {0}", (int)ptr1 + ", " + (int)ptr2);
     Console.ReadKey();
    }
}
```

Variable m and n integers are initialized with 10 and 20 respectively. ptr1 and ptr2 is used to store the memory address of m and n. By referring to the code you can see the way of initializing two pointers in one line. Then the data and addresses are printed separately.

The output is as follows:

```
Data:  10, 20
Address: -1937138880, -1937138872
```

Pointers are basically use for saving the memory and it helps in faster execution time since data are manipulated with the addresses and gets the direct access to memory locations.

Exercises to Practice

1. Write down three variables as integers (use any number you like). First, print out the values of their physical address (take a look at example 1), and then print out their original values **using pointers** (take a look at example 2).
2. Write down a variable and print out its address using a pointer. Then, create another variable and do the same. Now, swap the two variables' **physical addresses.** (hint: use **int* pointer1 = &variable2** and vice-versa).

Date and Time

C# programming language is having a **DateTime** structure to work with date and time. The syntax of creating DateTime object is as follows:

```
DateTime dt = new DateTime();//sets a default time of
01/01/0001 00:00:00
```

By using different constructors, we can set the **DateTime** struct using a **DateTime** object that initializes the values. Given below are some examples of different constructors use for setting the date and time.

```
using System;

public class Program
{
    public static void Main()
    {
        //assigns default value 01/01/0001 00:00:00
        DateTime dt1 = new DateTime();
        Console.WriteLine(dt1);

        //assign year, month, day
        DateTime dt2 = new DateTime(2015, 12, 31);
        Console.WriteLine(dt2);

        //assign year, month, day, hour, min, seconds
        DateTime dt3 = new DateTime(2015, 12, 31, 5, 10, 20);
        Console.WriteLine(dt3);

        //assign year, month, day, hour, min, seconds, UTC timezone
        DateTime dt4 = new DateTime(2015, 12, 31, 5, 10, 20, DateTimeKind.Utc);
        Console.WriteLine(dt4);
    }
}
```

In the first constructor date and time is set and the default value gets displayed.

In the second constructor only the date is specified, but the time is not. So, the default value will be printed for the time.

In the other constructors, both the time and date is specified and the date and time will be displayed accordingly.

So the code output will be as follows:

```
1/1/0001 12:00:00 AM
12/31/2015 12:00:00 AM
12/31/2015 5:10:20 AM
12/31/2015 5:10:20 AM
```

There is a special case where if there is a valid string for date and time, we can change the string to a DateTime object. Given below is a sample code for that.

```
using System;

public class Program
{
    public static void Main()
    {
        var str = "10/10/2022";
        DateTime dt;

        var isValidDate = DateTime.TryParse(str, out dt);
        if (isValidDate)
            Console.WriteLine(dt);
        else
            Console.WriteLine($"{str} is not a valid date string");
    }
}
```

Here, we use TryParse() and TryParseExact() methods to see if the string is a valid expression.

isValidDate is a boolean that returns true if the string represents a valid date.

So given below is the output of the above sample code.

```
10/10/2022 12:00:00 AM
```

Classes

Once you've understood everything else there is about C# and you've come to classes, you're well on your way to become a great coder. Now, pay special attention to this subject, as classes are an **absolute necessity** for becoming a good programmer.

Think of classes as "prototypes". We've covered integers, strings, booleans, and much more. What if you could create your own data type? This is exactly what classes allow you to do.

Classes allow you to create new instances of variables (called **objects**) that follow the exact blueprint you defined. A class consists of **properties** (variables) and **methods** (functions inside of the class). There isn't much to learn about classes theoretically, but there is much, much to practice about them.

Examples of Classes

Creating a New Class and Constructing Objects

Let's say you have a bike that you want to somehow define programmatically. This is what classes allow you to do. Take a look at the following example.

```
public class Bike {
      String color;
      int size;
      int age;
      int topSpeed;
}
```

Now, to **construct** an instance of a class (i.e. an object) you need a **constructor**. Let's see how they're made:

```
public Bike(String color, int size, int age, int
topSpeed) {
      this.color = color;
      this.size = size;
      this.age = age;
      this.topSpeed = topSpeed;
}
```

In this constructor, the keyword **this** refers to the current object we're creating. Then, we're manually assigning values to the new object. Now, how can you use this constructor to create a new object?

```
Bike myDadsBike = new Bike("Green", 10, 12, 14);
```

So, we made a new bike called "myDadsBike" that has a **Green color**, is of **size 10,** and is **12 years old.** The last value (14) refers to the top speed this bike can reach in mp/h. If you don't know some of these values, you can set them equal to 0.

Accessing An Object's Values and Printing Them

So far, you've probably understood that classes allow you to create your own prototype for a variable that's totally different from anything we've encountered so far. Why work manually with a variable called bikeColor, bikeSpeed, or bikeSize, when you can put them together in an object called myBike and have them in one place.

Now, let's try to access an object's value and print it:

```
Console.WriteLine(myDadsBike.color);
```

If you try compiling this code, you will get an error saying that you've violated the class's access-level. What does this mean? This means that you cannot access a class or its objects **unless** you've got the permission to do so. So, how can we get the permission to access a variable inside of the class?

- It's simple → just write the keyword **public** right before the "String color" code.

This would look something like this:

```
public class Bike
{
      public String color;
      int size;
      int age;
      int topSpeed;
}
```

Now, we will get the following output:

```
Green
```

Now, let's look at another simple example

```
class Vehicle
{
 string color = "blue";}
```

In this example, Vehicle **class** is created where it can create different objects in the same class. And vehicle has different features like color, weight, model etc. where these are named as **attributes.** Also, car has different functions like driving, parking, braking etc. where they are named as **methods** in C# programming language. Given below is an example where vehicle class can create an object to access the data from the class.

```
using System;

namespace MyApplication
{
  class Vehicle
  {
    string color = "blue";

    static void Main(string[] args)
    {
      Vehicle myObj = new Vehicle();
      Console.WriteLine(myObj.color);
    }
  }
}
```

In this example, Vehicle class is created and a new object called "myObj" is created to get the data from the class. Here dot syntax (.) is used with the object to access the variables/fields inside a class. Also, there can be many objects created for the same class to access the details from the class. Here myObj.color is used to access the color of the vehicle and will be printed as the output.

```
blue
```

Constructor

A special kind of a method known as "Constructor" is used to initialize the objects. With the defining of the constructor, we get the opportunity to initialize the object when it is created.

```
using System;

namespace MyApplication
{
  // Create a Fruits class
  class Fruit
  {
    public string item;  // Create a field

    // Create a class constructor for the Fruit class
    public Fruit()
    {
      item = "Mango"; // Set the initial value for model
    }

    static void Main(string[] args)
    {
      Fruit myObj = new Fruit();  // Create an object of the Car Class (this will call
      Console.WriteLine(myObj.item);  // Print the value of model
    }
  }
}
```

In the example, Fruit class is created, and a **string variable** called item is created. Since the constructor is a special method with the same name of the class, a constructor is created here with the name of class name "Fruits". Inside the constructor, item variable is initiated with "Mango". When the main method is called by creating an object, the constructor also gets called automatically and sets the initial value. Code output is as follows.

Mango

Refer the below examples and identify the advantage of using a constructor in initializing the variables.

```
using System;

namespace MyApplication
{
  class Car
  {
    public string model;
    public string color;
    public int year;
    static void Main(string[] args)
    {
      Car Nissan = new Car();
      Nissan.model = "Leaf";
      Nissan.color = "White";
      Nissan.year = 2010;

      Car Toyota = new Car();
      Toyota.model = "Camry";
      Toyota.color = "Black";
      Toyota.year = 2005;

      Console.WriteLine(Nissan.model);
      Console.WriteLine(Toyota.model);
    }
  }
}
```

```
using System;

namespace MyApplication
{
  class Car
  {
    public string model;
    public string color;
    public int year;

    public Car(string modelName, string colorName, int modelYear){

        model = modelName;
        color = colorName;
        year = modelYear;
    }

    static void Main(string[] args)
    {
      Car Nissan = new Car("Leaf", "White", 2010);
      Car Toyota = new Car("Camry", "Black", 2005);

      Console.WriteLine(Nissan.model);
      Console.WriteLine(Toyota.model);
    }
  }
}
```

Both these two codes give the same output as follows:

```
Leaf
Camry
```

Here you can see that without using the constructors, when creating a new object all the variables should be initialized and it makes a lengthy code. When having a constructor, we can easily initialize the variables of the objects as required and make the code look less complicated and neat.

Special keywords known as “Access Modifiers” are used in object-oriented programming languages that set accessibility of classes, methods and other members. Access modifiers are specially used syntax which facilitate the encapsulation of components.

Modifier	Description
public	Code is allowed to be access for all classes
private	Code is only accessible in the same class
protected	Code is accessible within the same class or a class inherited from the same class
internal	Limits the access of the code within the current project assembly

Most of the object-oriented programming languages have four main concepts: **Encapsulation, Polymorphism, Inheritance** and **Abstraction.**

Encapsulation

Encapsulation is a concept used in Object-oriented programming in order to protect the variables, methods and other data in a class from hiding the data or not allowing users to change the details of the code. This can be simply considered as a capsule which covers the drug inside it. By referring to the below example, let's try to understand this encapsulation concept.

```
using System;

namespace MyApplication
{
  class Vehicle
  {
    private string model;  // field
    public string Model    // property
    {
      get { return model; }
      set { model = value; }
    }
  }
  class Program
  {
    static void Main(string[] args)
    {
      Vehicle myObj = new Vehicle();
      myObj.Model = "Suzuki Estilo";
      Console.WriteLine(myObj.Model);
    }
  }
}
```

In the example, a string variable "model" is created with the access modifier of **private** keyword. So, this variable cannot be accessed by any other class to change the value. So, for initializing and assigning the values for private variable, special methods named as **get** and **set** are used. Here, **model** private variable value is set and get by a method called **Model** (which is the same name as variable). Here **get** method is used to return the value of model variable. **Set** method is used to assign a value to the variable **model**. In the program class in the example, an object named as **'myObj'** is created in **Vehicle class.** Then using the **Model method**, variable **model** is set with the value of "Suzuki Estilo" which helps to access and change the private variable in the **Vehicle class**. Then, the output is as follows:

```
Suzuki Estilo
```

Inheritance

Inheritance is a concept in object-oriented programing where there are **derived classes (child classes)** which are inherited with the attributes, methods from a **base class (parent class).** This concept helps to reduce the replicate of the codes again and again in different classes. Given below is an example to get a clear idea about this concept.

```
using System;

namespace MyApplication
{
  class Vehicle  // Base class
  {
    public string brand = "Toyota";  // Vehicle field
    public void drive()              // Vehicle method
    {
      Console.WriteLine("I can drive fast!");
    }
  }
  class Car : Vehicle  // Derived class
  {
    public string modelName = "Lexus";  // Car field
  }
  class Program
  {
    static void Main(string[] args)
    {
      // Create a myCar object
      Car myCar = new Car();

      // Call the drive() method (From the Vehicle class) on the myCar object
      myCar.drive();

      // Display the value of the brand field (from the Vehicle class) and the value of the
modelName from the Car class
      Console.WriteLine(myCar.brand + " " + myCar.modelName);
    }
  }
}
```

In this example, **Vehicle** is the **Base Class** and there are different attributes like **Brand** which is initialized as "Toyota" and a method with the name of **drive**. There is another derived class named **Car** which is having a different variable named **modelName**. Since Car class is a derived class of Vehicle, it can access all the attributes and methods in the Vehicle class as well. So in the main method, an object is created and call the drive method and value of brand field from Vehicle class. So the output is as follows:

```
I can drive fast!
Toyota Lexus
```

Inheritance concept is mainly used in the code where it is required to have code re-usability. In the place where same code is repeated in different classes, we can get the same properties inherited from the base class hence reducing the repeatability of the code.

Polymorphism

Polymorphism is also one of the main concepts in object-oriented programming where it considered about something which occurs in several different forms. Polymorphism occurs where many classes are related to each other by inheritance.
Given below is an example for an instance where we use polymorphism.

```
using System;

namespace MyApplication
{
  class Animal  // Base class (parent)
  {
    public void animalMove()
    {
      Console.WriteLine("The animal can move");
    }
  }

  class Dog : Animal  // Derived class (child)
  {
    public void animalMove()
    {
      Console.WriteLine("The dog moves by walking");
    }
  }

  class Fish : Animal  // Derived class (child)
  {
    public void animalMove()
    {
      Console.WriteLine("The fish move by swimming");
    }
  }

  class Program
  {
    static void Main(string[] args)
    {
      Animal myAnimal = new Animal();  // Create a Animal object
      Animal myDog = new Dog();  // Create a Dog object
      Animal myFish = new Fish();  // Create a Fish object

      myAnimal.animalMove();
      myDog.animalMove();
      myFish.animalMove();
    }
  }
}
```

In this example, there are three classes called Animal which is the base class and two derived class called Dog and Fish. Here there are same method named as "animalMove" in all three classes. And an object is created from each class and animalMoove method is called. The following output is received.

```
The animal can move
The animal can move
The animal can move
```

After referring to the output we can say that it is not what is expected by creating three objects for different classes. But it happening for a reason. Since all the methods are having the same name from the base class, every method with the same name in derived classes were replaced by the base class method. That is the reason for getting this output mentioned above.

Let's refer the below example and analyze the output.

```
using System;

namespace MyApplication
{
  class Animal  // Base class (parent)
  {
    public virtual void animalMove()
    {
      Console.WriteLine("The animal can move");
    }
  }

  class Dog : Animal  // Derived class (child)
  {
    public override void animalMove()
    {
      Console.WriteLine("The dog moves by walking");
    }
  }

  class Fish : Animal  // Derived class (child)
  {
    public override void animalMove()
    {
      Console.WriteLine("The fish move by swimming");
    }
  }

  class Program
  {
    static void Main(string[] args)
    {
      Animal myAnimal = new Animal();  // Create a Animal object
      Animal myDog = new Dog();  // Create a Dog object
      Animal myFish = new Fish();  // Create a Fish object

      myAnimal.animalMove();
      myDog.animalMove();
      myFish.animalMove();
    }
  }
}
```

This is similar to the previous code. But there are few keywords which were not in the previous code.

- There is a keyword **Virtual** in animalMove method in the **Animal class (base class)**
- There is a keyword **override** in animalMove method in **derived classes**

By using these keywords base class methods will not override the derived class methods as in the previous example. The output will be as follows:

```
The animal can move
The dog moves by walking
The fish move by swimming
```

Abstraction

Abstraction is also a key concept in object-oriented programming where data is hidden from user and only the important data is shown to the user. Here, **Abstract** keyword is used for classes and methods.

- **Abstract class:** This class is a restricted one which does not allow to create the objects. This must be inherited from another class to access this abstract class
- **Abstract method:** This can only be used in an abstract class and it doesn't have a method body and it is provided from the derived class.

Let's consider the below example to understand the use of abstract classes and methods.

```
using System;

namespace MyApplication
{
  // Abstract class
  abstract class Human
  {
    // Abstract method (does not have a body)
    public abstract void humanName();
    // Regular method
    public void age()
    {
      Console.WriteLine("15 years old");
    }
  }

  // Derived class (inherit from Human)
  class Child : Human
  {
    public override void humanName()
    {
      // The body of humanName() is provided here
      Console.WriteLine("Name: John");
    }
  }

  class Program
  {
    static void Main(string[] args)
    {
      Child myChild = new Child();  // Create a Child object
      myChild.humanName();
      myChild.age();
    }
  }
}
```

In this example, it can be seen that there is an **abstract class** called Human (It is also the base class). In Human class there are both regular and abstract methods. Child class which is a derived class from Human class is used to access this **abstract class (Human class).** By using the derived class, we can call the regular method and abstract method in abstract class. The output is as follows:

```
Name: John
15 years old
```

Exercises to Practice

1. Create a class named **Car** that has the following properties inside: color, manufacturer, yearOfManufacturing, engineType (if you're not sure about the details, you can leave them blank). Then, create at least 3 objects with a **constructor** and place the objects in an array (hint: check **lesson arrays**)
2. Create another class called **MobilePhone** and think of at least three properties to put inside. Create a constructor for the class. Then, make at least five objects of the phone class and change some of their properties (hint: use the **public** keyword as in the last example).

Lists

List is a collection of strongly typed objects which can be accessed using the index. Also lists are having different methods for sorting, searching and modifying. It is also considered to be a generic version of ArrayList that comes under the namespace of *System.Collection.Generic.*

Given below is a simple example code of how to create a list consisting with even numbers below 10.

```
using System;
using System.Collections.Generic;

public class Program
{
    public static void Main()
    {
        // adding elements using add() method
        List<int> evenNumbers = new List<int>();
        evenNumbers.Add(2);
        evenNumbers.Add(4);
        evenNumbers.Add(6);
        evenNumbers.Add(8);

        Console.WriteLine("No of elelemts: "+ evenNumbers.Count + " even 
numbers");
    }
}
```

In this example, List is initiated with the type of elements that is planned to be stored in it. Since in the example, there we going to store numbers, we have used int type for the List. And by using **Add()** method we can store new elements to the list. And by **Count()** method we can count the number of elements in the List. The output is as follows:

```
No of elelemts: 4 even numbers
```

Let's consider another example of creating a **string type list** to store the main cities in the country.

```
using System;
using System.Collections.Generic;

public class Program
{
    public static void Main()
    {
        // adding elements using add() method
        List<string> cities = new List<string>();
        cities.Add("Colombo");
        cities.Add("Matara");
        cities.Add("Galle");
        cities.Add("Kandy");

        Console.WriteLine("No of elelemts: "+ cities.Count);
    }
}
```

In this example, List is defined for string since the storing elements are names of the cities. Using the Add() method elements are added to the list same as in the previous example. Given below is the output of this simple code:

```
No of elelemts: 4
```

Same as in arrays using index, we can access the elements of the list. Given below is an example for that.

```
using System;
using System.Collections.Generic;

public class Program
{
    public static void Main()
    {
        // adding elements using add() method
        List<string> cities = new List<string>();
        cities.Add("Colombo");
        cities.Add("Matara");
        cities.Add("Galle");
        cities.Add("Kandy");

        Console.WriteLine("No of elelemts: "+ cities.Count);
        Console.WriteLine("Elements of the List are: ");
        Console.WriteLine(cities[0]);
        Console.WriteLine(cities[1]);
        Console.WriteLine(cities[2]);
        Console.WriteLine(cities[3]);
     }
}
```

Here cities[0] represent for the first element of the list and other elements are named as cities[1], cities[2], cities[3] respectively. So the output is as follows:

```
No of elelemts: 4
Elements of the List are:
Colombo
Matara
Galle
Kandy
```

If you need to insert a new element to the list in middle, then you need to use the **Insert()** method as in the following example.

```
using System;
using System.Collections.Generic;

public class Program
{
    public static void Main()
    {
        var fruits = new List<string>(){ "Mango", "Apple", "Banana", "Grapes" };

        fruits.Insert(1, "Oranges");// inserts "Oranges" at 1st index: after Mango.

        foreach (var num in fruits)
            Console.WriteLine(num);
    }
}
```

In this example code, fruits list is created with some string values. And we have a requirement of adding “Oranges” as the second element of the list. For that we use Insert(1,”Oranges”) method. Here 1 is the position of the element in the list. Then every element is printed in fruits list will be printed after adding “Oranges”.

```
Mango
Oranges
Apple
Banana
Grapes
```

There is a separate method for removing the elements from a list. Given below is an example where **Remove()** methods are used.

```
using System;
using System.Collections.Generic;

public class Program
{
    public static void Main()
    {
        var fruits = new List<string>(){ "Mango", "Apple", "Banana", "Grapes" };

        fruits.Remove("Mango"); // removes Mango element from a list

        fruits.RemoveAt(2); //removes the 3rd element (index starts from 0)


        foreach (var num in fruits)
            Console.WriteLine(num);
    }
}
```

There are two basic methods for removing the elements from a list. They are

- **Remove(*element*):** All the elements with this name will be removed from the list
- **RemoveAt(*number*):** Element with the position as in *number* will be removed from the list

In this example, by **fruits.Remove("Mango")** will remove the Mango from the list and by **fruits.RemoveAt(2)** will remove the 3rd element of the list (new list which is after removing Mango). The 3rd element in the new list is Grapes. So the output is as follows:

```
Apple
Banana
```

Dynamic Variables

Dynamic variables are having the facility of changing the types at run time based on the assigned value. Dynamic variables are normally defined with the **dynamic keyword**. The syntax is as follows:

dynamic myDynamicVar = 10; *here myDynamicVar is the variable name*

Normally dynamic type escapes at compile time and gets its type resolved at run-time. The following example shows how that the dynamic variable changes at run-time when the values are assigned to those variables.

```
using System;

public class Program
{
    public static void Main()
    {
        dynamic MyDynamicVar = 15;
        Console.WriteLine("Value: {0}, Type: {1}", MyDynamicVar, MyDynamicVar.GetType());

        MyDynamicVar = "Hello World!!";
        Console.WriteLine("Value: {0}, Type: {1}", MyDynamicVar, MyDynamicVar.GetType());

        MyDynamicVar = true;
        Console.WriteLine("Value: {0}, Type: {1}", MyDynamicVar, MyDynamicVar.GetType());

        MyDynamicVar = DateTime.Now;
        Console.WriteLine("Value: {0}, Type: {1}", MyDynamicVar, MyDynamicVar.GetType());
    }

}
```

In the example code, a dynamic variable with the name of **MyDynamicVar** is initialized here. Then different values are assigned to that variable and see how the variable type changes with the assigning value during run-time.

In the first line, variable is assigned with 15 hence it is an integer type. Then “Hello World!!” which is a string. And true value is assigned to MyDynamicVar variable hence making the variable type Boolean. At last dynamic variable is assigned with a DateTime making the variable type as DateTime.

Given below is the output of the code.

```
Value: 100, Type: System.Int32
Value: Hello World!!, Type: System.String
Value: True, Type: System.Boolean
Value: 9/10/2022 7:01:38 PM, Type: System.DateTime
```

Conclusion

We'd like to genuinely thank you for paying attention and reading this book. The team behind it spent hours building & composing it, so we hope that it helped out.

If you went over and understood most of the contents of this book, you now great knowledge in C# and an amazing foundation when it comes to programming in general.

So far in this book, we covered all of the major concepts of programming, including:

- Creating a work environment to start coding,
- The basics of C#,
- Conditionals,
- Variables,
- Arrays,
- Loops,
- Strings,
- Pointers,
- Classes,
- and more

If you enjoyed this book, please don’t hesitate to give us feedback. Thank you for your time!

Book 2:
Coding for Kids Ages 8-12

Introduction

It was a cool, windy evening in Chicago. I was enjoying the playoffs on television. Suddenly, I heard a crackle on the TV, and the picture started getting fuzzy. A couple of minutes later, the whole screen went green. No picture, no game. It was frustrating to have the TV go out in the middle of the game.

Hearing my groan of annoyance and frustration, my wife, Candy asked me what happened. 'Well. The TV screen just went blank. Right in the middle of the game'. My 9-year-old son, Steve, who just walked in the room, said 'That's an easy fix'. Steve switched the television off and made a few adjustments to the satellite box. And two minutes later, he switched the television on, and it was working. Like magic!!!

Next, we have the case of Abby. She was a tennis player in Madison high school. She had been struggling for months since she recovered from an elbow injury. She'd lost 3 tournaments this year which she had won the previous year. She was upset, but she realized that the loss happened for a reason. It wasn't bad luck or lack of skill. It was due to certain circumstances. She decided that she needed to change things quickly. She spent more time analysing replays of her game and how it had changed in the last six months. She figured out that her grip on the racket had changed since the injury and her forehand was badly affected. She changed her grip at practice and instantly felt she was playing a lot better. At the next tournament, she won easily. Abby was back on track.

Now, let's look at the final example of Matthew. Matthew was a 12-year-old in a small town in rural Wyoming. He had interest in science and technology, but there wasn't much opportunity to explore this in his community. One day, someone donated a dozen computers in his school, and he was one of the lucky ones to be able to take it home. The computer was pre-installed with C++. He was intimidated with the idea of coding. However, with the help of a few books in the library, he got started. He did some basic projects and eventually became the coding whiz of the school. His classmates loved his games and animations and asked him to teach them how to code. Matthew eventually went to college for computer science, and now works for a very high salary as a programmer in Silicon Valley.

All the above situations are hypothetical ones, where the innate ability of Matthew, Abby and Steve led to wonderful outcomes. They had the grit and determination to deal with adversity and learn quickly. However, there are other skills that each of them have shown that can be learnt with programming.

Steve had been learning programming for the last couple of years, and his problem-solving skills were advanced. He was able to break things apart, fix them and repair items like televisions and computers easily.

Abby had also learnt coding recently. She was really good at spotting mistakes in the code and fixing them. This had translated into real life in different situations, with an ability to spot details that others struggled with.

Matthew's life had changed due to programming. That was his only outlet for his skills and creativity in a community that didn't have many opportunities. He now has his dream career and hopes to inspire many more in his situation to do the same.

These above three examples show how coding can completely change one's mindset, problem solving abilities, creativity; and greatly improve one's quality of life.

What is Programming?

Programming is the creation of a systematic set of instructions that a computer can understand and execute. These instructions are called code, and they are written in a language that's known as a programming language. There are many extraordinary programming languages, each with their own personal syntax and capabilities.

Benefits of Programming

Programming is like a paintbrush for the digital world. It lets you to create and form thoughts into something tangible, something that can be shared and experienced by using others.

With programming, you have the strength to build and layout digital landscapes, from the tiniest of small print to the grandest of software designs. You can create interactive experiences that captivate audiences. You can automate tedious tasks, making them extra efficient and freeing up time for more important pursuits.

Programming is a great tool for problem-solving. It allows you to take complex issues and break them down into manageable pieces. It's like a jigsaw puzzle, the place you coalesce blocks collectively to build something greater. With programming, you can flip data into knowledge, and that knowledge into action. You can communicate with machines and make them do your bidding. It's like a secret language that only a select few are privy to, and with that knowledge, you can liberate hidden tasks.

Programming is a medium through which you can express your creativity, fix problems, and change the world. It's a tool that empowers you to carry your ideas to reality and make a real impact on the world.

It is an in-demand skill, with job possibilities in a diverse range of industries. From bookkeeping to cybersecurity, programming is a versatile tool that can lead to a beneficial career. Programmers are well-paid, and the demand for expert programmers is growing. According to the Bureau of Labor Statistics, the median salary for computer programmer in the United States is $88,240. It is not uncommon for people with 5 years of work experience to have a salary of $150000 or more.

Programming can be used to automate repetitive tasks, making them more efficient and less time-consuming. This can be utilized in a variety of industries, from manufacturing to finance.

It is a field that is constantly evolving, with new technologies and languages emerging all the time. Learning to code is a journey, and there is always something new to learn, which can be interesting and motivating.

Programming is also a collaborative effort and learning to program can help you learn how to work in a team. Understanding how to speak and work with others is a necessary skill, and programming can help you enhance that skill.

Programming abilities can also be used to start your very own business. Whether you choose to create an app, internet site or software, programming is an indispensable tool for constructing and launching a successful start-up. The world is lit with startups that have been launched by programming and grown into billion dollar businesses, like Facebook, Google, Amazon etc.

Programming empowers you to take control of technology and use it to obtain your goals. Instead of being a passive consumer of technology, you can become an energetic creator and use technology to make a tremendous have an impact on in your lifestyles and the lives of others.

Why Choose C++

Imagine you are a sculptor, with a block of stone in front of you. C++ is like the chisel in your hand, a precision device that approves you to carve and form your masterpiece with precision and control.

With C++, you have the energy to shape and form your code with great efficiency, making it run quicker and smoother. It's a low-level language, which has better communication with the machine. It allows you to fine-tune your program's performance, like a sculptor cautiously chiselling away the excess marble.

Think of other programming languages as paint brushes, they are amazing for creating colorful, expressive pieces; but they may additionally lack the precision and power of a chisel. C++ is like a Swiss Army knife of programming languages, it has equipment for unique purposes, like object-oriented and procedural programming.

C++ additionally has a significant and energetic community of developers, who continuously enhance and update the language, making it extra strong and versatile. This neighbourhood is like a crew of specialist sculptors, who are constantly inclined to share their knowledge and strategies with you.

C++ is a powerful, versatile programming language that is extensively used in enterprise and academia. It provides a solid foundation in programming standards and can be used to create a wide variety of software, including working systems, games, and simulations. Additionally, C++ is a compiled language, which potential that it can be optimized for performance and is commonly faster than interpreted languages. A compiled languages converts the entire code into machine language; and the computer runs the machine language. This is much faster than an interpreted language, which converts each line into machine language at run time.

C++ supports each object-oriented and procedural programming paradigm, making it flexible and versatile.

C++ is extensively used in industry and academia and is supported with the aid of most important running systems, giving it a high level of portability.

It's well worth noting that C++ is not always the best programming language for every application, and different languages may be better proper for certain tasks. However, C++ is a powerful and versatile language that can be used to create a broad range of software, and its strengths make it a popular choice among developers.

C++ Installation

Code Blocks is a software that we will use to execute C++ code and view the output. It is a beginner user-friendly IDE that is great to get started with it.

Steps

1. Browse to http://www.codeblocks.org/downloads/binaries/

Download the version that's best suited for your operating system by clicking on one of the links below:

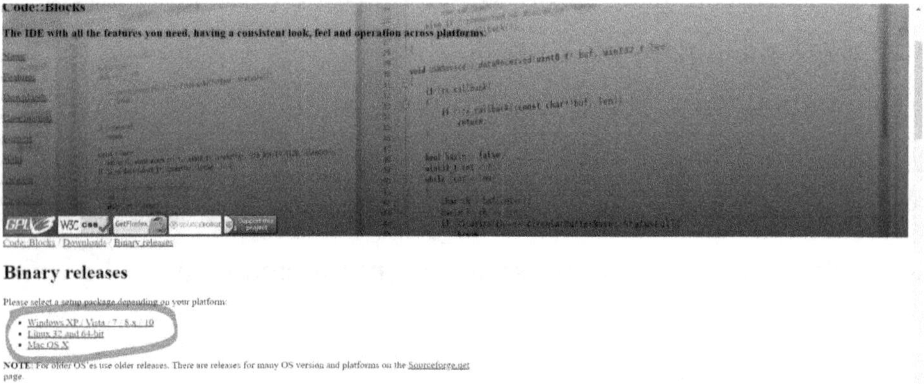

2. Install the program.
3. Once installed, open the Code::Blocks software below from the Start Menu.

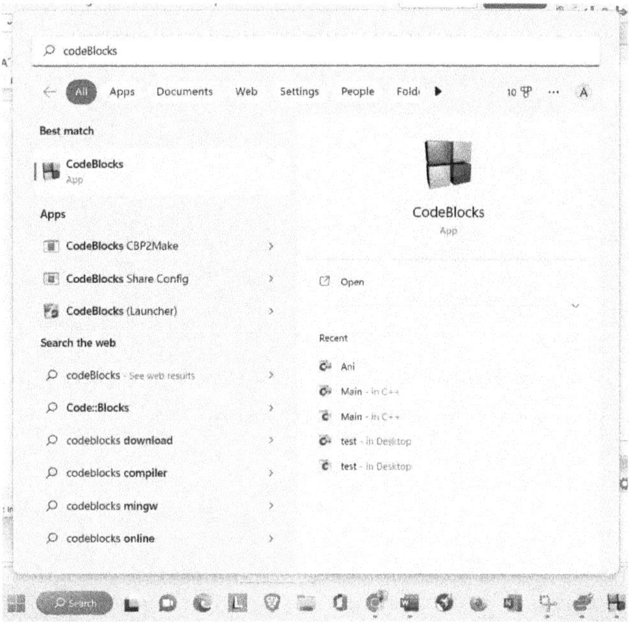

4. Open a new file as shown below.

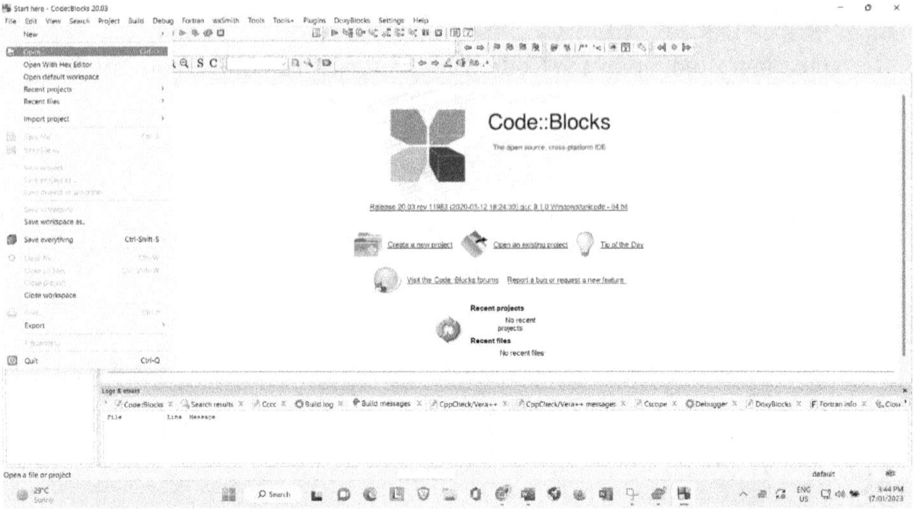

5. We're now going to test out some basic code below. Copy the code below highlighted in yellow and paste it in the file.

```
#include <iostream>
int main()
{
   std::cout << "Hello, World!" << std::endl;
   return 0;
}
```

It should look like this below:

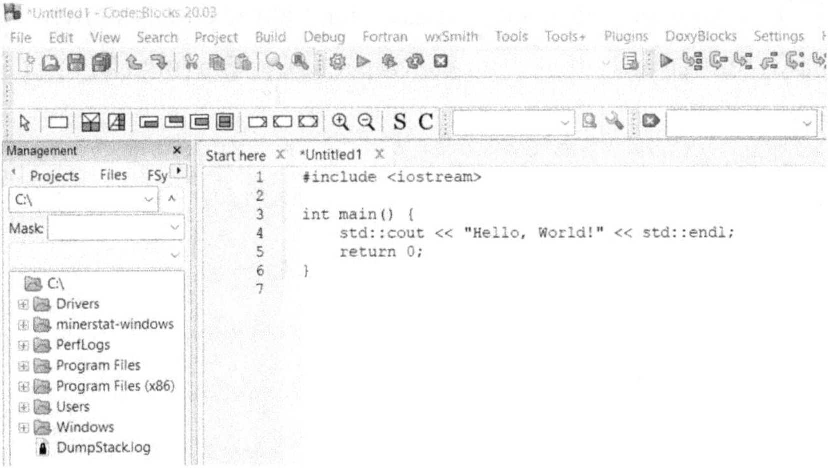

6. Now, click "**File > Save File As**"

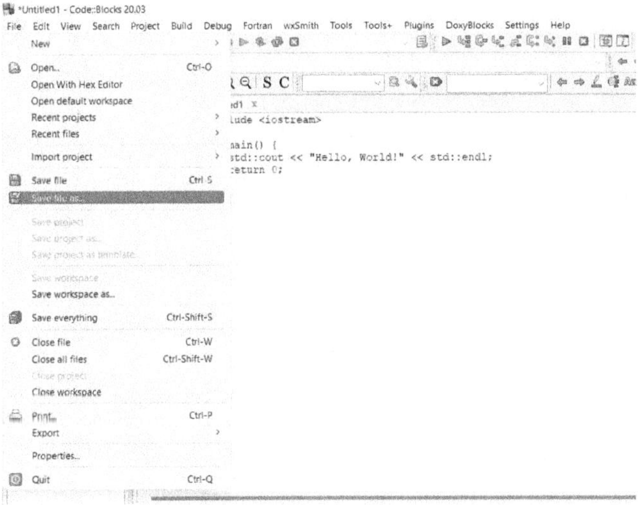

7. Name, the file and make sure it has a ".cpp" at the end as shown below. This ensures that you're saving it as C++ file (instead of a C file).

8. Now, build the code as shown below:

9. The log at the bottom shows whether build was successful. In this case, 0 errors with a successful build, as shown in picture below.

10. Once build is complete, run the code as shown below.

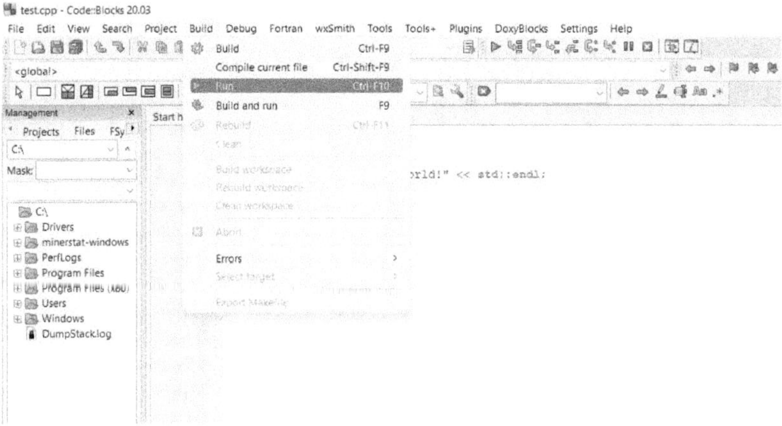

11. An output window should pop up with the message “Hello World” as shown below.

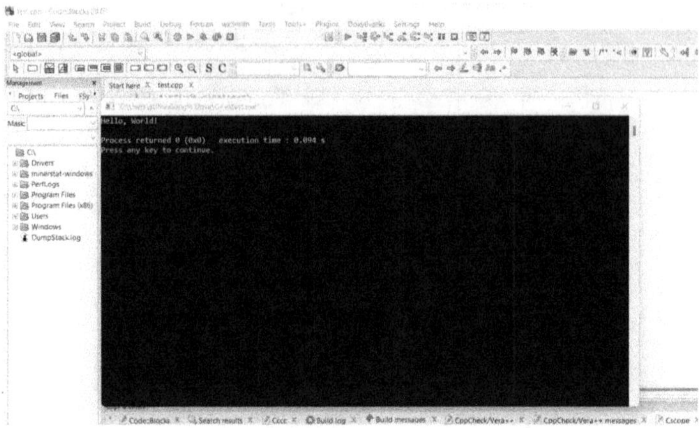

12. Press any key to exit window.

Simple C++ Programs to Start

In this chapter, we're going to go over a couple of basic programs to get you started. And explain every single line of the code. This will help you understand the purpose and objective of the code.

Program 1: "Hello World"

The first program is a "Hello World". It's the first program that most programmers write. It helps beginner programmers get started with the syntax and should help you execute your first program in C++. If the code seems familiar, it's the same code that we went over in the "C++ Installation" chapter. Now, you'll be able to understand what the code means.

```
#include <iostream>

int main()

{

  std::cout << "Hello, World!" << std::endl;

  return 0;

}
```

```
1   #include <iostream>
2
3   int main() {
4       std::cout << "Hello, World!" << std::endl;
5       return 0;
6   }
7
```

The purpose of the program above is to print the words “Hello World” on the screen.

The first line **“#include <iostream>”** imports a library called iostream into the program. It basically means that you can now use all the commands within iostream. **Iostream** contains two popular commands that this program will use, called **cout** and **endl**.

Cout allows you to print an output on the screen; and **endl** allows you to move to the next line of the output.

In Line 3, we have “**int main()**” which is used to start the actual program. The program executes every line after **int main()** which are included between the curly braces that look like “**{}**”. These 2 braces indicate the start and end of the program.

In line 4, **"std::cout << "Hello, World!" << std::endl;"** uses the "cout" object from the iostream library to output the string "Hello, World!" to the console. The "**<<**" operator is used to insert the string into the output stream. The "**std::endl**" is used to insert a newline character after the string, so the next output will appear on a new line.

In line 5, "**return 0**" indicates that the program is complete by returning 0 to the operating system.

When we run the program, we get the message "**Hello World**", as shown below.

Output:

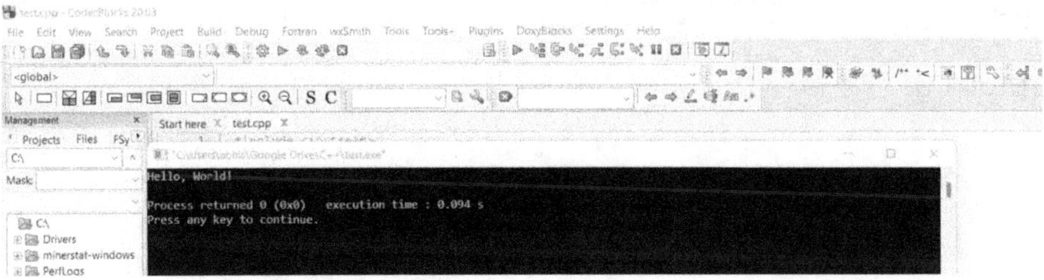

std::cout vs cout: Which One Do I Use?

Throughout the rest of the book, you will notice **std::cout** being used to print characters on the screen, instead of **cout**.

This is because **cout** is a member of the **std namespace**. If we don't use **std::cout** then there is a possibility of a naming conflict if other namespaces are used.

This is the same reason that we use **std::endl** instead of **endl**; and **std::string** instead of **string** in the rest of the book.

Program 2:

Program 2 is very similar to Program 1. Instead of printing out "Hello World", it prints out "Welcome to Coding in C++"

```
#include <iostream>


int main()
{
   std::cout << "Welcome to coding in C++" << std::endl;
   return 0;
}
```

The only difference is in line 5. The text between << and << is **"Welcome to Coding in C++".**

So, the code prints out "Welcome to Coding in C++"

Output:

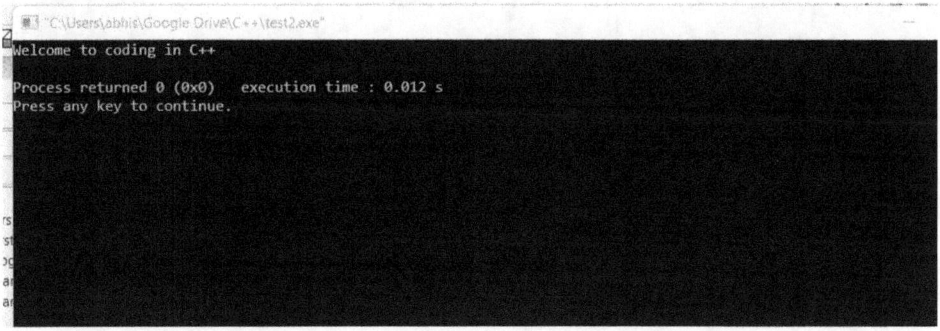

Problems to Practice

1. Write a program that prints your name on the screen.
2. Write a program that prints your name and age on the screen.

Variables

A variable is the most fundamental concept in programming.
It is basically a place to store a value. Think of it as a box where you can store something. In programming, you can store either a number, a string or a character.
A variable that can store a number is called an integer variable.
A variable that can store a string is called a string variable.
The value of a variable can change within a program. Variable in C++ are used to store and manipulate data.
In C++, we declare variables using the **var** command in iostream library.
Here's an example where we create a integer variable **num** and store the number 22 in it.

```
#include <iostream>

int main() {
    int num = 22;
    std::cout << "The value of variable num is: " << num << std::endl;
    return 0;
}
```

In line 4, **"int num=22"** creates an integer variable **num** and assigns it a value of **22**.

In line 5, we print the value of num. See output below.

```
"C:\Users\abhis\Google Drive\C++\var.exe"
The value of variable num is: 22

Process returned 0 (0x0)   execution time : 0.169 s
Press any key to continue.
```

Now, let's add a couple of lines to above program to change the value of the variable.

```
1  #include <iostream>
2
3  int main() {
4      int num = 22;
5      std::cout << "The value of variable num is: " << num << std::endl;
6      num = 55;
7      std::cout << "The new value of num is: " << num << std::endl;
8      return 0;
9  }
10
```

```
"C:\Users\abhis\Google Drive\C++\var.exe"
The value of variable num is: 22
The new value of num is: 55

Process returned 0 (0x0)   execution time : 0.053 s
Press any key to continue.
```

We add lines 6 and 7. In line 6, “num=55” changes the value of num to 55, and the new value of num now is 55. In line 6, we print the new value of num. See output below.

User Inputted Variable

The command **“cin”** from iostream library is used to accept an input from the user. It is shown below:

cin >> x

The above line accepts x as an input from the user.

The input can be used in a C++ program.

In the example below, we’ll prompt you to pick a number, and print the number on the screen.

```
1  #include <iostream>
2
3  int main() {
4      int yournumber;
5      std::cout << "Enter any number: ";
6      std::cin >> yournumber;
7      std::cout << "The number that you entered is: " << yournumber << std::endl;
8      return 0;
9  }
10
```

In line 5, we print the words **“Enter any number”** on the screen.

In line 6, you type in a number, and it stores it in the variable “**yournumber**”.

In the line 7, the number is printed on the screen.

See output below.

Output:

```
"C:\Users\abhis\Google Drive\C++\userinputvar.exe"
Enter any number: 78
The number that you entered is: 78

Process returned 0 (0x0)   execution time : 4.635 s
Press any key to continue.
```

User Input with 2 variables

In the next example, we'll accept two variables, one for a name and another for age, and print out both. **name** is a string variable and **age** is an integer variable.

```
1  #include <iostream>
2  #include <string>
3
4  int main() {
5      std::string id;
6      int age;
7
8      std::cout << "What's your name: ";
9      std::cin >> id;
10
11     std::cout << "How old are you?";
12     std::cin >> age;
13
14     std::cout << "You are " << id << " and your age is " << age << " years." << std::endl;
15     return 0;
16 }
17
```

In line 2 of above code, **"#include <string>"** allows you to use all string commands, including creation of string commands.
In line 5, we create a string variable called **id** to hold your name.
In line 7 and 8, you input your name and store it in the **id** variable.

In line 8 and 9, you store your age in the **age** variable.

Finally in line 14, we print out the name and age you entered; as shown in output below.

```
"C:\Users\abhis\Google Drive\C++\nameage.exe"
What's your name: Steven
How old are you?12
You are Steven and your age is 12 years.

Process returned 0 (0x0)   execution time : 10.363 s
Press any key to continue.
```

Problems to Practice

1. Write a program that creates two variables. The first variable holds your favorite color, and the second variable holds your name. Print out both your name and color in the same line.
2. Write a program that creates a variable that describes where you are going on your next vacation. Print out the variable on the screen.

Boolean Variables

A Boolean is a variable type that checks it a statement is true or false.
The Boolean contains either the value 'true' or 'false'.
It is declared as:
bool a = 'true'; or
bool a = 'false';
A 'true' value in C++ is output as 1 on the screen, while a 'false' value is output as 0.
It can also be assigned to a value through a statement:
bool a,b;
a = (5<7);
b = (9<0);
a is 'true'. When it is output on the screen, **a** returns a value of **1**, which stands for 'true' in C++.
b is false. When it is output on the screen, **b** returns a value of **0**, which stands for 'true' in C++.
Now, let's look at an example that defines this more clearly.

Boolean Example

In the code below, two integer variables **num1** and **num2** are assigned in lines 7-8. Two string variables are assigned in lines 9-10.

3 boolean variables a, b and c are declared in line 6.

Boolean variable **a** in line 11 checks if num1 is equal to num2. In line 14, it returns 0 if false and 1 if true.

Boolean variable **b** in line 12 checks if num1 is less than num2. In line 15, it returns 0 if false and 1 if true.

Boolean variable **c** in line 13 checks if str1 is equal to num2. In line 16, it returns 0 if false and 1 if true.

```
1  #include <iostream>
2
3  int main() {
4  int num1,num2;
5  std::string str1, str2;
6  bool a,b,c,d;
7  num1 = 7;
8  num2 = 10;
9  str1 = "Fear";
10 str2 = "Yell";
11 a = num1==num2;
12 b = num1<num2;
13 c= str1==str2;
14 std::cout << "Is num1 equal to num2? (1 for true and 0 for false) = " <<a << std::endl;
15 std::cout << "Is num1 less than num2? (1 for true and 0 for false) = " << b << std::endl;
16 std::cout << "Is str1 equal to str2? (1 for true and 0 for false) = " <<c << std::endl;
17 return 0;
18 }
19
```

Output

In the output below, **a** is false and returns 0 as **num1** is not equal to **num2**.

b is true and returns 1 as **num1** is less than **num2**.

c is false and returns 0 as **str1** is not equal to **str2**.

```
"C:\Users\abhis\Google Drive

Is num1 equal to num2? (1 for true and 0 for false) = 0
Is num1 less than num2? (1 for true and 0 for false) = 1
Is str1 equal to str2? (1 for true and 0 for false) = 0

Process returned 0 (0x0)   execution time : 0.043 s
Press any key to continue.
```

Problems to Practice

1. Write a program takes utilizes a Boolean variable to check if a student's grade is pass or fail. The pass mark is 60 out of a 100.

String Variables

A string variable is a variable types that holds only characters or a sequence of characters. It is part of the <string> C++ standard library. The <string> library is used to create and manipulate string variables; and it's accessed using the line below:

```
#include <string>
```

The variable is assigned as below:

```
string a = “xyz”;
```

The above line assigns the value “xyz” to string a.

You can change the string to a value of “bdc” using line below..

```
a=”bdc”;
```

Basic String Example

In our first example, the user inputs his name and it's stored in a string variable called name and the string variable is printed on the screen.

```
#include <iostream>
#include <string>

int main() {
    std::string name;
    std::cout << "What's your name? ";
    std::cin >> name;
    std::cout << "Hi, " << name << "!" << std::endl;
    return 0;
}

```

A string variable called **name** is declared on line 5.

In lines 6-7, the user enters his **name** into the string variable.

In line 8, the string variable is printed on the screen.

Output:

"C:\Users\abhis\Google Drive\C++\string_basic.exe"

```
What's your name? Tim
Hi, Tim!

Process returned 0 (0x0)   execution time : 1.987 s
Press any key to continue.
```

In example above, the user enters his name as Tim.

Tim is stored in variable **name** and printed on the screen.

Joining Strings

Strings in C++ can be joined together by using the '+' operator.

In the below example, the user inputs two strings and combines them into a single larger string variable. The combined string is printed on the screen.

```
1  #include <iostream>
2  #include <string>
3
4  int main() {
5      std::string string1;
6      std::string string2;
7
8      std::cout << "Enter the first string: ";
9      std::cin >> string1;
10
11     std::cout << "Enter the second string: ";
12     std::cin >> string2;
13
14     std::string combstring = string1 + string2;
15     std::cout << "The joined string is: " << combstring << std::endl
16
17     return 0;
18 }
19
```

Two string variables, **string1** and **string2** are created in lines 5 and 6.

In Lines 8-9, the user inputs the 1st string and it's stored in string variable **string1**.

In Lines 11-12, the user inputs the 2nd string and it's stored in string variable **string2**.

In Line 13, the two strings are joined together and combined in string variable **combstring**. **combstring** is printed to the screen in Line 14.

Output:

```
"C:\Users\abhis\Google Drive\C++\Double_Strings.exe"
Enter the first string: abc
Enter the second string: xyz
The joined string is: abcxyz

Process returned 0 (0x0)   execution time : 4.223 s
Press any key to continue.
```

The user inputs the first string as **'abc'**; and the 2nd string as **'xyz'**.

The combined string is '**abcxyz'**, which is stored in variable **combstring** and printed on the screen.

Length of string

In C++, the length of a string is calculated using the getline and length functions. In the below code, the user enters a string and the program outputs the length of the string.

```
1   #include <iostream>
2   #include <string>
3
4   int main() {
5       std::string string1;
6
7       std::cout << "Enter the string: ";
8       std::getline(std::cin, string1);
9
10
11      std::cout << "The length of the string is: " << string1.length() << std::endl;
12
13
14
15      return 0;
16  }
17
```

In the program in line 8, the user enters the string using getline.

The reason we use getline instead of a normal cin prompt is that getline takes into account all spaces that are in the string. If we just use cin, the string stops at the first space, and we get an incorrect length.

In line 11, the string is printed on the screen as shown in output below, using **string1.length()**.

Output:

In the output below, the user enters the string **"I won the race"** and it is stored in string1. The **getline** function gets the entire length of the string and the **string1.length()** prints the length as **14**.

If we used **cin** instead of getline, then we get a length of 1 as the first space starts after 1 letter.

"C:\Users\abhis\Google Drive\C++\String_length.exe"

```
Enter the string: I won the race
The length of the string is: 14

Process returned 0 (0x0)   execution time : 3.240 s
Press any key to continue.
```

Substrings

In C++, a substring is a portion of a larger string. The location of the substring is found using the find() function. In below code, the program accepts two strings as input. It then looks to find the location of the smaller string in the larger one. The location is called the index of the string, which is the position within the string.

```
1  #include <iostream>
2  #include <string>
3
4  int main() {
5      std::string string1, substring;
6      std::cout << "Enter the main string: ";
7      std::getline(std::cin, string1);
8      std::cout << "Enter the substring to be found: ";
9      std::getline(std::cin, substring);
10
11     int index = string1.find(substring);
12     if (index >=0) {
13         std::cout << "The substring \"" << substring << "\" was found at index " << index << " in the main string." << std::endl;
14     } else {
15         std::cout << "The substring \"" << substring << "\" was not found in the main string." << std::endl;
16     }
17
18     return 0;
19 }
20
```

In the example, the user enters the longer string in lines 5-6. The string is stored in string variable **string1**.

In Lines 7-8, the program accepts the 2nd smaller string, and stores it in the variable **substring**.

In line 11, the program finds the position of the substring within the main string using the main function. The position is stored in an integer variable called **index**. If the substring is not found, it returns a value of **-1** for index.

The program then prints out the value index if it is greater than or equal to 0. If it is less than 0, then the program outputs that the substring was not found.

Output:

```
"C:\Users\abhis\Google Drive\C++\substring.exe"
Enter the main string: I won the game
Enter the substring to be found: won
The substring "won" was found at index 2 in the main string.

Process returned 0 (0x0)   execution time : 8.172 s
Press any key to continue.
```

In above example, substring **won** is found at index 2 in the main string **“I won the game”**.

```
"C:\Users\abhis\Google Drive\C++\substring.exe"
Enter the main string: I won the game
Enter the substring to be found: lost
The substring "lost" was not found in the main string.

Process returned 0 (0x0)   execution time : 4.873 s
Press any key to continue.
```

In above example output, substring **lost** is not found in the main string **“I won the game”**, so index is **-1**. Substring was not found.

Replace Strings

In C++, you can also replace certain words within a string. This is done using a function called **insert()**. In the code below, the program accepts two user inputs as string variables, **string1** and **substr**. **String1** is the larger string and **substr** is the string we want to insert within the string. The program then accepts an integer variable called **index**. This is the location within the string that we want to insert the substring.

```
1  #include <iostream>
2  #include <string>
3
4  int main() {
5      std::string string1, substr;
6      int index;
7      std::cout << "Enter the main string: ";
8      std::getline(std::cin, string1);
9      std::cout << "Enter the substring to be inserted: ";
10     std::getline(std::cin, substr);
11     std::cout << "Enter the index location at which the substring should be inserted: ";
12     std::cin >> index;
13
14     string1.insert(index, substr);
15     std::cout << "The new string is: " << string1 << std::endl;
16
17     return 0;
18 }
19
```

In line 14, **substr** is inserted into **string1** at index location. The new string **string1** is printed out in line 15.

Output:

```
"C:\Users\abhis\Google Drive\C++\strreplace.exe"

Enter the main string: Cakes, sugar and tea
Enter the substring to be inserted: the
Enter the index location at which the substring should be inserted: 14
The new string is: Cakes, sugar athend tea

Process returned 0 (0x0)   execution time : 57.674 s
Press any key to continue.
```

In the sample output, the main string string 1 is **"Cakes, sugar and tea"**. The substring is **"the"** When the substring is inserted at index 14, we get **"Cakes, sugar atthend tea".**

Address

The below code is a good application of strings. Strings are used to get all elements of an address and print it out. The first line, second line, city, state, zip code and country are all entered as separate variables and printed on the screen. The inputs are entered in lines 6-17, and the outputs are printed out in lines 19-25.

A sample of the output is shown on the output below.

```
1   #include <iostream>
2   #include <string>
3
4   int main() {
5       std::string street1, street2, city, state, zip, country;
6       std::cout << "Enter first line of the street address: ";
7       std::getline(std::cin, street1);
8       std::cout << "Enter second line of the street address: ";
9       std::getline(std::cin, street2);
10      std::cout << "Enter the city: ";
11      std::getline(std::cin, city);
12      std::cout << "Enter the state: ";
13      std::getline(std::cin, state);
14      std::cout << "Enter the country: ";
15      std::getline(std::cin, country);
16      std::cout << "Enter the zip code: ";
17      std::getline(std::cin, zip);
18
19      std::cout << "Address: " << std::endl;
20      std::cout << street1 <<", " <<  std::endl;
21      std::cout << street2 <<", " <<  std::endl;
22      std::cout << city << ", " << std::endl;
23      std::cout << state << " - ";
24      std::cout << zip << ". " << std::endl;
25      std::cout << country << std::endl;
26      return 0;
27  }
28
```

Output:

```
"C:\Users\abhis\Google Drive\C++\address.exe"
Enter first line of the street address: 11
Enter second line of the street address: Smith Avenue
Enter the city: Chicago
Enter the state: Illinois
Enter the country: USA
Enter the zip code: 61122
Address:
11,
Smith Avenue,
Chicago,
Illinois - 61122.
USA

Process returned 0 (0x0)   execution time : 39.309 s
Press any key to continue.
```

Replace a Phrase

In C++, you can replace certain letters within a string with another string. This is done using the **replace()** function. In the below code, the program accepts three string variables as input. The first variable, **str**, is the main string. The second variable is called **phrase**, and it is the phrase that needs to be replaced. The third variable is called **new_phrase**, and it is the phrase that replaces the old one in **str**.

```
1   #include <iostream>
2   #include <string>
3
4   int main() {
5       std::string str, phrase, new_phrase;
6       std::cout << "Enter the main string: ";
7       std::getline(std::cin, str);
8       std::cout << "Enter the phrase to be replaced: ";
9       std::getline(std::cin, phrase);
10      std::cout << "Enter the new phrase: ";
11      std::getline(std::cin, new_phrase);
12
13      std::size_t index = str.find(phrase);
14      while (index <str.length()) {
15          str.replace(index, phrase.length(), new_phrase);
16          index = str.find(phrase, index + new_phrase.length());
17      }
18      std::cout << "The new string is: " << str << std::endl;
19
20      return 0;
21  }
22
```

In Line 13, the program checks if the phrase is located in **str** using the **find** function. It stores the index in an integer variable called **index**.

In Line 14, the program creates a while loop that runs while the **index** is smaller than the length of **str**. This is to ensure that all instances of phrase are found in **str**.

The first line in the loop in Line 15 replaces the **phrase** with **new_phrase** at the index. This **index** is the location of the phrase within str.

In Line 16, the program checks if there are any indexes within str that has the string variable phrase. If yes, the while loop continues till the entire string is checked.

Output:

```
"C:\Users\abhis\Google Drive\C++\phrase_replace.exe"
Enter the main string: the fox ate the hen yesterday
Enter the phrase to be replaced: the
Enter the new phrase: a
The new string is: a fox ate a hen yesterday

Process returned 0 (0x0)   execution time : 18.697 s
Press any key to continue.
```

In the above sample output, str is **"the fox ate the hen yesterday"**. Phrase is **"the",** and new phrase is **"a"**. So the program replaces every "the" with "a"; and we see that in the new output **"a fox ate a hen yesterday"**.

Problems to Practice

1. Write a program that accepts a 10-letter word from the user. If the length is 10, print out the words. Otherwise, print an error message.
2. Write a program that takes in 2 names as string variables and print out a sentence that combines the two names.
3. Write a program that takes in 5 string variables from a job candidate that store the candidate's name, occupation, zip code, salary and educational qualification. Print out all the information like a mini resume.
4. Write a program that takes in a sentence as an input and replaces all instances of curse words with ****
5. Write a program that finds the index of all instances of the word "help" in a sentence.

Conditionals

A conditional is a method to compare variables, and to make decisions in programming. It is a significant part of C++ programming. They are used to control the flow of the program and to respond to different situations.

The if else statement is the most commonly most conditional in C++. It's defined as below...

```
If (a==b)
{
//code 1
}
Else
{
//code 2
}
```

In the above code, it checks if the variable a is equal to variable b. If they are equal, then it executes code 1, else it executes code 2.

Let's look at a C++ example below.

If Else Example 1

```
1   #include <iostream>
2
3   int main() {
4       int a = 8;
5       int b = 15;
6       std::cout << " a = 8 "<< std::endl;
7       std::cout << " b = 15 "<< std::endl;
8       if (a > b) {
9           std::cout << "a is greater than b" << std::endl;
10      } else if (a < b) {
11          std::cout << "a is less than b" << std::endl;
12      } else {
13          std::cout << "a is equal to b" << std::endl;
14      }
15
16      return 0;
17  }
18
```

In line 4 and 5, it sets the values of variables a and b to 8 and 15 respectively. In lines 6 and 7, it prints the values on to the screen. In line 8, it checks if the value of a is greater than b. If so, it executes the code in brackets between lines 8 and 10.

If a is less than b, it executes the code in brackets between 10 and 12.

If neither of the above two conditions are true, it means that a=b, and it executes the code in brackets between lines 12 and 14.

Output:

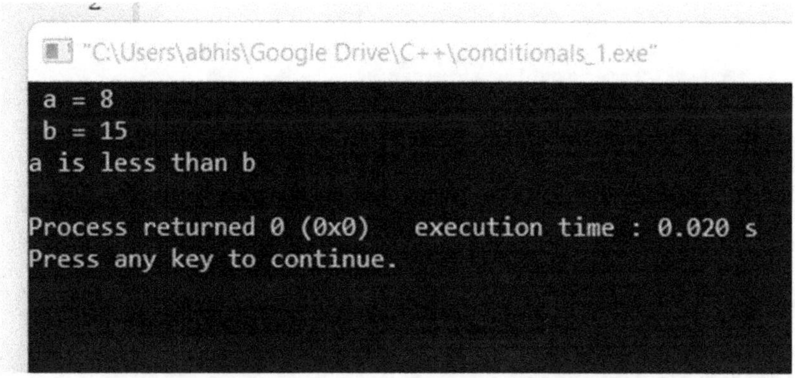

In the output, it executes code between lines 8 and 10, as **a is less than b.**

If Else Example 1

In the next example, the program accepts value of two variables as inputs from the user; and it prints out the larger number using conditionals.

In lines 6,7 it accepts the value of the first number and stores it in integer variable **a**.

In lines 8,9 it accepts the value of the second number and stores it in integer variable **b**.

```
1   #include <iostream>
2
3   int main() {
4       int a, b;
5
6       std::cout << "Enter the first number: ";
7       std::cin >> a;
8
9       std::cout << "Enter the second number: ";
10      std::cin >> b;
11
12      if (a > b) {
13          std::cout << "The larger number is: " << a << std::endl;
14      } else if (a<b){
15          std::cout << "The larger number is: " << b << std::endl;
16      } else {
17          std::cout << "Both numbers are equal" << std::endl;
18      }
19
20      return 0;
21  }
```

In line 12, it checks if the value of a is greater than b. If so, it executes the code in brackets between lines 12 and 14.

If a is less than b, it executes the code in brackets between 14 and 16.

If neither of the above two conditions are true, it means that a=b, and it executes the code in brackets between lines 16 and 18.

Output:

"C:\Users\abhis\Google Drive\C++\conditionals_2.exe"

```
Enter the first number: 10
Enter the second number: 8
The larger number is: 10

Process returned 0 (0x0)   execution time : 4.904 s
Press any key to continue.
```

In the output for above example, the user enters 10 and 8 as the first and second numbers.

It executes code between lines 12 and 14, as **a is greater than b.** It prints out **10** as the larger number.

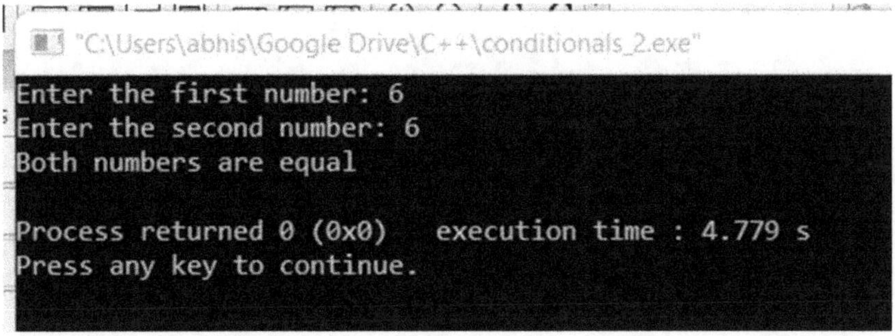

In the next example, the user enters 6 for both numbers. The program executes code between 16-18, and prints out that both numbers are equal.

If Then Example 3

In this example, the user guesses a number between 1 and 10. The if statement checks if it is equal to a randomly generated number.

If it is the same, then the program outputs a congratulation message. Otherwise, it says that you guessed wrong.

```
1   #include <iostream>
2   #include <cstdlib>
3   #include <ctime>
4
5   int main() {
6       int secret, guess;
7       secret = rand() % 10 + 1;
8       std::cout << "Guess a number between 1 and 10: ";
9       std::cin>>guess;
10          if (guess == secret) {
11              std::cout << "Congratulations! You guessed the number!" << std::endl;
12          } else{
13              std::cout << "Wrong! The correct number is " << secret << std::endl;
14          }
15      return 0;
16  }
17
```

In line 7, the program uses **rand()** function to generate a random number between 1 and 10. The random number is stored in an integer variable called **secret**.

In line 8-9, the program accepts a user input integer variable called **guess**.

The If condition in line 10 checks if the guess variable is equal to secret. If the condition is true, then it executes line 10-12. Otherwise, it executes line 12-14.

Output:

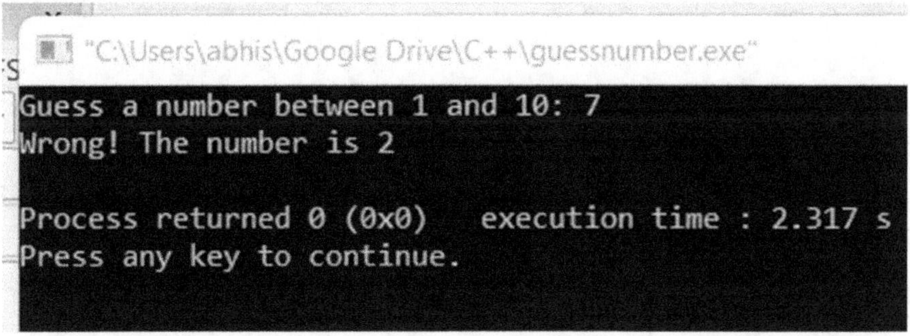

In the example output above, the random number secret generated is 2. The user guesses 7, so it executes line 12 -14 and prints out that you generated the wrong number.

Math Quiz with Conditionals

In below example, the program asks the user what the answer to two match problems are. It then checks whether the answers are correct using if conditionals. If the answer is correct, it prints out that the answer is correct, otherwise it tells the user that the answer is incorrect.

```
1   #include <iostream>
2   #include <cstdlib>
3   #include <ctime>
4
5   int main() {
6           int answer;
7           // Problem 1
8           std::cout << "Problem 1 "<< std::endl;
9           std::cout << "What is 7 + 10? ";
10          std::cin >> answer;
11
12          if (answer == 17)
13          {
14              std::cout << "Correct!" << std::endl;
15          } else {
16              std::cout << "Incorrect. The correct answer is " << 17 << std::endl;
17          }
18
19          int answer2;
20          // Problem 2
21          std::cout << "Problem 2 "<< std::endl;
22          std::cout << "What is 14 * 3? ";
23          std::cin >> answer2;
24
25          if (answer2 == 42)
26          {
27              std::cout << "Correct!" << std::endl;
28          } else {
29              std::cout << "Incorrect. The correct answer is " << 42 << std::endl;
30          }
31
32
33      return 0;
34  }
35
```

In lines 8-10, the program prints the question in problem 1 and gets the user to input the answer in integer variable **answer**. In line 12, it checks if the **answer** is 17. If the answer is correct, it prints out “Correct”, otherwise it prints out “Incorrect. The answer is 17.”

The exact same process is done for problem 2 between lines 21-30.

Output:

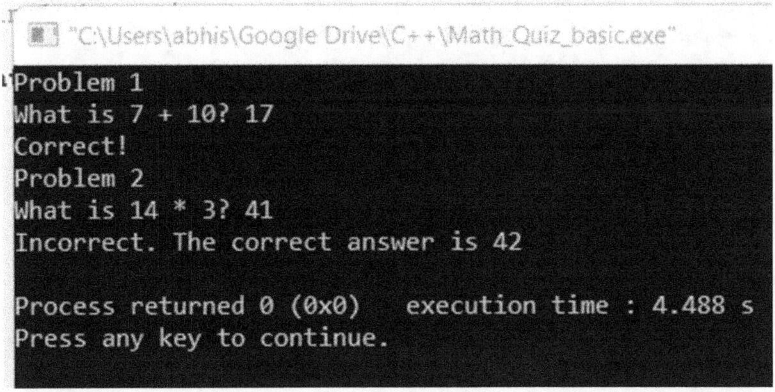

In output below, the user gets the first answer correct.

The second answer is wrong as he guesses 41 instead of 42.

Math Quiz with Random Numbers

The above program is modified to use random variables, and have the user guess the answer.

```
1  #include <iostream>
2  #include <cstdlib>
3  #include <ctime>
4
5  int main() {
6      int score = 0;
7      int sum1, sum2,diff1,diff2, answer;
8
9          sum1 = rand() % 100 + 1;
10         sum2 = rand() % 100 + 1;
11
12         std::cout << "What is " << sum1 << " + " << sum2 << "? ";
13         std::cin >> answer;
14
15         if (answer == sum1 + sum2)
16         {
17             std::cout << "Correct!" << std::endl;
18             score++;
19         } else {
20             std::cout << "Incorrect. The correct answer is " << sum1 + sum2 << std::endl;
21         }
22
23         diff1 = rand() % 100 + 1;
24         diff2 = rand() % 100 + 1;
25
26         std::cout << "What is " << diff1 << " - " << diff2 << "? ";
27         std::cin >> answer;
28
29         if (answer == diff1 - diff2)
30         {
31             std::cout << "Correct!" << std::endl;
32             score++;
33         } else {
34             std::cout << "Incorrect. The correct answer is " << diff1 - diff2 << std::endl;
35         }
36
37     return 0;
38 }
39
```

In this program, two random numbers between 1 to 100 are generated and stored in variables **sum1** and **sum2**; as seen in lines 9-10.

The user is then asked to find the answer to the sum of the two above variables, and the input is stored in integer variable **answer** in line 13. An if condition is used to check if the **answer** is correct in line 15. If the answer is correct, the program prints out "**Correct**", as in line 17. Otherwise, it prints out "**Incorrect**" And notifies the user of the correct answer is line 20.

The exact same process is done again with two new random integer variables **diff1** and **diff2**. This time the user is asked to input the difference of the two variables and the answer is checked again with another if condition.

Output:

```
"C:\Users\abhis\Google Drive\C++\Math_squiz.exe"
What is 42 + 68? 100
Incorrect. The correct answer is 110
What is 35 - 1? 34
Correct!

Process returned 0 (0x0)   execution time : 9.792 s
Press any key to continue.
```

In answer below, the two random variables sum1 and sum2 are 42 and 68. The user inputs 100 instead of 110 as the sum and so the user gets an incorrect answer.

In the second question, the two variables diff1 and diff2 are 35 and 1 respectively. The user inputs the correct answer of 34 and so gets a "Correct!" message.

Switch Case

Switch Case is another way of using conditionals in C++. It basically checks a variable's value using **switch** and then chooses among a bunch of **cases** based on the switch that happened. The program executes the **case** that is chosen. It's defined as below.

```
Switch (var)
{
Case 1: //code A
Case 2: //code B
Case 3: //code C
}
```

In the above example, it executes code A if **var** is equal to 1; code B if **var** is equal to 2 and code C if **var** is equal to 3.

Switch Case Example

In below example, a user inputs the month as a number from 1-12. Based on the number input, it chooses a month using switch case.

In line 6-7, the user inputs a number, and it is stored in variable **month**.

In line 8, switch is applied to variable month.

Based on the input number, it executes code in corresponding case. For example, if variable is 3 it executes code between line 15 and 17. In these lines, string variable **monthName** is assigned to **March**. **break** in line 17 function exits the switch loop.

```
#include <iostream>
#include <string>
int main() {
    int month;
    std::string monthName;
    std::cout << "Enter a number for the month (1-12): ";
    std::cin >> month;
    switch (month) {
        case 1:
            monthName = "January";
            break;
        case 2:
            monthName = "February";
            break;
        case 3:
            monthName = "March";
            break;
        case 4:
            monthName = "April";
            break;
        case 5:
            monthName = "May";
            break;
        case 6:
            monthName = "June";
            break;
        case 7:
            monthName = "July";
            break;
        case 8:
            monthName = "August";
            break;
```

```
33          case 9:
34              monthName = "September";
35              break;
36          case 10:
37              monthName = "October";
38              break;
39          case 11:
40              monthName = "November";
41              break;
42          case 12:
43              monthName = "December";
44              break;
45          default:
46              monthName = "Invalid month";
47      }
48
49      std::cout << monthName << std::endl;
50      return 0;
51  }
52
```

If numbers between 1-12 are not chosen, the code executed is default: which is between 45 and 47. MonthName is **"Invalid Month"**.

In lines 49 and 50, the code prints out the month name.

Output:

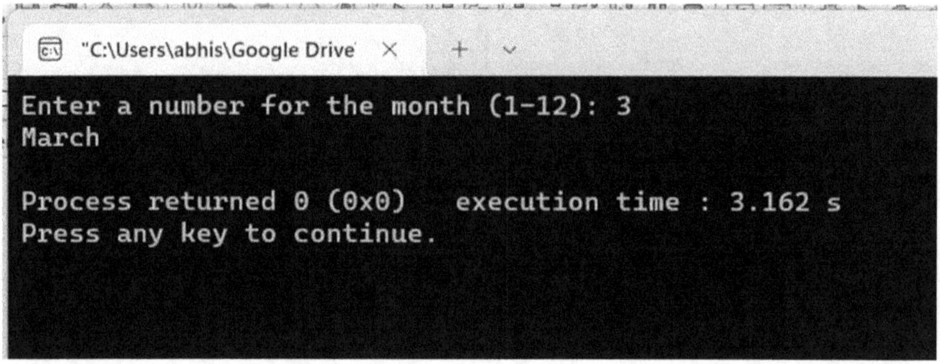

In above example code, user chooses 3 and it executes code between line 15 and 17. string variable **monthName** is assigned to **March**. It prints out **March** as shown above.

Problems to Practice

1. Write a program takes in a number and checks if it's positive, negative or zero.
2. Write a program that takes in a number and checks if it's even or odd (check remainder when divided by 2).
3. Write a program that has a user choose between 10 brands of car at an auto dealership and prints out the brand and price based on the choice that the user makes.

Loops

A loop is a repetition of commands within a program a certain number of times. Every repetition is called an iteration of the loop.

Let's say you are looking to print out your name 1000 times. One option is to just write `cout << "My name is xyz"` and do it a 1000 times. That would take you at least about 10 minutes at least to copy and paste. It also takes a decent amount of memory space and is a lot of lines of codes.

The better option is to use loops as below:

```
for (int i=1; i<1000;i++)
{
std::cout<<"My name is xyz";
}
```

The loop is declared above with the counter variable **i=1**. It executes code between the brackets while **i** is less than 1000. And it increments by 1 each time; thus printing "**My name is xyz**" 1000 times.

Loops Example 1

In the first example below, the program prints out all numbers between 1 and 20.

```
1  #include <iostream>
2
3  int main() {
4      for (int i = 1; i <= 20; i++) {
5          std::cout << i << " "<< std::endl;
6      }
7      return 0;
8  }
9
```

In line 4, the loop is declared above with the counter variable i=1. It executes code between the brackets while i is less than and equal to 20. Between the brackets in lines 4-6, it prints the value of counter variable i. So, it prints all the values of i while it increments by 1 between 1 and 20.

This is seen in output below.

Output:

```
"C:\Users\abhis\Google Drive\C++\fornext.exe"
1
2
3
4
5
6
7
8
9
10
11
12
13
14
15
16
17
18
19
20

Process returned 0 (0x0)   execution time : 0.024 s
Press any key to continue.
```

Loops Example 2

In below example, the user is asked to enter a number and it prints all the numbers between 1 and that number. In lines 5-6, the user inputs an integer variable **looplength**.

```
1   #include <iostream>
2
3   int main() {
4       int looplength;
5       std::cout << "Enter how many numbers to print (starting at 1): ";
6       std::cin>>looplength;
7       for (int i = 1; i <= looplength; i++) {
8           std::cout << i << " "<< std::endl;
9       }
10      return 0;
11  }
12
```

In line 7, the loop integer variable **i** is set between 1 and **looplength** and increments by 1. Inside the loop, the program prints the value of loop integer variable **i**.

As seen in output below, the user inputs a **looplength** value of 15. So, the program prints integers between 1 and 15.

Output:

"C:\Users\abhis\Google Drive\C++\looplength.exe"

```
Enter how many numbers to print (starting 0): 15
1
2
3
4
5
6
7
8
9
10
11
12
13
14
15

Process returned 0 (0x0)   execution time : 2.941 s
Press any key to continue.
```

While Loop

The while condition is another type of loop which the code executes while a certain condition is met.

In example below, the loop code within the brackets executes while i is less than and equal to 20. The loop variable is declared outside the loop as **i=1**. It increments inside the loop while printing value of **i** inside as well.

```
#include <iostream>

int main() {
    int i = 1;
    while (i <= 20) {
        std::cout << i << std::endl;
        i++;
    }
    return 0;
}
```

As seen in output below, it prints all integers between 1 and 20.

Output:

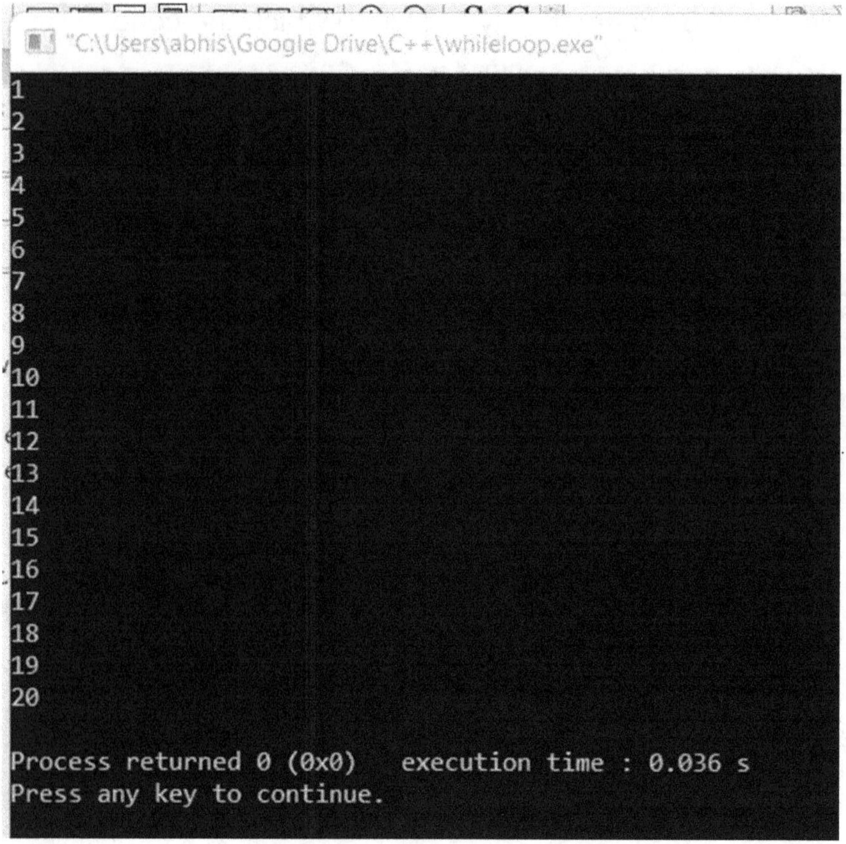
"C:\Users\abhis\Google Drive\C++\whileloop.exe"
1
2
3
4
5
6
7
8
9
10
11
12
13
14
15
16
17
18
19
20
Process returned 0 (0x0)   execution time : 0.036 s
Press any key to continue.

Math Quiz with Random Numbers in a Loop

This program is similar to the "Math Quiz with Random Numbers" program in the **conditionals** chapter. Make sure that you understand the program before looking at this. The program basically accepts two random numbers as inputs and calculates their sum. The user guesses the answer; and the program prints an output based on the answer.

The program below is similar, but it uses a for loop to repeat the process 5 times. 5 different sets of random numbers are generated in lines 9-10 and stored in **num1** and **num2** during each iteration of the loop. An integer variable **score**, declared in line 7, keeps track of the correct answers by the user.

In lines 12-13, the user inputs an **answer** for their sum. In lines 15-21, the program checks if the sum is correct. If the answer is correct, it congratulates the user and **adds 1 to the score variable**. Otherwise, it tells the user what the correct answer.

It repeats the process 5 times in total and prints out user **score** (number of correct answers).

```
#include <iostream>
#include <cstdlib>
#include <ctime>

int main() {
        int num1, num2, answer;
        int score = 0;
        for (int i = 0; i < 5; i++) {
         num1 = rand() % 100 + 1;
         num2 = rand() % 100 + 1;

         std::cout << "What is " << num1 << " + " << num2 << "? ";
         std::cin >> answer;

         if (answer == num1 + num2)
         {
             std::cout << "Correct!" << std::endl;
             score++;
         } else {
             std::cout << "Incorrect. The correct answer is " << num1 + num2 << std::endl;
         }

        }
        std::cout << "Your final score is " << score << "/5" << std::endl;
    return 0;
}
```

Output:

```
"C:\Users\abhis\Google Drive\C++\Math_Quiz_Random_Loop.exe"

What is 42 + 68? 110
Correct!
What is 35 + 1? 36
Correct!
What is 70 + 25? 95
Correct!
What is 79 + 59? 138
Correct!
What is 63 + 65? 128
Correct!
Your final score is 5/5

Process returned 0 (0x0)   execution time : 13.823 s
Press any key to continue.
```

In the above example, the user gets all correct answers, so the score variable gets to 5 and the final score is 5 out of 5.

Problems to Practice

1. Write a program that takes in two random numbers and has a user guess their product. Print out whether the user got the answer correct. Do this 5 times in a FOR loop and print out how many correct answers the user got.
2. Write a program that takes in two random whole numbers and figures out which number is higher. Divide the higher number by the lower number and have the user guess the remainder. Print out whether the user got the answer correct. Do this 5 times in a FOR loop and print out how many correct answers the user got.
3. Write a guessing game where the user has to guess a randomly generated number between 1 and 100. If the number is too high, say "too high", otherwise say it's "too low". Keep doing this till the user guesses correctly (Hint: use a while loop).

Timers and Clocks

Timers and clocks in C++ are mechanisms to find the amount of elapsed time between the start and end of a certain event.
This is great for performance analysis, gaming, animations, alarm clocks and optimization.
Several different libraries are used for different types of timers, such as <unistd>,<ctime>,<chrono> etc.

Countdown Clock
In the first example, we'll go through the **sleep()** function which is a sort of countdown clock. The sleep function pauses the program for a certain number of seconds.
The sleep function is part of the **<unistd.h>** library, which is invoked in Line 2 of below program.
The program below, in lines 6-7, accepts an integer variable **timetoalarm**, which holds the number of seconds the program is to pause.
In Line 9, the program invokes the sleep function. It pauses the program for **timetoalarm** seconds.
In Line 10, the program prints an output to the program which indicates that the sleep function has elapsed.

```
#include <iostream>
#include <unistd.h>

int main() {
    int timetoalarm;
    std::cout << "Enter the time for the alert (in seconds): ";
    std::cin >> timetoalarm;
    std::cout << "Timer set for " << timetoalarm << " seconds." << std::endl;
    sleep(timetoalarm);
    std::cout << timetoalarm<< " seconds over!" << std::endl;
    return 0;
}
```

Output:

In the code below, you will notice a pause of 6 seconds before the text "6 seconds over!" is printed on the screen.

```
"C:\Users\abhis\Google Drive\C++\Timer.exe"
Enter the time for the alert (in seconds): 6
Timer set for 6 seconds.
6 seconds over!

Process returned 0 (0x0)   execution time : 8.835 s
Press any key to continue.
```

Get Current Date and Time

In C++, we can get the information about the current date and time using the **time** and **localtime** function.

The code below prints today's date and time to the output screen. It uses the time function from the **<ctime library>** which is invoked in line 2.

In line 5, a **time_t** variable called **cTime** is assigned to the current time using the time function.

In line 6, the **localtime** function converts **cTime** into a **localtime** variable. This broken down **localtime** variable has year, month, day information that can be printed on the screen.

In lines 8-14, the different components of the **localtime** variable are printed on the screen. (Note that the year needs to have 1900 added to it, as the program only detects how many years past 1900 have passed. For example, if the date is 2020; the program would output 120. We need to add 1900 to ensure the correct date. For the same reason, the number 1 needs to be added to the month.)

```
1   #include <iostream>
2   #include <ctime>
3
4   int main() {
5       std::time_t cTime = std::time(nullptr);
6       std::tm* localtime = std::localtime(&cTime);
7
8       std::cout << "Today's date and time:" << std::endl;
9       std::cout << "Year: " << localtime->tm_year + 1900 << std::endl;
10      std::cout << "Month: " << localtime->tm_mon + 1 << std::endl;
11      std::cout << "Day: " << localtime->tm_mday << std::endl;
12      std::cout << "Hour: " << localtime->tm_hour << std::endl;
13      std::cout << "Minute: " << localtime->tm_min << std::endl;
14      std::cout << "Second: " << localtime->tm_sec << std::endl;
15
16      return 0;
17  }
18
```

Output:

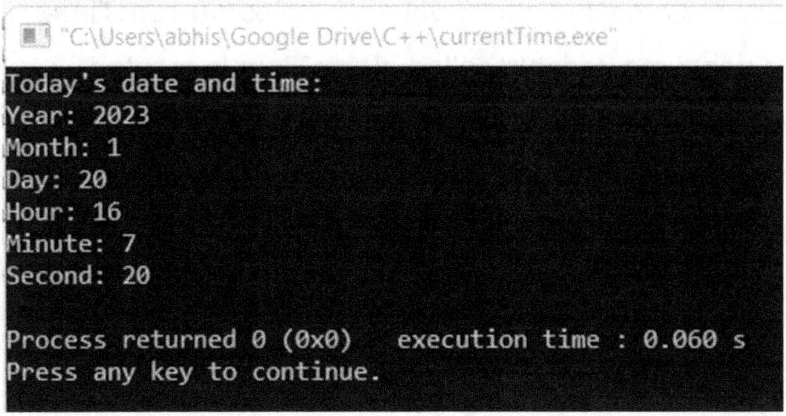

Alarm clock

An alarm clock is set to activate an alert at a particular date and time. There is no specific alarm clock in C++. However, in the program below, we use the **localtime** and **sleep** function to make an alarm clock. We use the **localtime** function to determine the difference in time between current time and alarm clock time; and then we use the sleep function to pause the program till alarm time.

The program uses functions from **<unistd.h>** and **<ctime>** which are invoked in lines 2-3 of the program.

In lines 7-10, the program accepts user input for hour and minute of time. In this program, we are doing an alarm within the same day as we don't want to keep the program running for multiple days.

In Lines 13-17, **time** and **localtime** functions are used to get the current time and stores it in a time variable called **currentTime**.

In Line 20, a new time variable called **alarmTime** is created which stores the time of the alarm.

In line 21, the program calculates the difference between **alarmTime** and **localtime** and stores it in a time variable called **timeUntilAlarm**.

In Line 26, the line uses the **sleep** function to pause the program till the alarm clock time.

In line 28, the program prints an output to the screen which indicates that it's time for the alarm.

```
1   #include <iostream>
2   #include <ctime>
3   #include <unistd.h>
4
5   int main() {
6       int ahour, aminute;
7       std::cout << "Enter the hour for the alarm (between 0-23): ";
8       std::cin >> ahour;
9       std::cout << "Enter the minute for the alarm (between 0-59): ";
10      std::cin >> aminute;
11
12      // Get current time
13      std::time_t currentTime = std::time(nullptr);
14      std::tm* localTime = std::localtime(&currentTime);
15      localTime->tm_hour = ahour;
16      localTime->tm_min = aminute;
17      localTime->tm_sec = 0;
18
19      // Calculate time until alarm
20      std::time_t alarmTime = std::mktime(localTime);
21      std::time_t timeUntilAlarm = alarmTime - currentTime;
22
23      std::cout << "Alarm set for " << ahour << ":" << aminute << "." << std::endl;
24      std::cout << "Time until alarm: " << timeUntilAlarm << " seconds." << std::endl;
25
26      sleep(timeUntilAlarm);
27
28      std::cout << "It's alarm time!" << std::endl;
29      return 0;
30  }
31
```

Output:

```
"C:\Users\abhis\Google Drive\C++\alarmclock.exe"

Enter the hour for the alarm (between 0-23): 16
Enter the minute for the alarm (between 0-59): 15
Alarm set for 16:15.
Time until alarm: 0 seconds.
It's alarm time!

Process returned 0 (0x0)   execution time : 4.976 s
Press any key to continue.
```

Stopwatch

A stopwatch in C++ is used to determine the amount of time elapsed between two events. Both events occur by pressing "Enter" on the keyboard. The stopwatch uses a function called **cin.get()** to detect when "Enter" is pressed on the keyword, to start and stop the clock.

It records the start time using **chrono::high_resolution_clock::now()** the first time the user presses enter. The stopwatch is now running. Now, the user presses enter again to stop the clock. The program records the end time. It computes the elapsed time between the start and end times as a duration in milliseconds using **chrono::duration_cast<std::chrono::milliseconds>(end - begin)**.

The output from chrono function is in milliseconds, so it has to be divided by 1000 before being output on the screen.

```cpp
#include <iostream>
#include <chrono>

int main() {
    std::cout << "Press Enter to Start the Clock." << std::endl;
    std::cin.get();

    auto begin = std::chrono::high_resolution_clock::now();

    std::cout << "Press Enter to stop the stopwatch." << std::endl;
    std::cin.get();

    auto end = std::chrono::high_resolution_clock::now();
    auto tme = std::chrono::duration_cast<std::chrono::milliseconds>(end - begin);

    std::cout << "Elapsed time: " << tme.count()/1000 << " seconds." << std::endl;
    return 0;
}

```

Output:

```
"C:\Users\abhis\Google Drive\C++\stopwatch.exe"
Press Enter to Start the Clock.

Press Enter to stop the stopwatch.

Elapsed time: 6 seconds.

Process returned 0 (0x0)   execution time : 8.073 s
Press any key to continue.
```

Problems to Practice

1. Write a program that takes in a person's name, birth month and birth date and prints all on the screen.
2. Write a program that takes in a person's birthday and calculates the number of days to the person's birthday.
3. Write a program that creates a timer for an athletic meet. It starts the timer when the race starts and stops when the race ends. Print out the time taken for the winner. (Basically, a stopwatch that stops when the first person crosses the line)

Doing Math with C++

The high processing capabilities of C++ make it the ideal programming language to complete all kinds of computations, from kindergarten Math problems to industry level computations.
In this chapter, we'll go over a few commonly used C++ internal math functions; and a few others that are not well known but very useful as well.
In all the programs in this chapter, we invoke the **cmath** library by using the line: **#include <cmath>**

Round Numbers

C++ has the ability to round decimal numbers to the nearest whole number. We use a function called **round()** function to achieve this.
This is shown in the example below:

```
1     #include <iostream>
2     #include <cmath>
3
4
5     int main() {
6         float dnum;
7         std::cout << "Enter a decimal number: ";
8         std::cin >> dnum;
9
10        std::cout << "Rounded to nearest whole number: " << round(dnum) << std::endl;
11
12        return 0;
13    }
14
```

In Line 2, the **cmath** library which contains all C++ Math functions is invoked.

In Line 7, the program declares a float variable called **dnum** which holds the decimal number value. A **float** variable is one which can hold decimal values. An integer variable can only hold whole number values.

In Lines 8 and 9, the program accepts a decimal number from the user and stores it in variable **dnum**.

In Line 11, the decimal number is rounded to the nearest whole number using **round(dnum)** and display it on the screen using **cout** command.

We can see the outputs below, for 2 instances of running the program. In the first instance, 5.45 gets rounded down to 5. In the second instance, 3.67 gets rounded to the closest whole number of 4.

Output:

```
"C:\Users\abhis\Google Drive\C++\roundnumber.exe"
Enter a decimal number: 5.45
Rounded to nearest whole number: 5

Process returned 0 (0x0)   execution time : 6.279 s
Press any key to continue.
```

```
"C:\Users\abhis\Google Drive\C++\roundnumber.exe"
Enter a decimal number: 3.67
Rounded to nearest whole number: 4

Process returned 0 (0x0)   execution time : 4.437 s
Press any key to continue.
```

Round Decimals Up and Down

C++ also has the ability to individually round decimals up or down. **Ceil()** rounds a decimal to the higher whole number, while **floor()** rounds a decimal down to a lower whole number.

The below program takes in a decimal number and stores it in a variable dnum. It calculates and prints out both the rounded up and rounded down whole number. As seen in the output below the code, 10.83 is rounded up to 11 and rounded down to 10.

```
#include <iostream>
#include <cmath>



int main() {
    float dnum;
    std::cout << "Enter a decimal number: ";
    std::cin >> dnum;

    std::cout << "Decimal Number Rounded up: " << ceil(dnum) << std::endl;
    std::cout << "Rounded down: " << floor(dnum) << std::endl;

    return 0;
}
```

Output:

```
"C:\Users\abhis\Google Drive\C++\roundupdown.exe"
Enter a decimal number: 10.83
Decimal Number Rounded up: 11
Rounded down: 10

Process returned 0 (0x0)   execution time : 6.560 s
Press any key to continue.
```

Calculate remainder

In C++, we calculate the reminder using a **modulus** operator which is represented by the **%** sign below. So, if 21 divided by 5 has remainder of 1, in C++ it would be:

21 % 5 = 1

In below example, the program takes in two integer variables **n1** and **n2** and finds the reminder when **n1 is divided by n2**.

In Line 10, the remainder is calculated using **n1%n2** and the output is printed on the screen.

```
1   #include <iostream>
2
3
4   int main() {
5       int n1, n2;
6       std::cout << "Enter numerator: ";
7       std::cin >> n1;
8       std::cout << "Enter denominator: ";
9       std::cin >> n2;
10      std::cout << "The remainder when "<< n1 << " is divided by "<< n2 << " is = " << n1 % n2 << std::endl;
11      return 0;
12  }
13
```

Output:

```
"C:\Users\abhis\Google Drive\C++\remainder.exe"
Enter numerator: 17
Enter denominator: 3
The remainder when 17 is divided by 3 is = 2

Process returned 0 (0x0)   execution time : 17.197 s
Press any key to continue.
```

In above example, n1 is 17 and n2 is 3 and the remainder when 17 is divided by 3 is 2, as shown in output.

```
"C:\Users\abhis\Google Drive\C++\remainder.exe"
Enter numerator: 45
Enter denominator: 6
The remainder when 45 is divided by 6 is = 3

Process returned 0 (0x0)   execution time : 11.069 s
Press any key to continue.
```

In above example, n1 is 45 and n2 is 6 and the remainder when 45 is divided by 6 is 3, as shown in above output.

Basic Math Operations

Basic arithmetic operations in C++ are conducted using their arithmetic sign.

Addition is done using “+”

Subtraction is done using “-“

Multiplication is done using “*”

Division is done using “/”

In below code, the program accepts two float variables **n1** and **n2**; and calculates their sum, difference, product and difference. The math operations are done in lines 10-13 and the output is printed on the screen.

```
1   #include <iostream>
2
3
4   int main() {
5       float n1, n2;
6       std::cout << "Enter first number: ";
7       std::cin >> n1;
8       std::cout << "Enter second number: ";
9       std::cin >> n2;
10      std::cout << n1 << " + " << n2 << " = " << n1 + n2 << std::endl;
11      std::cout << n1 << " - " << n2 << " = " << n1 - n2 << std::endl;
12      std::cout << n1 << " * " << n2 << " = " << n1 * n2 << std::endl;
13      std::cout << n1 << " / " << n2 << " = " << n1 / n2 << std::endl;
14      return 0;
15  }
16
```

Output:

```
"C:\Users\abhis\Google Drive

Enter first number: 5
Enter second number: 7
5 + 7 = 12
5 - 7 = -2
5 * 7 = 35
5 / 7 = 0.714286

Process returned 0 (0x0)   execution time : 7.285 s
Press any key to continue.
```

In above example, the two integers n1 and n2 are 5 and 7. The outputs when basic math operations are performed are shown above.

Exponent

In C++, an exponent or power is calculated using the **pow()** function. For example, if we want to calculate 2 raised to the power 5, we use:

pow(2,5) which gives an output of **32**.

In below code, the program accepts two float variables called **base** and **exp**. The **base** is the base of the exponent and **exp** is the power to which the base is raised.

In line 11, the program calculates the power of **base** raised to **exp** and stores it in a third float variable called **res**.

In line 12, the output **res** is printed on the screen.

```
1   #include <iostream>
2   #include <cmath>
3
4   int main() {
5       float base, exp;
6       std::cout << "Enter the base number: ";
7       std::cin >> base;
8       std::cout << "Enter the exponent: ";
9       std::cin >> exp;
10
11      float res = pow(base, exp);
12      std::cout <<base<<" raised to the power "<<exp<< " is " << res << std::endl;
13
14      return 0;
15  }
16
```

Output:

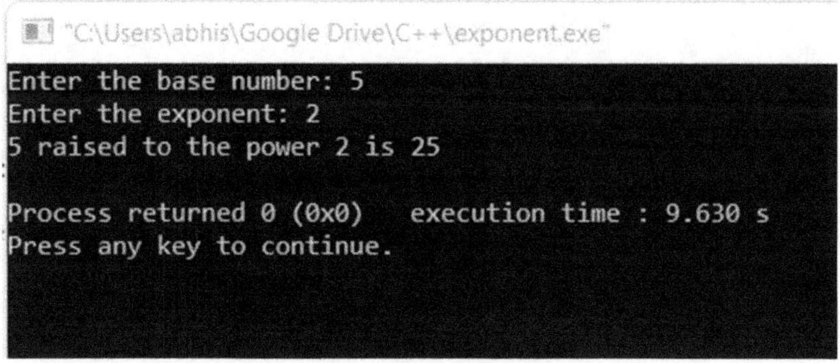

In above example, **base** is 5 and **pow** is 2. The output variable **res** is 5 raised to the power of 2, which is 25.

Logarithm

In C++, a logarithm is calculated using the **log()** function. There is no way to include base in the logarithm in C++. So the log of a number has to be divided by the log of its base. For example, the log of 20 to the base 2 is given by:

log (20) / log (2)

In the below code, the program accepts two float variables **num** and **base** in lines 6-9. The base is given by the variable **base**.

In line 11, the program calculates the log of num and stores it in a float variable called **logn**.

In line 12, the output is printed on the screen.

```cpp
#include <iostream>
#include <cmath>

int main() {
    float num, base;
    std::cout << "Enter the number: ";
    std::cin >> num;
    std::cout << "Enter the log base: ";
    std::cin >> base;

    float logn = log(num) / log(base);
    std::cout <<" The logarithm of "<<num<<" to the base "<<base<< " is " << logn << std::endl;

    return 0;
}
```

Output:

```
"C:\Users\abhis\Google Drive\C++\log.exe"
Enter the number: 100
Enter the log base: 10
 The logarithm of100 to the base 10 is 2

Process returned 0 (0x0)   execution time : 2.748 s
Press any key to continue.
```

In above output, **num** is 100 and **base** is 10. The output **logn** calculates the log, which is 2.

Square root

In C++, the square root of a number is calculated using the **sqrt()** function.

In the below code, the program accepts a float variable called **num**.

In line 9, the program calculates the square root of num and stores it in a float variable called **res**.

In line 10, the output is printed on the screen.

```
1   #include <iostream>
2   #include <cmath>
3
4   int main() {
5       float num;
6       std::cout << "Enter the number: ";
7       std::cin >> num;
8
9       float res = sqrt(num);
10      std::cout <<" The square root of "<<num<< " is " << res << std::endl;
11
12      return 0;
13  }
14
```

Output:

```
"C:\Users\abhis\Google Drive\C++\squareroot.exe"
Enter the number: 36
 The square root of 36 is 6

Process returned 0 (0x0)   execution time : 6.520 s
Press any key to continue.
```

In above example, the variable **num** is 36 and **res** is 6, which is output to the screen.

Trigonometry

C++ has a wide range of trigonometrical functions. In this book, we'll go over a few basic functions. The sine, cosine and tangent of an angle is given by **sin()**, **cos()** and **tan()** functions respectively. The angle must be in radians. For example, if we wanted to calculate sine of 30 degrees, we use:

sin (30*M_PI/180) instead of **sin (30)**

where M_PI is 3.142 in C++

In code below, the program accepts the angle in degrees and stores it in a float variable called **angle**.

In line 8, the value of the angle is converted to radians and stored in a double variable called **angle_radian**.

In line 9-11, the program calculates the values of sine, cosine and tangent of angle and stores the values in double variables **sine**, **cosine** and **tangent**.

In lines 12-14, the values are output on the screen.

```
1   #include <iostream>
2   #include <cmath>
3
4   int main() {
5       float angle;
6       std::cout << "Enter the angle (in degrees): ";
7       std::cin >> angle;
8       double angle_radian = angle*M_PI/180;
9       float sine = sin(angle_radian);
10      float cosine = cos(angle_radian);
11      float tangent = tan(angle_radian);
12      std::cout <<" The sine of "<<angle<< " is " << sine << std::endl;
13      std::cout <<" The cosine of "<<angle<< " is " << cosine << std::endl;
14      std::cout <<" The tangent of "<<angle<< " is " << tangent << std::endl;
15      return 0;
16  }
17
```

Output:

```
"C:\Users\abhis\Google Drive\C++\sincostan.exe"

Enter the angle (in degrees): 30
 The sine of 30 is 0.5
 The cosine of 30 is 0.866025
 The tangent of 30 is 0.57735

Process returned 0 (0x0)   execution time : 3.284 s
Press any key to continue.
```

In above code, the user inputs a value of 30, and the program calculates and prints out the sine, cosine and tangent of 30 degrees.

Hypotenuse

The hypotenuse of a right-angled triangle is calculated using the square root function **sqrt()**. The Sqrt function is used on the sum of the squares of the two sides of the right angle.

In below code, the program accepts two float variables **side1** and **side2**. These are the two sides of the right angle.

The hypotenuse is stored in a third float variable and is stored in a variable called **hypotenuse**.

In line 12, the value of the hypotenuse is calculated and stored in **hypotenuse** variable.

In line 13, this is output onto the screen.

```cpp
#include <iostream>
#include <cmath>

int main() {
    float side1, side2, hypotenuse;
    std::cout << "Enter the base of the right angled triangle: ";
    std::cin >> side1;
    std::cout << "Enter the vertical side of the right angled triangle: ";
    std::cin >> side2;


    hypotenuse  = sqrt(side1*side1+side2*side2);
    std::cout <<" The hypotenuse of the triangle is " << hypotenuse << std::endl;

    return 0;
}
```

Output:

"C:\Users\abhis\Google Drive\C++\hypotenuse.exe"

```
Enter the base of the right angled triangle: 5
Enter the vertical side of the right angled triangle: 12
 The hypotenuse of the triangle is 13

Process returned 0 (0x0)   execution time : 3.533 s
Press any key to continue.
```

In above sample code, **side1** and **side2** are 5 and 12.

The hypotenuse is calculated as square root of 5 squared plus 12 squared, which comes to an answer of 13.

Problems to Practice

1. Write a program that takes in 3 numbers as integer values; and calculates their sum, difference, product, and quotient.
2. Write a program that takes in 2 numbers and finds the quotient and remainder when 1st number is divided by the 2nd number.
3. Write a program that takes in the radius of a circle as a float variable and finds the area of the circle ($A=pi*r^2$).
4. Write a program that takes in an angle and one side of a right-angled triangle as two float variables. Calculate the values of the two missing sides. (Use sine and cos values of angle)
5. Write a program that takes in an angle and hypotenuse of a right-angled triangle as two float variables. Calculate the values of the two missing sides. (Use sine and cos values of angle)
6. Write a program that takes in a number as a float variable and finds the cube of the number. (Use an exponent of 3 for cube)
7. Write a program that takes in a number as a float variable and find the cube root. (Use an exponent of 1/3 for cube root)
8. Write a program that takes in the value of a hypotenuse and one side of a right-angled triangle. The program finds the value of the missing side and prints it out.

Arrays

An array is a collection of elements of a particular data type.
Each element is indexed and can be accessed by using its index.
It has a fixed number of elements that is defined by the user.
Arrays are great tools to manipulate and store data effectively, as they are great for fast access to data and iteration.
In C++, arrays are defined as below:

int arr[6]={10,20,30,40,50,60};

arr is an integer array of 6 elements shown above.
The first index in a C++ array is always 0.
So, in the above example, if we want to change the second element to 15:

arr[1]=15;

Then the array arr becomes:

arr[6] = {10,15,30,40,50,60}

Basic Array

In our first example, we create an array of 15 elements and print out all numbers from 0-14 using the indexes of the array.

In the code below, the array **arr** is defined in line 4 as an integer array of 15 elements.

In lines 5-7, each element of the array is assigned as a number from **0 to 14** in ascending order. This is done using a for loop where the loop indexes from 0 to 14.

In lines 8-10, the elements of the array are printed out using a for loop.

This is shown in output below the code.

```
1   #include <iostream>
2
3   int main() {
4       int arr[15];
5       for (int i = 0; i < 15; i++) {
6           arr[i] = i;
7       }
8       for (int i = 0; i < 15; i++) {
9           std::cout << "Array Element "<<i<<" = "<<arr[i] << std::endl;
10      }
11      return 0;
12  }
13
```

Output:

```
"C:\Users\abhis\Google Drive\C++\Basicarray.exe"
Array Element 0 = 0
Array Element 1 = 1
Array Element 2 = 2
Array Element 3 = 3
Array Element 4 = 4
Array Element 5 = 5
Array Element 6 = 6
Array Element 7 = 7
Array Element 8 = 8
Array Element 9 = 9
Array Element 10 = 10
Array Element 11 = 11
Array Element 12 = 12
Array Element 13 = 13
Array Element 14 = 14

Process returned 0 (0x0)   execution time : 0.053 s
Press any key to continue.
```

Basic Array 2

In the next example, the size of the array is input by the user. An array of the desired size is created. Then the user fills out all the elements of the array.

In line 6, the program accepts the size of the array from the user and stores in an integer variable called **sizeofArray**.

In line 8, the program creates an integer array called **myArr** of length **sizeofArray**.

In lines 10-12, each element of the array is filled by the user after prompted by the program.

In lines 15-17, the elements of the array are printed on the screen.

```
1   #include <iostream>
2
3   int main() {
4       int sizeofArray;
5       std::cout << "Enter the size of the array: ";
6       std::cin >> sizeofArray;
7
8       int myarr[sizeofArray];
9
10      for (int i = 0; i < sizeofArray; i++) {
11          std::cout << "Enter element " << i+1 << ": ";
12          std::cin >> myarr[i];
13      }
14
15      std::cout << "The elements of the array are: ";
16      for (int i = 0; i < sizeofArray; i++) {
17          std::cout << myarr[i] << " ";
18      }
19
20      return 0;
21  }
22
```

Output:

```
"C:\Users\abhis\Google Drive\C++\Basicarray2.exe"
Enter the size of the array: 5
Enter element 1: 34
Enter element 2: 23
Enter element 3: 45
Enter element 4: 11
Enter element 5: 4
The elements of the array are: 34 23 45 11 4
Process returned 0 (0x0)   execution time : 10.261 s
Press any key to continue.
```

In output above, the size of the array is entered as 5, which creates an array **myArr[5]**. The 5 elements of **arr** are 34,23,45,11 and 4.

The array is then printed on the screen.

Reverse Name

In C++, a string is just an array of characters. Each element of the string is a character and can be accessed by the index. For example,

string name = “Tim”

name is an array of 3 characters. So, name[0]=”T”.

If we do name[1]=”o”, then:

name = “Tom”

In below program, we use this fact to reverse a string array. The string array is a name input by the user.

In line 7, the program accepts a name from the user and stores it in a string array called **name**.

In line 11-13, the program has a for loop that goes from name.length-1 to 0. So, if the name is "tommy", name.length is 5. So, the for loop goes from 4 to 0. It runs 5 times in total.

In line 12, **cout<<name[i]** prints the character of the array that is based on the loop index.

The loop, in effect, prints out the name in reverse.

```
1   #include <iostream>
2   #include <string>
3
4   int main() {
5       std::string name;
6       std::cout << "Enter your first name: ";
7       std::cin >> name;
8       std::cout << std::endl;
9
10      std::cout << "Name reversed is ";
11      for (int i = name.length() - 1; i >= 0; i--) {
12          std::cout << name[i];
13      }
14      std::cout << std::endl;
15
16      return 0;
17  }
18
```

Output:

In the output below, **"tommy"** is entered by the user. The program prints out **"ymmot"**, which is the reverse of the string.

```
"C:\Users\abhis\Google Drive\C++\reversename.exe"
Enter your first name: tommy

Name reversed is ymmot

Process returned 0 (0x0)   execution time : 12.033 s
Press any key to continue.
```

Guess US State Capitals

In below example, we play a game of US Capitals. The user is prompted with a question on the capital of a country. Based on the output, the program either prints out that the user is correct; or prints the correct answer.

The program uses two arrays, called **states[]** and **capitals[]**, which are defined in lines 9 and 10.

Both these arrays are in the **appendix** of this book and can be copied and pasted into the program.

In line 12, the program determines the size of the array **states[]** and stores in an integer variable called **numStates**.

In line 14, two string variables **state** and **correctedCapital** are created. **state** holds the value of a random state that the program gets from the array; and **correctedCapital** is the capital of that **state**. The program basically gets a random state from the array using the **rand()** function. To invoke the rand function, we also invoke the random library in line 3.

Since we want to run this quiz 5 times, the program runs a for loop 5 times in line 15.

Inside the loop in line 16, a random number is generated between 1 and **numStates** and stored in integer variable **randomIndex**.

In line 17, the state based on **randomIndex** is generated and stored in string variable **state**. In line 18, the capital of state is stored in string variable **correctedCapital**.

In line 20, the user enters his guess for the capital of state and the answer is stored in string variable **userGuess**.

An if loop is used to check if **userGuess** is correct. If it correct, a **"Correct"** message is printed on the screen. An integer variable **score** is increased by 1. The score variable keeps track of the number of correct answers by the user.

Otherwise, an incorrect message with the correct answer is printed on the screen.

This sequence is run 5 times until the for loop is over.

In line 30, the program the number of correct answers by the user.

```cpp
#include <iostream>
#include <string>
#include <random>


int main() {
    int score = 0;
    std::string states[] = {"Alabama","Alaska","Arizona","Arkansas","California","Colorad
    std::string capitals[] = {"Montgomery","Juneau","Phoenix","Little Rock","Sacramento",


    int numStates = sizeof(states) / sizeof(states[0]);

    std::string state, correctCapital;
    for (int i = 0; i < 5; i++) { // play 10 rounds
        int randomIndex = rand() % numStates + 1;
        state = states[randomIndex];
        correctCapital = capitals[randomIndex];
        std::cout << "What is the capital of " << state << "? ";
        std::string userGuess;
        std::cin >> userGuess;
        if (userGuess == correctCapital) {
            std::cout << "Correct!\n";
            score++;
        } else {
            std::cout << "Incorrect. The correct answer is " << correctCapital << ".\n";
        }
    }

    std::cout << "Your final score is " << score << " out of 5.\n";

    return 0;
}
```

Output:

```
What is the capital of Texas? Austin
Correct!
What is the capital of Maine? idk
Incorrect. The correct answer is Augusta.
What is the capital of Oklahoma? Oklahoma City
Incorrect. The correct answer is Oklahoma City.
What is the capital of Alaska? Incorrect. The correct answer is Juneau.
What is the capital of Massachusetts? Boston
Correct!
Your final score is 2 out of 5.

Process returned 0 (0x0)   execution time : 21.106 s
Press any key to continue.
```

In above output, the user is asked 5 questions on capitals of US states.
He answers 5 but only gets 2 of them correct, which are the capitals of Texas and Oklahoma City.

Problems to Practice

1. Write a program that creates a string array of 5 names. It then asks the user to enter 5 names into the array. The program then prints out the final array of 5 names.
2. A class has 20 students who just completed a Physics test. Create two arrays, one a string array that contains names, and another one which is an integer array that contains Physics marks. The program prompts the user to enter names and Physics marks of all students. At the end, the program prints out the average score, the highest score and the person with the highest score.
3. Write a program that takes in an array and creates a new array of half the length with every odd character. It then prints out the new array.
4. Write a program that creates an array of world countries and capitals. Create a game where it asks the user 5 times the capital of a certain country and adds the number of times the user guesses correct. At the end, it prints out the number of times the user guessed right.

Pointers

A pointer is a variable that holds the memory location of another variables. It is a special feature of C and C++, though a few other languages hold it.

Let's say we have a variable x, and we define that as equal to 10 in C++ using:

int var = 10;

var has a value of 10 but it is assigned to a particular space in the computer memory. To access this value, we use:

int* pvar = &var;

pvar holds the memory location so if we print **pvar** on the screen we get something like **0c76fe89.**

If we only know the name of the pointer but not the variable, we can use ***pvar** to get the value of what is stored in the pointer location. In this case, both ***pvar** and **var** have a value of 10.

Pointers are great because they allow for efficient use of computer memory and allow for faster computer processing.

While we won't go into the advanced programs that pointers are used for, we'll go over the basics of pointers with some simple examples so we can see how they are used.

The main difference between a variable and a pointer is that if the value of the variable changes, the value of the pointer remains the same. For example, if we do:

x=20;

the value of **pvar** still remains 0c76fe89. We can also change the value of x by changing the value of ***pvar.**

*pvar =30;

Means that the value of x also changes to 30.

Pointer Basic Example 1

A pointer is a variable that holds the memory location of another variable.

In the below example, **num** is the variable and is assigned to a value of 20 in line 4.

In line 5, a pointer variable **pnum** is assigned the memory location of **num**.

In line 6, 7 and 8; the program prints the value of **num**, **pnum** and ***pnum** respectively. As seen in output below the code, **pnum** has the memory location of num, while ***pnum** holds the value of **num**.

In line 9, the program uses ***pnum** to change the value of the variable to 100. This also changes the value of **num** as shown in the output below the code.

```cpp
#include <iostream>

int main() {
    int num = 20;
    int* pnum = &num;
    std::cout << "num = " << num << std::endl;
    std::cout << "pnum = " << pnum << std::endl;
    std::cout << "*pnum = " << *pnum << std::endl;
    *pnum = 100;
    std::cout << "num = " << num << std::endl;
    return 0;
}
```

Output:

In the beginning num has a value of 20, while **pnum** has a value of **0x61f214**. ***pnum** holds the value of num, so it prints out 20. After the program assigns ***pnum** a value of 100, we see that **num** is changed to 100.

"C:\Users\abhis\Google Drive\C++\Pointerexample.exe"

```
num = 20
pnum = 0x61fe14
*pnum = 20
num = 100

Process returned 0 (0x0)   execution time : 0.059 s
Press any key to continue.
```

Making it Point to a Different Variable

A common strategy in high computation problems is to use the same pointer for multiple variables. This makes the program run faster as it uses less memory.

In below code, the program uses the same pointer for multiple variables. The two variables are **num1** and **num2** assigned to values of **20** and **40** respectively.

In line 6, the pointer first points to **num1**. In lines 7-10, the values of **num1**, **num2**, **pnum** and ***pnum** are printed. **pnum** holds the memory address, while ***pnum** holds the value of **num1**, which is **20**.

Then, in line 12, the same pointer **pnum** points to **num2**. In lines 13-17, the same values are printed again. This time, ***pnum** is now 40 as that is the value of num2. But we notice that the memory location **pnum** is the same. It is the same memory address, but it now points to num2.

This is shown in the output below.

```cpp
#include <iostream>

int main() {
    int num1 = 20;
    int num2 = 40;
    int* pnum = &num1;
    std::cout << "num1 = " << num1 << std::endl;
    std::cout << "num2 = " << num2 << std::endl;
    std::cout << "pnum = " << pnum << std::endl;
    std::cout << "*pnum = " << *pnum << std::endl;

    pnum=&num2;
    std::cout << "Now pnum points to num2" << std::endl;
    std::cout << "num1 = " << num1 << std::endl;
    std::cout << "num2 = " << num2 << std::endl;
    std::cout << "pnum = " << pnum << std::endl;
    std::cout << "*pnum = " << *pnum << std::endl;


    return 0;
}
```

Output:

```
"C:\Users\abhis\Google Drive\C++\Pointerexample2.exe"
num1 = 20
num2 = 40
pnum = 0x61fe14
*pnum = 20
Now pnum points to num2
num1 = 20
num2 = 40
pnum = 0x61fe10
*pnum = 40

Process returned 0 (0x0)   execution time : 0.056 s
Press any key to continue.
```

Pointers to Swap Variables

Swapping variables is a good way to utilize pointers. Instead of changing memory locations, the same memory locations can be used which allows for faster processing.

In the below code, two integer variables **x** and **y** have values of 50 and 25 before swapping as output in line 11.

The swapping process occurs in lines 3-6 in the function called **swap**. The function accepts the memory values of x and y as shown in line 13. **&x** and **&y** are the memory locations.

In line 4, the value of a (represented by a*) is sent to a temporary variable called **temp**.

In line 5, ***a** is assigned to ***b**. This means that the memory location that used to hold the value of a now holds the value of b.

In line 6, ***b** holds the value of temp. This means the memory location of b now holds temp, which is the value of a.

So, the values that a and b hold are swapped, while keeping the memory locations the same.

This is shown when the values are printed on the screen in line 15 in the output below the code.

```cpp
#include <iostream>

void swap(int* a, int* b) {
    int temp = *a;
    *a = *b;
    *b = temp;
}

int main() {
    int x = 50, y = 25;
    std::cout << "Before swapping: x = " << x << ", y = " << y << std::endl;

    swap(&x, &y);

    std::cout << "After swapping: x = " << x << ", y = " << y << std::endl;

    return 0;
}
```

Output:

"C:\Users\abhis\Google Drive\C++\pointerswap.exe"

```
Before swapping: x = 50, y = 25
After swapping: x = 25, y = 50

Process returned 0 (0x0)   execution time : 0.054 s
Press any key to continue.
```

Problems to Practice

1. Write a program that uses pointers to find sum of two integer variables. It adds the pointer values instead of the variable values.
2. Write a program with a function that takes in 3 numbers and arranges them in ascending order. It uses pointers to temporarily store values while swapping values.
3. Do the same as the above program to find the maximum value of an array of numbers.

Vectors

A vector is a collection of elements of the same data type. The number of elements in the vector is dynamic, meaning that it changes with every element that is added.

It is contained in the library class <vector> and can be invoked by

#include <vector>

A vector is defined as below:

vector<string> names;

The above line defines a vector of strings called names. When initialized, it contains 0 names. We can add names to the vector using push_back (which adds items to the back of the vector) or push_front(which adds items to the front of the vector)

Names.push_front("Abhi")

Adds Abhi to the front. So, the vector now has a length of 1.

Names.push_back("Bob")

Adds Bob to the back, which makes it the second element. Now, the vector has a length of 2. The 2 elements in order are "Abhi" and "Bob".

We can also remove items from the vector using pop_back or pop_front.

Names.pop_front() would remove "Abhi" while

Names.pop_back() would remove "Bob".

Vector of Numbers

In the first vector program below, we create a vector of numbers and insert numbers into it in a while loop based on user input. The while loop checks if the user wants to continue adding numbers; and does so while the user says yes.

In line 5, the program declares a vector of integers called **numbers**.

In line 6, a character variable called **choice** is declared with a value of 'y'. The variable **choice** is used as a parameter for the while loop in line 8. The while loop runs as long as choice is equal to 'y'. In lines 11-12, the user inputs another value for **choice**, and the user inputs 'y' to continue adding numbers in the while loop.

In line 7, an integer variable called **newNumber** is created, and this variable holds the value of numbers that are input by the user. In line 10, the user inputs the value of **newNumber**. This value is added to the vector in line 11. The process in lines 9-11 occurs as long as the user wants to keep entering new numbers.

In lines 17-19, the programs output the values in vector **numbers** using a for loop. **numbers.size()** in line 17 is the length of the vector; and each element of the vector is accessed using **numbers[i]** in line 18.

```
#include <iostream>
#include <vector>

int main() {
    std::vector<int> numbers;
    char choice = 'y';
    int newNumber;
    while (choice == 'y') {
        std::cout << "Enter a number: ";
        std::cin >> newNumber;
        numbers.push_back(newNumber);
        std::cout << "Add another number? (y/n) ";
        std::cin >>choice;
    }

    std::cout << "The numbers in the list are: ";
    for (int i = 0; i < numbers.size(); i++) {
        std::cout << numbers[i] << " ";
    }
    std::cout << std::endl;

}
```

Output:

In the sample output below, the users enters five numbers 5,10,45,78,34 and then hits a value of ‘n’ for choice to exit the while loop. The vector numbers are output as **[5 10 45 78 34]**. In the example, we see that vectors are superior to arrays as the length of the array is constant and cannot adjust based on user preference. Vectors allow for dynamic allocation which is great for our example below where we don’t know how many numbers are going to be entered by the user.

```
"C:\Users\abhis\Google Drive\C++\vectornumbers.exe"
Enter a number: 5
Add another number? (y/n) y
Enter a number: 10
Add another number? (y/n) y
Enter a number: 45
Add another number? (y/n) y
Enter a number: 78
Add another number? (y/n) y
Enter a number: 34
Add another number? (y/n) n
The numbers in the list are: 5 10 45 78 34

Process returned 0 (0x0)   execution time : 15.589 s
Press any key to continue.
```

Vector of Names

In below example, a vector of names is created. Two names are added, and one is removed. The vector is printed after each set of operations. This is a great example of how vectors are applied. If we used arrays for below example, we would have to change the size of the array each time a member was added or removed. In the case of vectors, it dynamically allocates the size.

In below code in line 5, a string vector called **vectornames** is created and has 5 names in it.

In line 7-11, the size of the vector and the list of names are printed.

In lines 14 and 15, two names, **Alice** and **Mike** are added to the vector.

In lines 16-20, the size of the vector and list of names are printed again. We see that the size of the vector increases to **7** and the two new names are added at the end (as **push_back** is used for both)

Now, one name is removed from the back of the vector using **pop_back** in line 23.

The size of the vector and list of names are again printed in lines 24-28. We see that the size is reduced to 6, and the last name Alice is removed from the vector.

All the outputs are shown in the output screen below the code.

```
1   #include <iostream>
2   #include <vector>
3
4   int main() {
5       std::vector<std::string> vectornames = {"Alex", "Tim", "John", "Matthew", "Finny"};
6
7       std::cout << "Size: " << vectornames.size() << std::endl;
8       std::cout << "Contents: "<< std::endl;
9       for (int i = 0; i < vectornames.size(); i++) {
10          std::cout << vectornames[i] << " "<< std::endl;;
11      }
12      std::cout << std::endl;
13
14      vectornames.push_back("Mike");
15      vectornames.push_back("Alice");
16      std::cout << "Size 2: " << vectornames.size() << std::endl;
17      std::cout << "Contents2: "<< std::endl;
18      for (int i = 0; i < vectornames.size(); i++) {
19          std::cout << vectornames[i] << " "<< std::endl;;
20      }
21      std::cout << std::endl;
22
23      vectornames.pop_back();
24      std::cout << "Size 3: " << vectornames.size() << std::endl;
25      std::cout << "Contents 3: "<< std::endl;
26      for (int i = 0; i < vectornames.size(); i++) {
27          std::cout << vectornames[i] << " "<< std::endl;;
28      }
29
30      return 0;
31  }
32
```

Output:

```
"C:\Users\abhis\Google Drive\C++\vectorexample.exe"
Size: 5
Contents:
Alex
Tim
John
Matthew
Finny

Size 2: 7
Contents2:
Alex
Tim
John
Matthew
Finny
Mike
Alice

Size 3: 6
Contents 3:
Alex
Tim
John
Matthew
Finny
Mike

Process returned 0 (0x0)   execution time : 0.054 s
Press any key to continue.
```

Vector for student roll

In the next vector example, vectors are used to create a list of students and grades for a university. 5 vectors are created for names, math grades, science grades, social science grades and averages. The names, math grades, science grades, social science grades are input by the user in a while loop, and the average is calculated using the grades.

The vectors **names**, **mathGrades**, **scienceGrades**, **socialScienceGrades** and **averages** are created in lines 6-10. Names is a string vector and averages is a float vector, and the other three are integer vectors.

A character variable **choice** defined in line 12, is used to determine whether the while loop continues. It continues as long as the user enters a value of 'y' for **choice** in line 36.

In lines 20 to 30, the user inputs values for **newName**, **newMathGrade**, **newScienceGrade** and **newSocialScienceGrade**.

In line 32, **newAverage** is calculated using the three grades. All the new data is added to the vectors in line 31 and 33. This process continues till all the student data has been entered, and then user enters a value of 'n' for choice.

```
1   #include <iostream>
2   #include <string>
3   #include <vector>
4
5   int main() {
6       std::vector<std::string> names;
7       std::vector<int> mathGrades;
8       std::vector<int> scienceGrades;
9       std::vector<int> socialSciencesGrades;
10      std::vector<float> averages;
11
12      char choice = 'y';
13      while (choice == 'y') {
14          std::string newName;
15          int newMathGrade;
16          int newScienceGrade;
17          int newSocialSciencesGrade;
18          float newAverage;
19
20          std::cout << "Enter student name: ";
21          std::cin >>newName;
22          names.push_back(newName);
23          std::cout << "Enter math grade: ";
24          std::cin >>newMathGrade;
25          mathGrades.push_back(newMathGrade);
26          std::cout << "Enter science grade: ";
27          std::cin >>newScienceGrade;
28          scienceGrades.push_back(newScienceGrade);
29          std::cout << "Enter social sciences grade: ";
30          std::cin >>newSocialSciencesGrade;
31          socialSciencesGrades.push_back(newSocialSciencesGrade);
32          newAverage = (newMathGrade + newScienceGrade + newSocialSciencesGrade) / 3;
33          averages.push_back(newAverage);
34
35          std::cout << "Any more students? (y/n) ";
36          std::cin >> choice;
37      }
38
```

The number of students is now printed out in line 39 using **names.size()**.

The student's name and average are printed using the for loop in lines 42-44.

```
39      std::cout << "Number of students in class: " << names.size() << std::endl;
40      std::cout << "Student Roll: "<< std::endl;
41      for (int i = 0; i < names.size(); i++) {
42          std::cout << "Name:" << names[i] << " "<< std::endl;
43          std::cout << "Average:" << averages[i] << " "<< std::endl;
44      }
45
46      return 0;
47  }
48
```

Output:

In sample output, names and grades are input for 3 students, Timmy, Matthew and Aaron.

And the student's name and average is printed out at the end after all data has been entered.

"C:\Users\abhis\Google Drive\C++\vector_students.exe"

```
Enter student name: Timmy
Enter math grade: 78
Enter science grade: 67
Enter social sciences grade: 89
Any more students? (y/n) y
Enter student name: Matthew
Enter math grade: 25
Enter science grade: 76
Enter social sciences grade: 87
Any more students? (y/n) y
Enter student name: Aaron
Enter math grade: 99
Enter science grade: 34
Enter social sciences grade: 77
Any more students? (y/n) n
Number of students in class: 3
Student Roll:
Name:Timmy
Average:78
Name:Matthew
Average:62
Name:Aaron
Average:70

Process returned 0 (0x0)   execution time : 52.833 s
Press any key to continue.
```

Problems to Practice

1. Write a program that adds in bank customers data that is entered by the user. Have separate vectors for customer name, customer account balance, customer interest rate and customer credit rating.
2. Write a program that takes in data for gym memberships, with separate vectors for customer name, customer id number, customer joining date and membership expiration date. Calculate the days to expiration for each customer and put that in a separate vector.
3. Write a program that creates a vector for a grocery store. Each spot in the grocery store is an element on the vector, and it contains the name of the food in that grocery spot. The item can be removed a changed. If new spots are created to hold more items, new spots are added.

Maps

A map is a collection of a certain data type which is referenced by a key instead of an index.

A map is declared as shown below:

map<string, int> employeepay;

The line above declares a map called **employeepay**. Within the brackets, we see two variables. The first variable is a string and is the key to the map. The second variable is an integer variable and is the value in the map. In this case, the integer variable contains the salary of the employee. A map is assigned as shown below:

employeepay["Jim"]=52000;

In the above case, **Jim** is the string key to the **employeepay** integer value of **52000**.

A map is great when items are stored in an unordered fashion. In such cases, it's easier and more beneficial to access data using a map key instead of an index.

Map values can be accessed using square brackets [] or .at() function as shown below:

cout<<employeepay["Jim"]; or cout<<employeepay.at("Jim");

Both output a value of 52000.

The elements in a map are sorted by their keys. If the key is a string, they are sorted in ascending order.
The data is allocated in a dynamic fashion just like vectors, with the size changing each time an element is added or removed.
The main difference with vectors is that vectors are referenced by an index, while maps use a key.

Map Example 1

In our first example, we create two integer maps of weights and heights. Each map is accessed with a string key that represents the name of the person. The map values are assigned and printed out to show the basics of how a map works.
In code below, the two maps weight and height, are created in lines 5-6.
The maps are assigned integer data values in lines 8-9, and some of the values are printed out in lines 20-33.

```
#include <iostream>
#include <map>

int main() {
    std::map<std::string, int> weight;
    std::map<std::string, int> height;

    weight["Steve"] = 85;
    height["Steve"]=72;

    weight["Abhi"] = 73;
    height["Abhi"]=70;

    weight["Bob"] = 93;
    height["Bob"]=80;

    weight["Zach"] = 65;
    height["Zach"]=66;

    std::cout << "Abhi's " << "weight is "<<weight.at("Abhi") << std::endl;
    std::cout << "Steve's " << "height is "<<height.at("Steve") << std::endl;
    std::cout << "Bob's " << "height is "<<weight["Steve"] << std::endl;


    return 0;
}
```

Output:

The printed map values are shown below:

```
"C:\Users\abhis\Google Drive

Abhi's weight is 73
Steve's height is 72
Bob's height is 85

Process returned 0 (0x0)   execution time : 0.043 s
Press any key to continue.
```

Printing out the Entire Map

To print the entire map, we use a for loop known as a range based for-loop. A range based for loop is used to access all elements in a map, as seen in lines 20-24.

In line 20, the **const auto &pair : weight** means that the variable **pair** will be used to access weight elements.

pair.first is the key to the map and **pair.second** is the value of the map that the key relates to.

So, **pair.first** is used to get the person's name and **pair.second** is the person's weight.

Since the second map height has the same key as the first map weight, we can use **pair.first** as the key. Using the key, we can access height using **height[pair.first]**. Using this, all key items are printed in lines 21-23 in the for loop. This is shown in the output below the code.

```
#include <iostream>
#include <map>

int main() {
    std::map<std::string, int> weight;
    std::map<std::string, int> height;

    weight["Steve"] = 85;
    height["Steve"]=72;

    weight["Abhi"] = 73;
    height["Abhi"]=70;

    weight["Bob"] = 93;
    height["Bob"]=80;

    weight["Zach"] = 65;
    height["Zach"]=66;

    for (const auto &pair : weight) {
        std::cout << pair.first << "'s weight: " << pair.second << std::endl;
        std::cout << pair.first << "'s height: " << height[pair.first] << std::endl;
        std::cout << std::endl;
    }


    return 0;
}
```

Output:

One thing to note is that the data in the map is stored in the order of the keys. If the key is a string as in this example, the data is stored in alphabetical order. That's why Abhi's weight and height are printed first and Zach's are printed last.

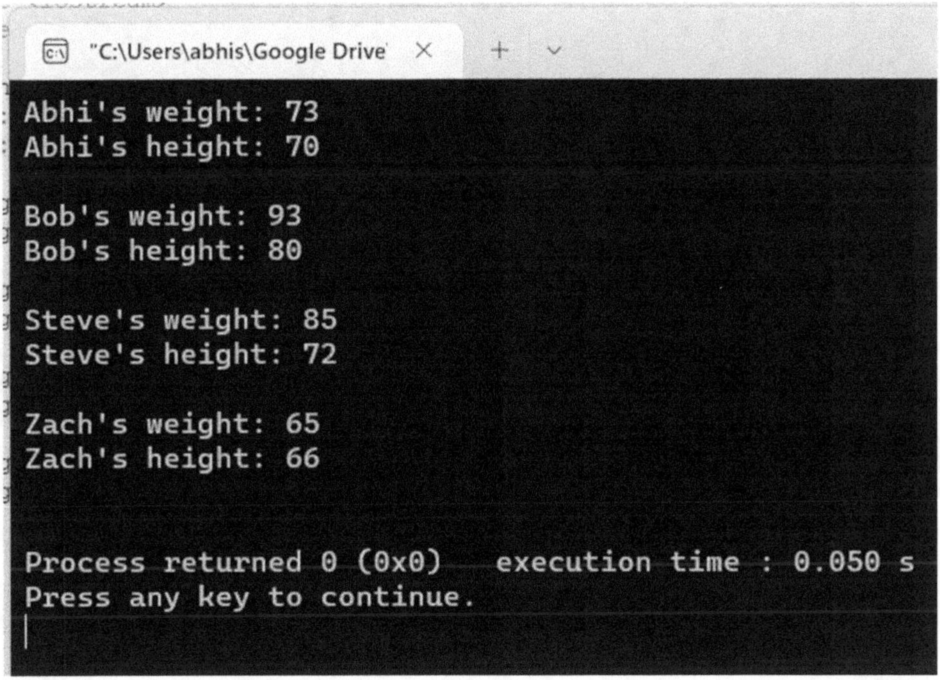

Removing Elements from a Map

Map data can easily be erased using the **erase()** function. This is seen in line 26 below when **Abhi's** weight is erased.

The new map data is printed out in lines 29-31.

As seen, even though the **height** data is not erased, it is not printed out for **Abhi** as it doesn't have access to the map key for pair defined in line 30. Pair.first has been erased for **Abhi,** so height[pair.first] does not print.

```cpp
#include <iostream>
#include <map>

int main() {
    std::map<std::string, int> weight;
    std::map<std::string, int> height;

    weight["Steve"] = 85;
    height["Steve"]=72;

    weight["Abhi"] = 73;
    height["Abhi"]=70;

    weight["Bob"] = 93;
    height["Bob"]=80;

    weight["Zach"] = 65;
    height["Zach"]=66;

    for (const auto &pair : weight) {
        std::cout << pair.first << "'s weight: " << pair.second << std::endl;
        std::cout << pair.first << "'s height: " << height[pair.first] << std::endl;
        std::cout << std::endl;
    }

    weight.erase("Abhi");

    std::cout <<"New Map Data:"<< std::endl;
    for (const auto &pair : weight) {
        std::cout << pair.first << "'s weight: " << pair.second << std::endl;
        std::cout << pair.first << "'s height: " << height[pair.first] << std::endl;
        std::cout << std::endl;
    }


    return 0;
}

```

Output:

"C:\Users\abhis\Google Drive

```
Abhi's weight: 73
Abhi's height: 70

Bob's weight: 93
Bob's height: 80

Steve's weight: 85
Steve's height: 72

Zach's weight: 65
Zach's height: 66

New Map Data:
Bob's weight: 93
Bob's height: 80

Steve's weight: 85
Steve's height: 72

Zach's weight: 65
Zach's height: 66



Process returned 0 (0x0)   execution time : 0.047 s
Press any key to continue.
```

Searching for Elements in a Map

Elements in a map can be searched using the find function and assigned it to an iterator. An iterator in C++ is an object that acts as a pointer and allows the user to access elements in maps, lists etc.

```
#include <iostream>
#include <map>

int main() {
    std::map<std::string, int> weight;
    std::map<std::string, int> height;

    weight["Steve"] = 85;
    height["Steve"]=72;

    weight["Abhi"] = 73;
    height["Abhi"]=70;

    weight["Bob"] = 93;
    height["Bob"]=80;

    weight["Zach"] = 65;
    height["Zach"]=66;

    for (const auto &pair : weight) {
        std::cout << pair.first << "'s weight: " << pair.second << std::endl;
        std::cout << pair.first << "'s height: " << height[pair.first] << std::endl;
        std::cout << std::endl;
    }

    weight.erase("Abhi");

    std::cout <<"New Map Data:"<< std::endl;
    for (const auto &pair : weight) {
        std::cout << pair.first << "'s weight: " << pair.second << std::endl;
        std::cout << pair.first << "'s height: " << height[pair.first] << std::endl;
        std::cout << std::endl;
    }

```

First, the program accepts a name from the user and stores it in the string variable **nametofind** in line 38 below.

The line **auto it = weight.find(nametofind)** creates an iterator that points to the name on the map that matches **nametofind**. If it cannot find the name, it returns **weight.end()**.

The if loop in line 41 checks if the name is in the map by checking if it is equal to **weight.end().** If it finds the name, it prints out the weight using it->second. it->second points to the weight of **nametofind**.

Since the height of the person has the same key/name, the program uses **height(nametofind)** to find the height. This is seen in line 42.

If it cannot find the name, it prints out **"Name not found"** in line 44.

```
35      std::cout << std::endl;
36      std::string nametofind;
37      std::cout<<"Enter name to search: ";
38      std::cin>>nametofind;
39      auto it = weight.find(nametofind);
40
41      if (it != weight.end()) {
42          std::cout << nametofind << "'s weight is " << it->second << " and height is " << height[nametofind]<<std::endl;
43      } else {
44          std::cout << nametofind << " not found." << std::endl;
45      }
46
47      return 0;
48  }
49
```

Output:

In the sample outputs below, the program first searches for Bob's name on user request. It finds the name and prints out his weight and height.

Then, the program is run again, and it searches for Abhi's name. The name cannot be found as it was deleted in the program in line 26.

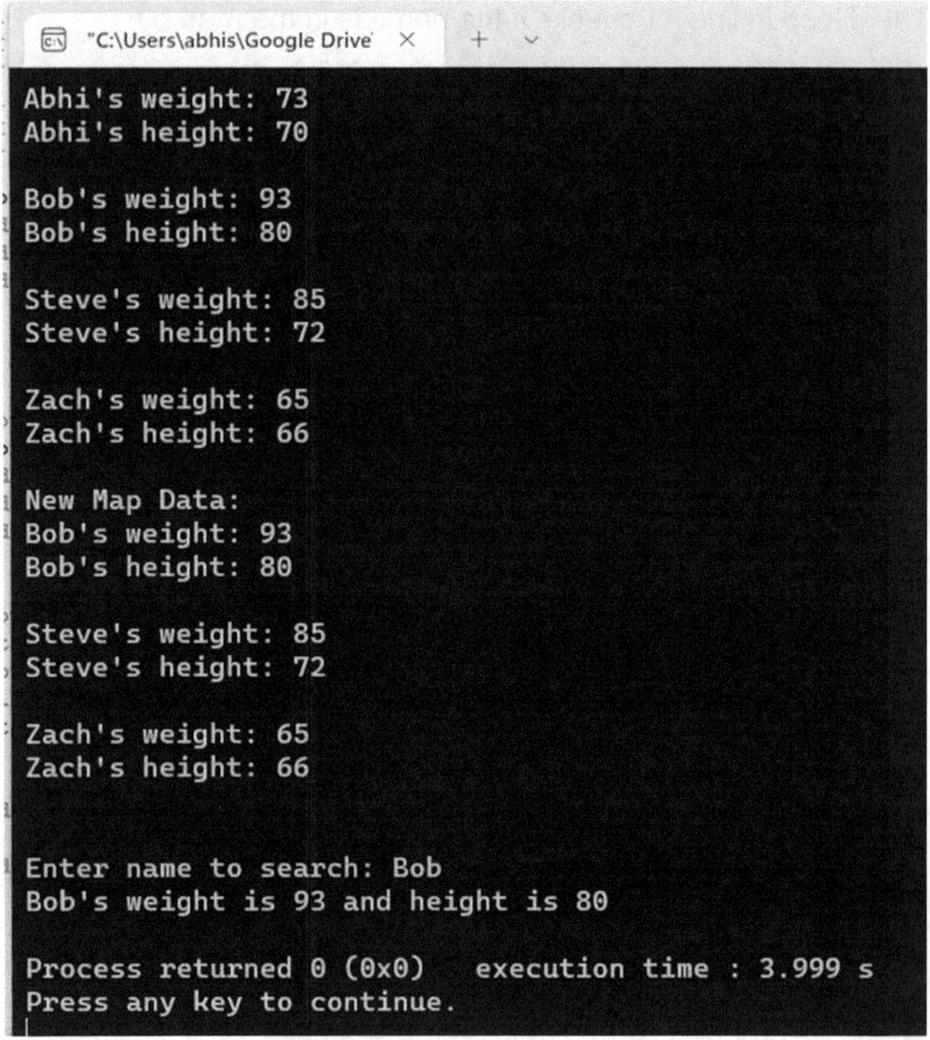
"C:\Users\abhis\Google Drive
Abhi's weight: 73
Abhi's height: 70
Bob's weight: 93
Bob's height: 80
Steve's weight: 85
Steve's height: 72
Zach's weight: 65
Zach's height: 66
New Map Data:
Bob's weight: 93
Bob's height: 80
Steve's weight: 85
Steve's height: 72
Zach's weight: 65
Zach's height: 66
Enter name to search: Bob
Bob's weight is 93 and height is 80
Process returned 0 (0x0)   execution time : 3.999 s
Press any key to continue.

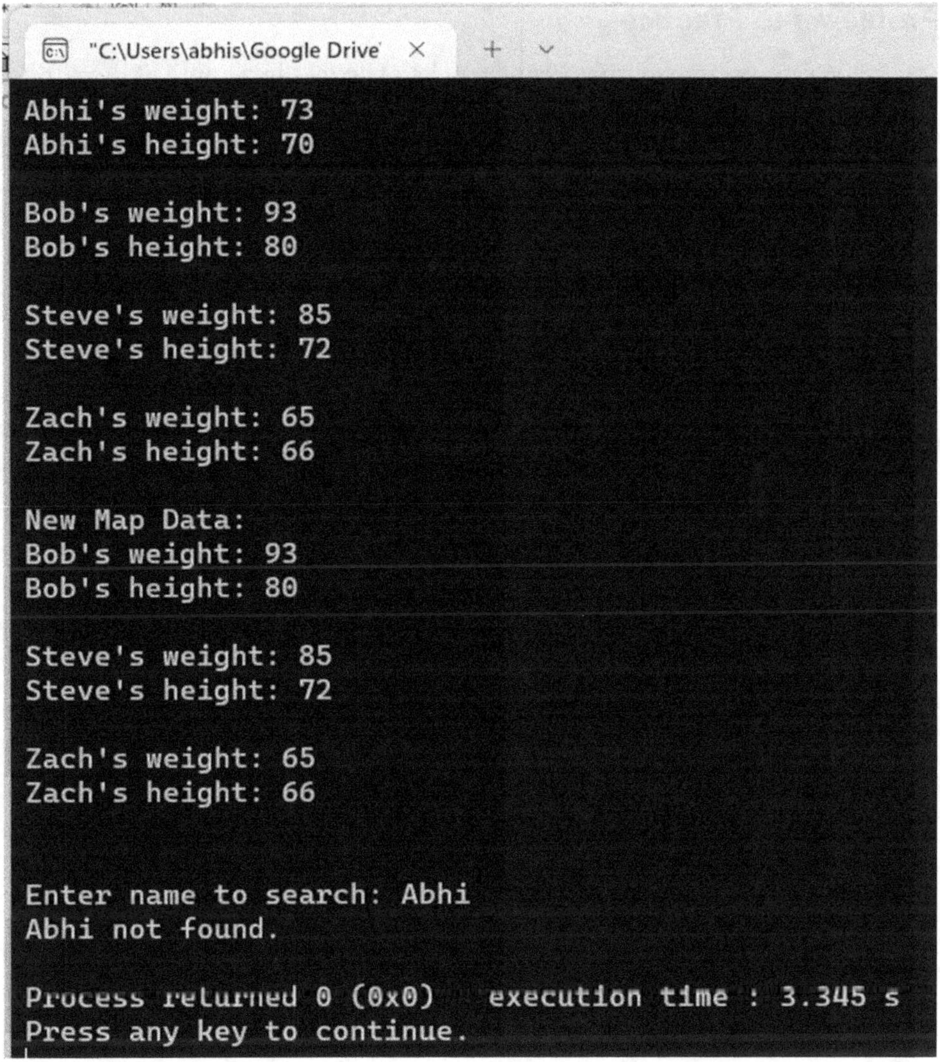
"C:\Users\abhis\Google Drive
Abhi's weight: 73
Abhi's height: 70
Bob's weight: 93
Bob's height: 80
Steve's weight: 85
Steve's height: 72
Zach's weight: 65
Zach's height: 66
New Map Data:
Bob's weight: 93
Bob's height: 80
Steve's weight: 85
Steve's height: 72
Zach's weight: 65
Zach's height: 66
Enter name to search: Abhi
Abhi not found.
Process returned 0 (0x0)   execution time : 3.345 s
Press any key to continue.

Problems to Practice

1. Write a program that keeps tracks of scores in a game of dice. It's a lot easier to use maps with keys as player names and just adding scores to each player.
2. Create a map that holds employee data and access employee data by employee id number. The maps contain employee names, salary, performance data.
3. Create a map that holds bank customer data with keys that can be accessed by bank customer number. The maps contain customer names, occupation, balance and credit rating.

Lists

A list is a C++ element that stores a series of elements. It is part of the standard library and can be accessed using **#include <list>.**

Lists are similar to arrays and maps. The main difference to arrays is that the length is dynamically allocated at runtime. So, the length of the list changes automatically at run time when elements are added or removed.

List elements are accessed using index elements. This differentiates them from maps that are accessed using keys.

A list has great utility when items have to processed in a particular order eg. customers in a queue, an online restaurant portal etc.

A list is defined as below:

list <string> names;

This creates a list of employees that contains string variables.

The variables are assigned using:

names.push_back("Sam") or names.push_front("Sam")

which pushes the item either to the back or front of the list respectively. Now, let's look at a few basic examples to understand this better.

List Example

In below example, list function is invoked from the C++ library in line 2.

In line 5, a list of strings called **queue1** is created.

In lines 6-8, three strings “Thomas”, “Bob” and “Madison” are added to list queue1. In line 9, “Alvis” is added to the front of the queue.

The list is printed using the for loop in lines 11 to 13.

The for loop defined in line 11 goes through **queue1** list elements and assigns each iteration to element **i**. **i** is printed out in line 12 each iteration.

```
1   #include <iostream>
2   #include <list>
3
4   int main() {
5       std::list<std::string> queue1;
6       queue1.push_back("Thomas");
7       queue1.push_back("Bob");
8       queue1.push_back("Madison");
9       queue1.push_front("Alvis");
10      std::cout << "Initial queue:"<<std::endl;
11      for (auto &i : queue1) {
12          std::cout << i << std::endl;
13      }
14      std::cout << std::endl;
15
16
17      return 0;
18  }
19
```

Output:

The output below has all the **queue1** list elements.

Madison is the last on the list since it is added using **push_back** and is the last element added.

Alvis is the last element added using **push_front** so it is the first on the list.

As shown below, lists are a great way to manipulate queues of data.

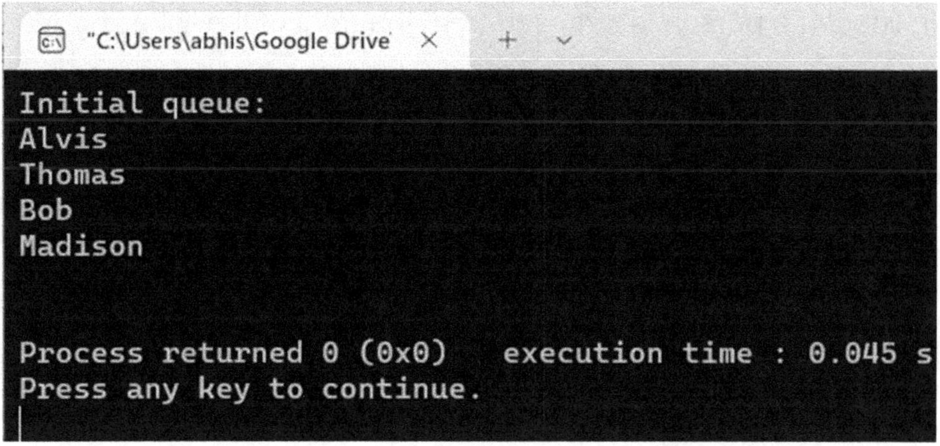

Adding and Removing Items from a List

In the next program, the first list example is modified by added 1 queue element and then removing one element. The list is printed after each change.

In line 16, a string called **Steve** is added to queue1 list to the 2nd spot. The **++queue.begin()** implies that Steve is added to beginning of the **queue + 1 person**, or **2nd person in the queue**. The queue is then printed in lines 18-20.

In line 24, a person is removed from the front of the list using **"pop_front"**. This removes **Alvis** as he is the first list member.

```
1   #include <iostream>
2   #include <list>
3
4   int main() {
5       std::list<std::string> queue1;
6       queue1.push_back("Thomas");
7       queue1.push_back("Bob");
8       queue1.push_back("Madison");
9       queue1.push_front("Alvis");
10      std::cout << "Initial queue:"<<std::endl;
11      for (auto &i : queue1) {
12          std::cout << i << std::endl;
13      }
14      std::cout << std::endl;
15
16      queue1.insert(++queue1.begin(), "Steve");
17      std::cout << "Queue after 1 person pushes Bob to get 2nd spot "<<std::endl;
18      for (auto &i : queue1) {
19          std::cout << i << std::endl;
20      }
21      std::cout << std::endl;
22
23
24      queue1.pop_front();
25      std::cout << "Queue after 1st person served"<<std::endl;
26      for (auto &i : queue1) {
27          std::cout << i << std::endl;
28      }
29      std::cout << std::endl;
30
31
32      return 0;
33  }
34
```

Output:

In the output below, we see **Steve** added as the second person the list to displace **Bob**.

Then, **Alvis** is removed when **pop_front** is used to remove the person in front of the list.

```
"C:\Users\abhis\Google Drive\C++\list.exe"
Initial queue:
Alvis
Thomas
Bob
Madison

Queue after 1 person pushes Bob to get 2nd spot
Alvis
Steve
Thomas
Bob
Madison

Queue after 1st person served
Steve
Thomas
Bob
Madison


Process returned 0 (0x0)   execution time : 0.059 s
Press any key to continue.
```

Auto Dealership List

In the next example, a list is used to service customers in an auto dealership. The person in the front is serviced when it's his turn and he's removed from the list using **pop_front()**. New customers are added to the back of the list using **push_back()**. The list **customerQueue** is created as a string list in line 4.

3 customer names are added as strings to **customerQueue** in lines 6-8, and this list is printed in lines 10-13.

One customer is serviced in line 15. This removes a person from the front of the list. The list is then printed in lines 17-20. In the output below the code, we see that **John Smith** is removed from the list.

Now, the program accepts a string called **newCustomer** from the user. **newCustomer** is added to the back of the **customerQueue**, and the list is again printed in lines 30-32.

```cpp
#include <iostream>
#include <list>
int main() {
    std::list<std::string> customerQueue;

    customerQueue.push_back("John Smith");
    customerQueue.push_back("Jane Doe");
    customerQueue.push_back("Bob Johnson");

    std::cout << "Current queue:" << std::endl;
    for (const auto& customer : customerQueue) {
        std::cout << customer << std::endl;
    }

    customerQueue.pop_front();
    std::cout << std::endl;
    std::cout << "Updated queue after serving 1st customer:" << std::endl;
    for (const auto& customer : customerQueue) {
        std::cout << customer << std::endl;
    }

    std::cout << std::endl;
    std::string newCustomer;
    std::cout << "Enter the name of the new customer: ";
    std::cin >>newCustomer;
    customerQueue.push_back(newCustomer);

    std::cout << std::endl;
    std::cout << "Updated queue:" << std::endl;
    for (const auto& customer : customerQueue) {
        std::cout << customer << std::endl;
    }
    return 0;
}

```

Output:

In the output below, we add Joe as the new customer, and Joe is added to the back of **customerQueue**.

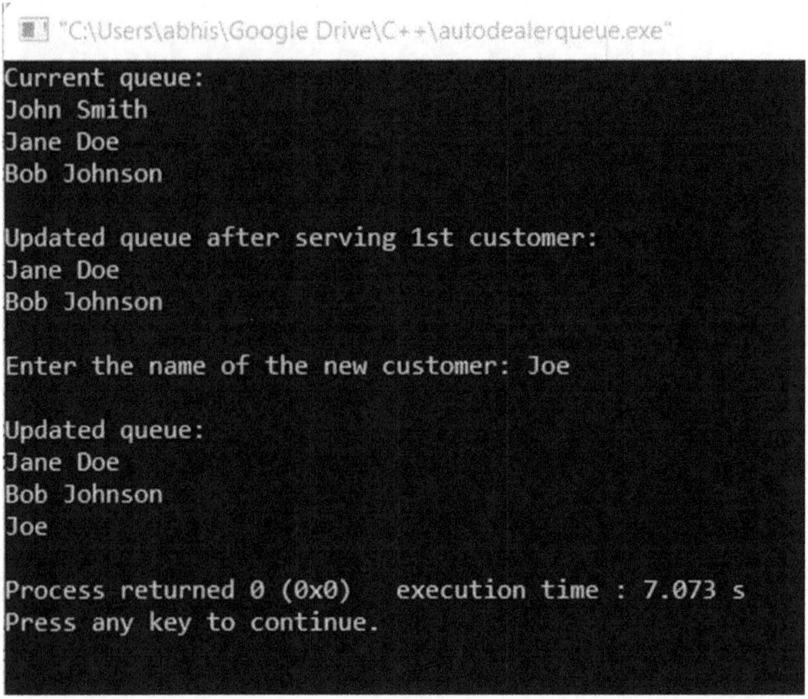

Problems to Practice

1. Write a program that represents a list of customers for an airport queue. It includes a list for customer name, customer check-in time and check out time. It can remove customers and add new customers; and it keeps track of total number of customers in the lounge at the same time.
2. Write a program that deals with customer complaints for an online business. There's a queue of complaints. Create two lists: one for customer names, another for customer products and the final one for refund amount. All of these are changed dynamically as customer complaints are dealt with.

Classes

What is an object?

An object is a data structure that contains data and functions that operate on the data. The data may be of the same of the same or different variable type. These objects are great to model real world applications.

For example, we may want to store car data, which consists of make, model, mileage, tyre diameter, engine rpm etc. And we may want to have functions that use the data to calculate other variables like reliability, weight etc.

What are classes?

Classes are the best blueprints for creating objects. Classes have a structure for creating a variety of data types and functions that utilize the data.

Classes can have both a public and private component. Private variables and functions cannot be accessed outside the class, while public variables and functions can be accessed outside the class using an object. Now, let's look at a simple example to make all a lot clearer.

A Basic Class

In this program, we create a class called Circle that has two public functions and one private variable. This private variable is an input when an instance of the class is created in the main program.

The class is first initialized in lines 4-6 with one input variable called **radius**. This is a private variable, meaning that it can only be accessed within the class. **getArea()** and **getCircumference()** are public functions within the class.

The private variable **radius** is created in line 15-17.

getArea() in lines 7-10 calculates the area of the circle with radius value of float variable **radius**.

getCircumference() in lines 11-14 calculates the circumference of the circle with radius value of float variable **radius**.

In the main program starting line 20, the user enters the value of radius, and it is stored in float variable **r**.

In line 24, an instance of the class called **myCircle** is created with an input radius of **r**.

MyCircle cannot access any private variable of the class, but it can access the public functions using **MyCircle.getArea()** and **MyCircle.getCircumference().**

The area obtained by **MyCircle.getArea()** is stored in a float variable called **area** in line 25, and it is printed on the screen in line 27.

The circumference obtained by **MyCircle.getCircumference()** is stored in a float variable called **crcm** in line 26, and it is printed on the screen in line 28.

```
1   #include <iostream>
2   class Circle {
3   public:
4       Circle(float radius):radius(radius)
5       {
6       }
7       float getArea()
8       {
9           return 3.14 * radius * radius;
10      }
11      float getCircumference()
12      {
13          return 2 * 3.14 * radius;
14      }
15  private:
16      float radius;
17  };
18
19  //now using this class
20  int main() {
21      float r;
22      std::cout << "Enter radius";
23      std::cin >> r;
24      Circle myCircle(r);
25      float area = myCircle.getArea();
26      float crcm = myCircle.getCircumference();
27      std::cout << "The area of the circle is: " << area << std::endl;
28      std::cout << "The circumference of the circle is: " << crcm << std::endl;
29      return 0;
30  }
31
```

Output:

All the data is seen in the output below the code. The user enters a radius value of 7. It is stored in float variable r.

The value of the area is calculated with this radius vale using **myCircle.getArea()** and output printed below.

The value of the area is calculated with this radius vale using **MyCircle.getCircumference()** and output printed below.

```
"C:\Users\abhis\Google Drive\C++\Rectangle.exe"

Enter radius 7
The area of the circle is: 153.86
The circumference of the circle is: 43.96

Process returned 0 (0x0)   execution time : 3.992 s
Press any key to continue.
```

Basic Class Example 2

In the next example, we create a class called Dog which has 4 public variables and 4 public functions. The class basically takes in the dog name, breed, location and age and prints them out using public member functions.

In the code below, the class is first initialized in line 8-9 as a class with four input variables.

The four public variables are declared in lines 4-7. They consist of 3 string variables **name**, **breed** and **location** and one integer variable **age**.

The four public functions are declared in lines 11-27. The functions are **getname(), getbreed(),getage()** and **getlocation().** They return the values of all the four variables mentioned.

The main program starts in line 31. An instance of the class is created in line 32. The instance is called **Dog1** and enters values for all 4 variables. **Dog1** has a name of "Cleo", a breed of "Dalmation", an age of 11, and a city of "Atlanta".

The four member functions of the class are accessed using **Dog1.getname(), Dog1.getbreed, Dog1.getage() and Dog1.getlocation()**. They are stored in string variables **dn**, **da**, **db** and **dl** in lines 33-36.

These values are printed out in lines 37-40.

This is seen in the output below the code.

```cpp
#include <iostream>
class Dog {
    public:
        std::string name;
        std::string breed;
        int age;
        std::string location;
        Dog(std::string name, std::string breed, int age, std::string location) : name(name), breed(breed), age(age), location(location)
        {
        }
        std::string getname()
        {
            return name;
        }
        std::string getbreed()
        {
            return breed;
        }
        int getage()
        {
            return age;
        }
        std::string getlocation()
        {
            return location;
        }
};


//now using this class
int main() {
Dog dog1("Cleo", "Dalmation", 11, "Atlanta");
std::string dn=dog1.getname();
std::string db=dog1.getbreed();
int da=dog1.getage();
std::string dl=dog1.getlocation();
std::cout << "The Dog's name is " << dn << std::endl;
std::cout << "The Dog's age is " << da << std::endl;
std::cout << "The Dog's breed is " << db << std::endl;
std::cout << "The Dog's location is " << dl << std::endl;

}
```

Output:

```
"C:\Users\abhis\Google Drive\C++\Dog_Class.exe"
The Dog's name is Cleo
The Dog's age is 11
The Dog's breed is Dalmation
The Dog's location is Atlanta

Process returned 0 (0x0)   execution time : 0.046 s
Press any key to continue.
```

Create a Bank Account

In the next example, we create a class called BankAccount that imitates the functions of a bank. The class has 3 public variables and 4 public member functions. It takes in customer name, bank balance and account number as public variables. The 4 class member functions are used to deposit money, withdraw money, print account balance and print account number.

In the program below, the class is initialized in line 8 as a class with 4 variables.

The three variables are declared in lines 4-6. There is one string variable **holdername** that holds the customer's name and two variables **balance** and **accountNum**. These hold the funds balance and account number respectively.

The deposit function in lines 11-14 accepts a float variable **amount** as input and adds that to the float variable **balance**. It basically performs the function of a customer deposit.

The withdraw function in lines 16-19 accepts a float variable **amount** as input and subtracts that from the float variable **balance**. It basically performs the function of a customer withdrawal.

The other two functions **getBalance()** and **getAccountNum()** basically output the **balance** and **accountNum** variables.

The main function starts in line 36. In line 37, an instance of the class called **BankAccount1** is created with a **balance** of 5000, a **holdername** of “John Smith” and **accountNum** of 007123.

These variables are printed out in lines 38-39 using the **getBalance()** and **getAccountNum()** functions in the class. The public variable **holderName()** is also used.

In line 41, a deposit of 500 is made; and the new balance is printed in line 42.

Two withdrawals are made in line 44 and 50. If statements are used to check if the withdrawal is more than the balance. If the withdrawal is more than the balance, an error message is printed. If not, the transaction is completed.

The final customer balance is printed in each case.

All the screen outputs are shown below the code, and you can run it yourself to verify.

```
1   #include <iostream>
2   class BankAccount {
3     public:
4         float balance;
5         int accountNum;
6         std::string holderName;
7
8       BankAccount(double balance, int accountNum, std::string holderName): balance(balance), accountNum(accountNum), holderName(holderName) {}
9
10
11      void deposit(float amount)
12      {
13          balance = balance + amount;
14      }
15
16      bool withdraw(float amount)
17      {
18          if (amount > balance) {
19              return false;
20          }
21      balance = balance - amount;
22      return true;
23      }
24
25      double getBalance() {
26          return balance;
27      }
28
29      int getAccountNum() {
30          return accountNum;
31      }
32
33  };
34
```

```cpp
int main() {
    BankAccount account1(5000, 007123, "John Smith");
    std::cout << "Account Holder: " << account1.holderName << std::endl;
    std::cout << "Initial balance for Account " << account1.getAccountNum() << ": " << account1.getBalance() << std::endl;

    account1.deposit(500);
    std::cout << "Balance after deposit: " << account1.getBalance() << std::endl;

    if (account1.withdraw(2000)) {
        std::cout << "Withdrawal successful. New balance: " << account1.getBalance() << std::endl;
    } else {
        std::cout << "Insufficient funds. Current balance: " << account1.getBalance() << std::endl;
    }

    if (account1.withdraw(1000)) {
        std::cout << "Withdrawal successful. New balance: " << account1.getBalance() << std::endl;
    } else {
        std::cout << "Insufficient funds. Current balance: " << account1.getBalance() << std::endl;
    }
    return 0;
}
```

Output:

In the output below, the program first prints out the account holder name John Smith and an account balance of 5000. After adding 500, the account balance printed out is now 5500.

After the first withdrawal of 2000, the account balance is now 3500.

After the second withdrawal of 1000, the account balance updates to 2500.

```
"C:\Users\abhis\Google Drive\C++\bankaccount.exe"
Account Holder: John Smith
Initial balance for Account 3667: 5000
Balance after deposit: 5500
Withdrawal successful. New balance: 3500
Withdrawal successful. New balance: 2500

Process returned 0 (0x0)   execution time : 0.057 s
Press any key to continue.
```

Problems to Practice

1. Write a program that adds a function to above bank program. It adds a reward of 10% to the balance to anyone who wishes to deposit more than 10000.
2. Create a class called Car that takes in car name, car brand, number of miles, weight and cost. Create member functions that can output all above data.
3. Create a class Rectangle that takes in a width and height and can return area and perimeter.
4. Create a class that simulates a bank loan. It takes in credit rating as either A, B, C, D. It takes in a name, a loan amount and an account number. It has 2 functions: one which calculates the annual interest rate; and one which output both interest rate and annual interest added.
    a. Credit rating of 'A' has interest rate of 2%; 'B' has 4% rate; C has 6% rate; D has an 8% rate
    b. Interest is calculate using simple interest formula of: Interest = (Loan Amount * Time * Interest Rate) / 100 ; Time is 1 year for annual interest rate.

Common C++ Code Errors

While running C++, it's normal to encounter errors in the code that need fixes. It's part of the fun of coding. Programmers of all levels encounter errors. However, there are a few basic errors that are most common in C++. We've listed out 5 errors that you are most likely to encounter in C++ as a beginner.

1. **Syntax Error**

This error refers to an error in the syntax of your code, such as a missing semicolon (;) after a statement.

The example below would have a syntax error due to the missing semicolon in line 4.

```
1   #include <iostream>
2
3   int main() {
4       std::cout << "Hello, World!" << std::endl
5       return 0;
6   }
7
```

2. **Undeclared Identifier**

This error occurs when a variable is used by a program that hasn't been defined yet.

In example below, variable **name** has not been defined, but the code tries to print its value in line 6. This would cause an undeclared identifier error.

```
1    #include <iostream>
2
3    int main() {
4
5        std::cout << "Hello, World!" << std::endl;
6        std::cout << "My name is " << name << std::endl;
7        return 0;
8    }
9
```

To prevent this, we change the code as follows, and declare a string **name** in line 6.

```
1    #include <iostream>
2
3    int main() {
4
5        std::cout << "Hello, World!" << std::endl;
6        std::string name="Dave";
7        std::cout << "My name is " << name << std::endl;
8        return 0;
9    }
10
```

3. Undefined reference

An undefined reference occurs when an item is referenced in the code that has not been defined.

In the below example, **printname()** has not been defined properly in line 3, but it is referenced in line 7.

```
#include <iostream>

void printname();
int main() {
    std::cout << "Hello, World!" << std::endl;
    std::string name="Dave";
    printname();
    return 0;
}

```

We correct this by properly defining **printname()** below. **Printname** is a function that accepts a string as a parameter and prints it out as seen lin lines 4-6.

```
1  #include <iostream>
2
3  void printname(std::string name)
4  {
5      std::cout << name << std::endl;
6  }
7  int main() {
8      std::cout << "Hello, World!" << std::endl;
9      std::string name="Dave";
10     printname(name);
11     return 0;
12 }
13
```

4. Uninitialized variable

An uninitialized variable error occurs when a variable is declared and referenced in the code but no value has been assigned to it yet. In the example below, integer variable **tst** has not been initialized in line 5 but is used in line 6.

```
1   #include <iostream>
2
3   int main()
4   {
5       int tst;
6       std::cout << "The value of tst is: " << tst << std::endl;
7       return 0;
8   }
9
```

To correct this, we add a value to **tst** in line 5.

```
1   #include <iostream>
2
3   int main()
4   {
5       int tst=5;
6       std::cout << "The value of tst is: " << tst << std::endl;
7       return 0;
8   }
```

5. Type Mismatch

A type mismatch error occurs when two variables of incompatible variable types are combined. For example, a string variable is set equal to an integer variable or vice versa.

In the code below, there is one integer variable x, and one string variable y. x is set equal to y in line 7. This returns a type mismatch error as the two variables are incompatible

```
1   #include <iostream>
2
3   int main()
4   {
5       int x = 10;
6       std::string y = "Steve";
7       x = y;
8       return 0;
9   }
```

Appendix

US States and Capitals array

```
std::string states[] =
{"Alabama","Alaska","Arizona","Arkansas","California","Colorado"
,"Connecticut","Delaware","Florida","Georgia","Hawaii","Idaho","Ill
inois","Indiana","Iowa","Kansas","Kentucky","Louisiana","Maine","
Maryland","Massachusetts","Michigan","Minnesota","Mississippi",
"Missouri","Montana","Nebraska","Nevada","New
Hampshire","New Jersey","New Mexico","New York","North
Carolina","North
Dakota","Ohio","Oklahoma","Oregon","Pennsylvania","Rhode
Island","South Carolina","South
Dakota","Tennessee","Texas","Utah","Vermont","Virginia","Washi
ngton","West Virginia","Wisconsin","Wyoming"};

std::string capitals[] = {"Montgomery","Juneau","Phoenix","Little
Rock","Sacramento","Denver","Hartford","Dover","Tallahassee","
Atlanta","Honolulu","Boise","Springfield","Indianapolis","Des
Moines","Topeka","Frankfort","Baton
Rouge","Augusta","Annapolis","Boston","Lansing","St.
Paul","Jackson","Jefferson City","Helena","Lincoln","Carson
City","Concord","Trenton","Santa
Fe","Albany","Raleigh","Bismarck","Columbus","Oklahoma
City","Salem","Harrisburg","Providence","Columbia","Pierre","Nas
hville","Austin","Salt Lake
City","Montpelier","Richmond","Olympia","Charleston","Madison",
"Cheyenne"};
```

Conclusion / Next Steps

Thank you for taking the team to read this book.

I hope you have found it useful; and learnt the basics of C++. If you've been through the exercises, you now understand the basics, and able to program much more advanced applications in the future.

If you liked my book and you'd like to learn more, check out my Author page below. I'll have another book out soon that shows how to create a shopping cart from scratch using html, css and JavaScript.

https://www.amazon.com/Bob-Mather/e/B07HHQZC4Y

I'd also recommend looking at the other books in the section, especially the ones on how Artificial Intelligence will take over the world.

If you'd like any clarification regarding the topics; or any suggestions; please email me at: abiprod.pty.ltd@gmail.com

I also do one-one coaching online if you are interested in personalized help.

Book 3:
Learn Python Using Soccer

Importance of Programming

It was a bright Sunday afternoon, and Lily decided to spend quality time with her daughter, Amy.

They eagerly opened the DIY Robotics kit that they had bought on Amazon. As they assembled the robot, Lily noticed a very puzzled look on her daughter's face. Some of the instructions seem to be missing, and one of the components seemed faulty. Not sure what to do Lily called on her cousin, Steve. Steve was a young kid as well in the same school, but he had spent a few months learning programming. He had not touched a robot just like Amy. But Steve approached the situation differently. He looked up instructions for a similar robotic kit online, and then viewed a map of the different items on YouTube. He figured out which component was faulty and found a replacement part. With Steve's help, they continued with the task of building the robot. Within a few hours, they completed the task with no issues. Steve's brief interaction with programming had improved his problem-solving skills by an immeasurable amount, and he was able to apply these principles to problems outside the computer screen.

Not only did Steve fix the robot, but he also ignited Amy's love for robotics, and Lily got to spend some bonding time with her daughter, Amy.

Now let's look at another example. James was a 10-year-old boy who dreaded doing his Math homework. His parents were worried about him falling behind the rest of the class and getting bad grades. They had tried a bunch of math tutors but none of them really seemed to help. None of them were able to hold James' attention. However, James had a passion for computer games, and he would spend hours playing them after school. James' uncle came up with the idea of teaching James how to program computer games to see if that would help James at school. James enrolled in a coding course which he attended every day after school. Even though James struggled initially, he grew to love the course. Over the weeks and months of the course, his problem solving and logical thinking improved tremendously. He was not only able to complete his homework, but he was also able to do it quickly. He was able to outcompete the rest of his class at Math and Physics, and also had learnt a skill that none of his classmates could do. And he had a lot of fun doing it.

Both James and Amy are good examples of how programming can change a kids' approach to solving a problem. The problem can be a Math problem, a physics problem, an engineering problem or even another programming problem. The logical approach to solving a problem can be used by anyone for the rest of their life, at school and at work.

In this book, we look to make programming a lot more fun using real world applications in the most popular sport in the world, and one of the fastest growing sports in the United States. We hope you have as much fun learning as we did from creating this book.

Why Python?

While the choice of whether to learn programming is not a difficult one, the choice of programming language is not that simple.
There are thousands of programming languages to choose from, and there are more being created every day. However, sticking to the most popular ones will yield the best results, as they have the most community support and online documentation.
The right programming language for you depends on what you are using it for. If you are looking to create high performance software applications and games, C++ would be the best choice. However, it is not recommended for beginners as it is a difficult program to learn.
If you're looking to create a website, Javascript is the best programming language as it integrates well with html and css elements.
However, the best programming language that is recommended for beginners is Python.
It is simple and readable. It is easy to read and write, which makes it ideal for beginners to start learning. Python can be used for a wide variety of applications, from web development to machine learning and scientific computing.

Python has a large helpful community around the web that helps beginners with answers to basic questions.

Python has a large and active community of developers, which means there is a wealth of third-party libraries and frameworks available. For example, Django and Flask are great libraries for web development, NumPy and pandas for data manipulation, and TensorFlow and PyTorch for machine learning.

Python is also an open-source program, which means it is free to use and modify without paying any licensing fees.

Python has excellent libraries like NumPy, Pandas, Schikit-learn etc. which make it the best language for data analysis and machine learning. As a result, Python programmers have a wealth of opportunities in the job market.

Why use Soccer for Python?

Anyone who's ever learnt programming knows that while it's really fascinating and interesting, it can get pretty difficult at times. It's tough when you get stuck on a certain problem and keep getting the same error. At times, it's a little tedious when you get to longer length programs.

It's important that you're programming on something that you're passionate about. It's tough when you're making generic "Hello World" programs like everyone else. That's why most people drop out of programming and never learn much.

That's the reason we came up with this topic for programming. Using soccer examples, we make coding a lot more interesting. However, if you're not interested in soccer, or don't like soccer, we don't recommend this book. This is mainly for soccer fans. You can check out our other books on Amazon.

Soccer is the most popular sport in the world, and among the fastest growing sports among the younger population in the US. We know we can inspire a huge population interested in this sport to get into programming and change their lives.

Most people have a basic knowledge of the rules and regulations of soccer. The familiarity can make it easier for beginners to grasp programming concepts. It can help increase engagement for those who are struggling through programming concepts. It makes programming less abstract and can bridge the gap between theory and practical learning.

Installing Python

Your first step in this journey is installing the Python program onto your computer.

Go to the website https://www.python.org/downloads/ and download the latest version of Python.

Windows Download

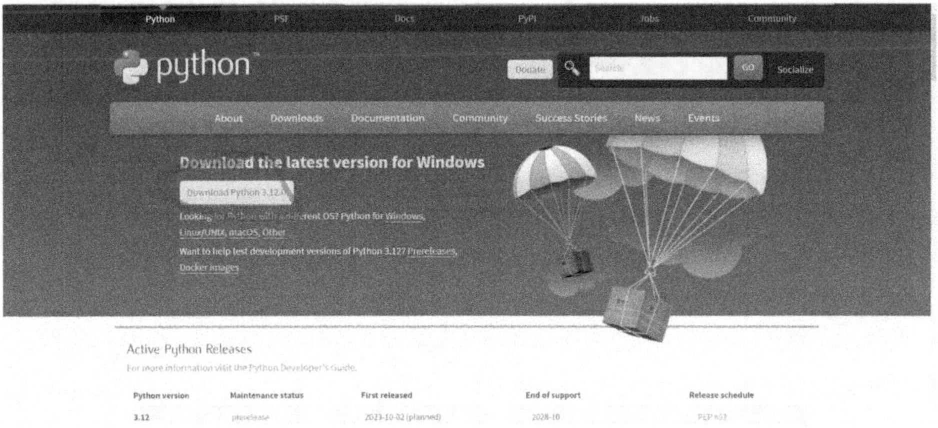

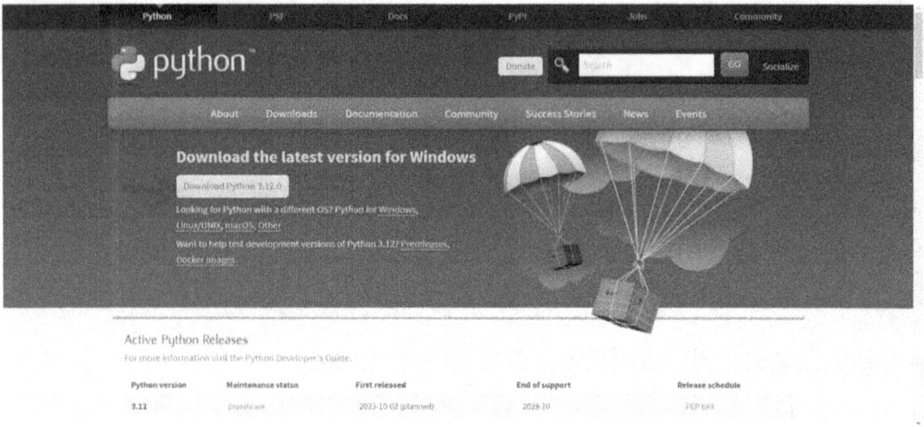

MAC Download

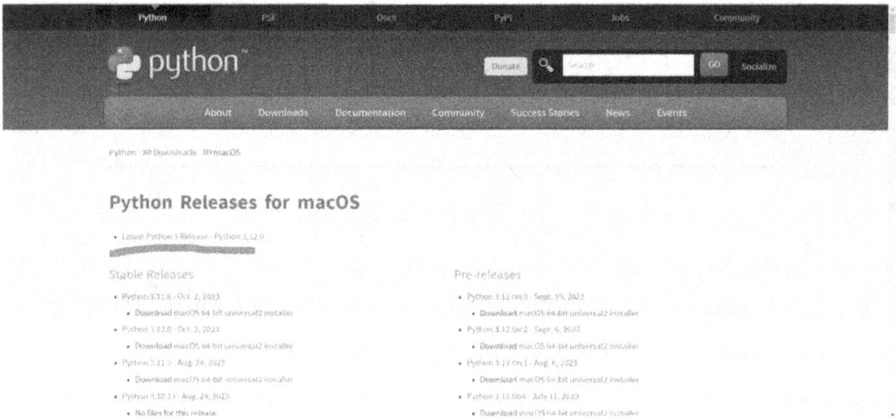

After downloading Python, install it on your computer as shown below.

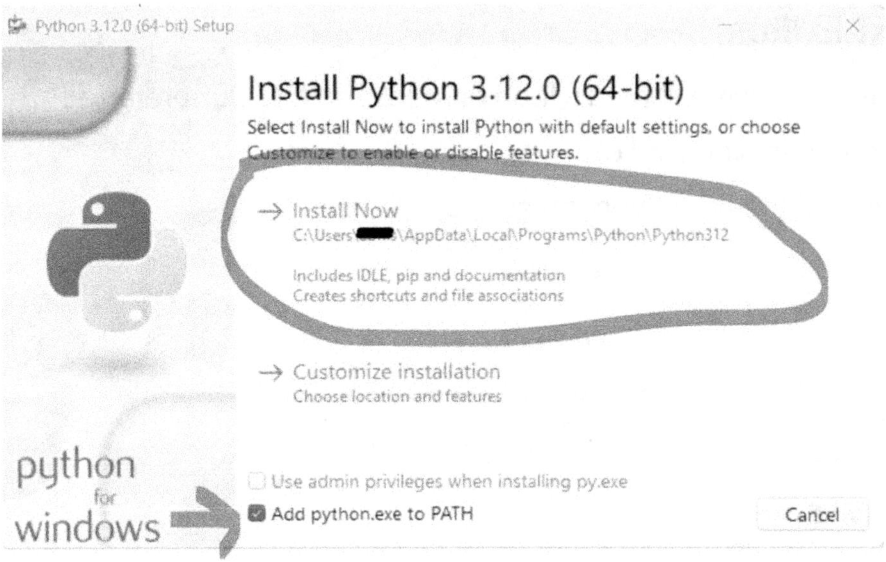
Python 3.12.0 (64-bit) Setup
Install Python 3.12.0 (64-bit)
Select Install Now to install Python with default settings, or choose
Customize to enable or disable features.
Install Now
C:\Users\[redacted]\AppData\Local\Programs\Python\Python312
Includes IDLE, pip and documentation
Creates shortcuts and file associations
Customize installation
Choose location and features
python
for
windows
Use admin privileges when installing py.exe
Add python.exe to PATH
Cancel

Text Editor

In this book, we will run Python on a text editor. Our preferred text editor is NotePad++.

Download the latest version at: https://notepad-plus-plus.org/downloads/ and install it.

Once Installed, you can type in "Notepad++" in the TaskBar and open up NotePad++ as below:

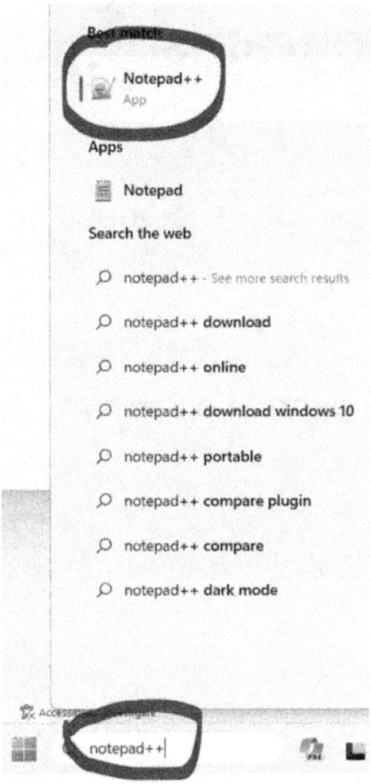

Best match
Notepad++
App
Apps
Notepad
Search the web
notepad++ - See more search results
notepad++ download
notepad++ online
notepad++ download windows 10
notepad++ portable
notepad++ compare plugin
notepad++ compare
notepad++ dark mode
notepad++

Your First Python Programs

In our first Python program, we will print the words “The beautiful game” onto the console screen.

First, open up **NotePad++.**

In NotePad++, type in **print(“The beautiful game”)** as shown below.

Now, save the file. Click “**File > Save As**”.

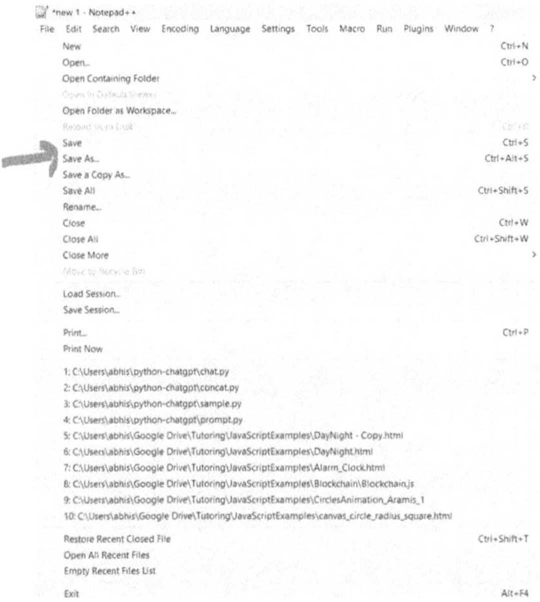

Choose Python file in “Save As Type”

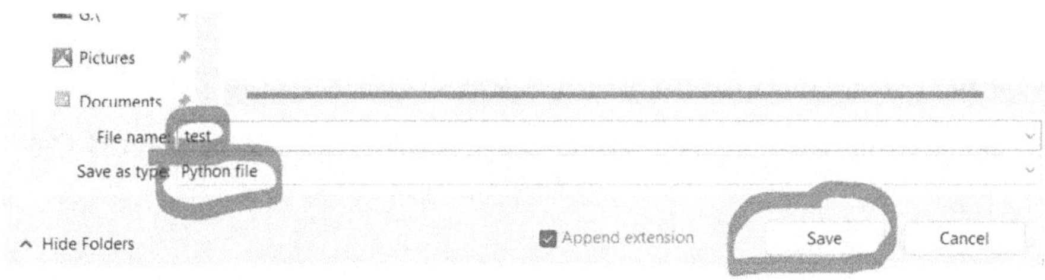

In this book, we are going to run all the files using Command prompt. To access **command prompt**, type in **cmd** in Taskbar search as shown below.

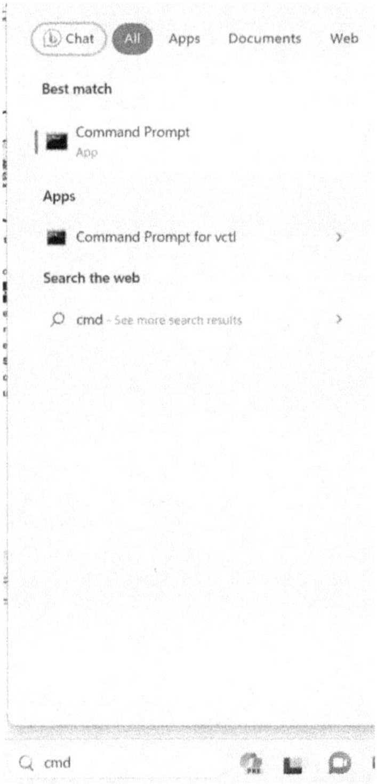

Browse to the correct folder in the user console. This path is going to be different for everyone based on where you saved the test.py file.

Once you get to the correct folder, run the program by typing in "python test.py"

And now you can see **“The beautiful game”** printed on the screen below.

Program 2

In the next program, we are going to print the sum of the numbers 4 and 5 on the screen.

Open up Notepad++ as before, and create a file called “test2.py” with 1 line. The line is print(4+5) as shown below.

Save the file.

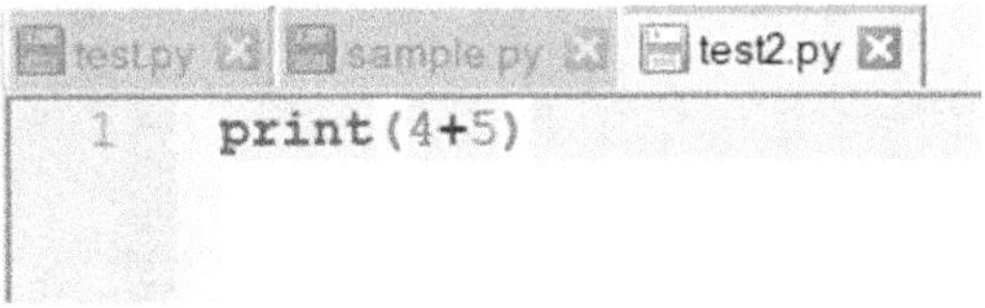

Run the program from Command console as shown below.

Once program is run, you can see the output of 9 on the screen.

Exercises to Practice

1. Write a program that prints the word “Joga Bonito” on the screen.
2. Write a program that prints your favorite player’s name on the screen.

Python Variables

A variable in programming is an item that stores a certain value. The value has to be a certain data type.

To describe it in soccer terms, a variable is like an equipment bag. A bag can store a certain type of equipment e.g. a round bag can only hold a soccer ball. A shoe bag can only hold soccer shoes. A soccer ball bag cannot hold shoes; and vice versa.

A variable can also change values within the program, as long as it's the same data type. So, we can replace the ball in a soccer bag and add a different one. Same thing with the equipment bag. So, in programming, a variable is of a certain data type and holds a certain value. The value can change within the program. So, let's take the example of an integer variable **n**. An integer variable can only hold numbers.

int-variable.py

```
n=75
print("The value of n is ");
print (n);
```

And print the value of n:

```
C:\Users\[redacted]\python-programs>python int-variable.py
The value of n is
75
```

Now, let’s change the value of variable **n** to 100.

int-variable.py int-variable-2.py

```
n=75
print("The 1st value of n is ");
print (n);
n=100
print("The 2nd value of n is ");
print (n);
```

```
C:\Users\[redacted]\python-programs>python int-variable.py
The value of n is
75

C:\Users\[redacted]\python-programs>python int-variable-2.py
The 1st value of n is
75
The 2nd value of n is
100
```

Now, let’s do the example of a string variable. A string variable holds a text character or a bunch of text characters.

Now, let’s create a variable called **player1** which holds string “Ronaldo”. Print out **player1** and we see that the program prints “Ronaldo”.

```
player1="Ronaldo"
print("The value of player1 is ");
print (player1);
```

```
C:\Users\[redacted]\python-programs>python string-variable.py
The value of player1 is
Ronaldo
```

Now, let’s change the value of variable **player1** to “Messi”. Print out player1 again and see that the value of **player1** has changed to “Messi”.

```
player1="Ronaldo"
print("The value of player1 is ");
print (player1);
player1="Messi";
print("The new value of player1 is ");
print (player1);
```

```
C:\Users\[redacted]\python-programs>python string-variable-2.py
The value of player1 is
Ronaldo
The new value of player1 is
Messi
```

In Python, you don't need to specify the data type when declaring a variable. Python automatically detects the type based on what is stored inside the variable.

For example, when we put Player1 = "Ronaldo", Python makes Player1 a string variable based on the word" Ronaldo" being a string.

Python Variable Data Types

Now, let's look at the different data types used in Python.

1. **Integer Data Type int:** The integer data type is used to store whole numbers like 0,1,2 etc.

    In the example goals, the variables **team1goals** and **team2goals** hold the integer values of the number of goals scored by Team 1 and Team 2. These values are printed on the screen below.

```
team1goals=2
team2goals=5
print("Team 1 Goals:")
print(team1goals)
print("Team 2 Goals:")
print(team2goals)
```

Output:

```
Team 1 Goals:
2
Team 2 Goals:
5
```

2. **Float Data Type:** A float data type is used to store decimal numbers. In the example below, **player1_average_goals_per_game** and **player2_average_gaols_per_game** are two float variables that hold the decimal values of the average goals per game for the two players.

```
player1_average_goals_per_game=1.4
player2_average_goals_per_game=0.7
print("Player 1 Goals Per Game:")
print(player1_average_goals_per_game)
print("Player 2 Goals Per Game:")
print(player2_average_goals_per_game)
```

Output:

```
Player 1 Goals Per Game:
1.4
Player 2 Goals Per Game:
0.7
```

3. **String Data Type:** A string variable is used to store single non-numeric character/characters. In the example below, string variables **player1name, player2name** and **player3name** store the names of players as strings. These are all printed as outputs on the screen.

```
player1name="Salah"
player2name="Ronaldo"
player3name="Onana"

print("Player 1 Name:")
print(player1name)
print("Player 2 Name:")
print(player2name)
print("Player 3 Name:")
print(player3name)
```

Output:

```
Player 1 Name:
Salah
Player 2 Name:
Ronaldo
Player 3 Name:
Onana
```

4. **Boolean Data Type**: A Boolean variable is one that can hold two values. These two values are **true** and **false**. Boolean variables are

used to perform checks, compare values of variables, compare names of variables etc.

In the below example, there are two integer variables **team1goals** and **team2goals** that hold values of goals scored by team1 and team2.

The Boolean variable **team1_win_boolean** compares the values of **team1goals** and **team2goals**. If team1goals is greater than team2goals, then **team1_win_boolean** returns a value of **true**. If not, it returns **false**.

In the below example, team1goals is less than team2goals, so team1_win_boolean is **false**.

```
team1goals=2
team2goals=5
print("Team 1 Goals:")
print(team1goals)
print("Team 2 Goals:")
print(team2goals)

team1_win_boolean=(team1goals>team2goals)
print("Is it true that Team1 won")
print(team1_win_boolean)
```

Output:

```
Team 1 Goals:
2
Team 2 Goals:
5
Is it true that Team1 won
False
```

In the next example, there are two integer variables **player1_average_goals_per_game** and **player2_average_goals_per_game** that hold values of average goals per game scored by player1 and player2.

The Boolean variable **player_goals_per_game_better** compares the values of **player1_average_goals_per_game** and **player2_average_goals_per_game**. If **player1_average_goals_per_game** is greater than **player2_average_goals_per_game**, then **player_goals_per_game_better** returns a value of true. If not, it returns false.

In the below example, **player1_average_goals_per_game** is greater than **player2_average_goals_per_game**, so **player_goals_per_game_better** is **true**.

```
player1_average_goals_per_game=1.4
player2_average_goals_per_game=0.7
print("Player 1 Goals Per Game:")
print(player1_average_goals_per_game)
print("Player 2 Goals Per Game:")
print(player2_average_goals_per_game)

player_goals_per_game_better=(player1_average_goals_per_game>player2_average_goals_per_game)
print("Is it true that player1 scored more goals")
print(player_goals_per_game_better)
```

Output:

```
Player 1 Goals Per Game:
1.4
Player 2 Goals Per Game:
0.7
Is it true that player1 scored more goals
True
```

Sample Outputs:

To add 2 decimal numbers we would need to use the **float() data type as it would output an incorrect whole number. This is shown** below, as 5.1+6.2 would produce an answer of 11 if variable data type **int** was used.

```
>>> int(5.1+6.2)
11
>>> float(5.1+6.2)
11.3
```

If we want to join two strings together and print, then we need to use str() function as using int or float would produce an error.

```
>>> int("Steve "+"won")
Traceback (most recent call last):
  File "<stdin>", line 1, in <module>
ValueError: invalid literal for int() with base 10: 'Steve won'
```

```
>>> str("Steve "+"won")
'Steve won'
```

There are other data types like double, tuple, dict etc. but these are beyond the scope of this beginners' book.

Converting Between Data Types

Why would I need to convert data types?

In some cases, certain tasks in Python only can happen with certain data types. For example, if we want to print a string and an integer in the same line, we can't use **print("The winner horse is horse number"+5)**

It produces the error below.

```
>>> print("The winning horse is horse number" + 5)
Traceback (most recent call last):
  File "<stdin>", line 1, in <module>
TypeError: can only concatenate str (not "int") to str
```

We need to convert the number 5 to a string as shown below.

```
>>> print("The winning horse is horse number " + str(5))
The winning horse is horse number 5
```

If we want to work with whole numbers, then we need to convert all decimals to int using **int()**. For example **int(5.2)** would produce 5.

The following functions help to convert between data types.
Str() converts any variable to a string data type
int() converts a variable into a integer data type
float() converts a variable into a float data type

Exercises to Practice

1. Create two integer variables called **manchesterunited** and **arsenal** and assign integer values to them equal to the number of goals scored in a match. Print out the values of each variable on the screen. Then, create a Boolean variable **compare_scores** to figure out who won the match, and print out the result using the value of the Boolean **compare_scores**.
2. Create two variables that store the average goals conceded by two goalkeepers. Print them on the screen. Then, create a Boolean variable **compare_averages** to figure out who is the better goalkeeper, and print out the result using the Boolean value.
3. Write a program that takes in two numbers and prints out their sum. The output message must be a combination of a string and a number. An example output would be "The sum of 2 and 5 is 7". The output statement would include the variables for 2,5 and 7.

Printing Data onto a Screen in Python

There are several ways to print data onto the screen in Python. For the purposes of this book we're going to go through 3 most commonly used ways to do so.

To demonstrate the differences in the 3 methods, we're going to print the line "Adam is 35 years old" on the screen in 4 different ways and each method is labelled on the screen.

```
1  print("Adam is 35 years old - 1st method")
2  
3  name = "Adam"
4  age = 35
5  
6  print(f"{name} is {age} years old - 2nd method")
7  
8  print(name+ " is "+ str(age) + " years old - 3rd method")
```

1st Method: Normal Printing

In line 1, we print the entire line on the screen by putting it inside the print function. This is the simplest method and easiest way if we know the exact string that we want to print.

2nd Method: Printing using f-Strings

In the next method, we declare two variables **name** and **age**. In lines 3 and 4, name is a string variable assigned to **"Adam"** and age is an integer variable assigned to **35**.

In line 6, we use a method known as **f-string** printing which allows us to include variable names in the print string. The values of the variables replace the variable names when the output is printed on the screen. This method is invoked by starting the print string with the value f right before the double quotation.

This method allows us the flexibility to print the string even if the name and age variables are changed to different values.

3rd Method: Printing using String Concatenation

In this method, multiple strings are added together and input on the screen. They are added together using the "+" sign as shown in line 8. Since age is an integer variable, it has to be converted into a string using **str(age)** before being included in the output.

The outputs for all three methods are shown below:

Output:

```
Adam is 35 years old - 1st method
Adam is 35 years old - 2nd method
Adam is 35 years old - 3rd method
```

4th Method: Printing at End of String

If there's a string in which a variable need to be printed at the end of the string, we can use the comma operator to do so. See example below.

```
age = 35
print("Adam's age = ",age)
```

Output:

```
Adam's age =  35
```

Exercises to Practice

1. Create two variables **player1** and **player2** that hold the names of two soccer players Messi and Ronaldo. Create another two integer variables **goals1** and **goals2** that hold the goals scored by Messi and Ronaldo. Messi has 819 goals, while Ronaldo has 830 goals. Print out on the screen "Ronaldo has 830 goals" and "Messi has 819 goals". Use the first three methods listed above.
2. Print out "Argentina won the 2023 world cup" using the first three methods in the chapter.
3. Print out "Ronaldo's age = 38" using the 4th method in the chapter.

Python Conditionals

A conditional in programming is a way to perform a check to see if a certain condition is met. If a certain condition is met, it can perform a certain task. If it is not met, it can perform a different task. It is a very useful way to automate tasks and eliminate manual checks.

In the example below, the program has two integer variables **players_on_subs_bench** and **minimum_subs_required**. If the number of players (**players_on_subs_bench**) on the bench was greater than or equal to minimum subs (**minimum_subs_required**), then it prints a start match message on the screen. Else it prints out that there are not enough players to start the match.

Players_on_subs_bench is assigned to a value of 1 in this program, and **minimum_subs_required** is assigned to a value of 5. Since **players_on_subs_bench** is the smaller value, it prints "Not enough players to start the match."

```
players_on_subs_bench = 1
minimum_subs_required=5

if players_on_subs_bench >= minimum_subs_required:
    print("Please start match.")
else:
    print("Not enough players to start the match.")
```

Output:

```
Not enough players to start the match.
```

Now, let's change the program to have more subs so it meets the conditions. **Players_on_subs_bench** is changed to a value of 6. Since **players_on_subs_bench** is the larger value now, it prints "Please start match."

```
players_on_subs_bench = 6
minimum_subs_required=5

if players_on_subs_bench >= minimum_subs_required:
    print("Please start match.")
else:
    print("Not enough players to start the match.")

```

Output:

```
Please start match.
```

Example 2:

The below program checks if the ball has crossed the goal line by checking exactly where the ball bounced. The integer variable **ballbouncepoint** stores the value of the ball bounce location.

If **ballbouncepoint** is greater than 700, it is judged to have crossed the line and goal is declared. If not, ball did not cross the line. No goal.

In below example, **ballbouncepoint** is below 700, so there is no goal printed as output on the screen.

```
ballbouncepoint = 600

if ballbouncepoint >= 700:
    print("Ball crossed line. Goal!!")
else:
    print("Ball did not cross line. No Goal!!")
```

Output:

```
Ball did not cross line. No Goal!!
```

In next example, **ballbouncepoint** is 750, which is more than the check of 700, so the output is **"Ball crossed line. Goal!!"** Goal is declared.

```
ballbouncepoint = 750

if ballbouncepoint >= 700:
    print("Ball crossed line. Goal!!")
else:
    print("Ball did not cross line. No Goal!!")
```

Output:

```
Ball crossed line. Goal!!
```

Example 3:

The below program checks the goals scored by team x and team y. These are stored in integer variables **team_x_score** and

team_y_score. The team with the larger score wins. These are checked using if-else conditionals in lines 4-9.

If **team_x_score** is larger then **team_y_score**, then print "Team X wins". If **team_y_score** is larger than **team_x_score** then print "Team Y wins". If neither is true, then it goes to line 9 and prints **"It's a draw".**

whowon.py

```
1   team_x_score = 1
2   team_y_score = 2
3
4   if team_x_score > team_y_score:
5       print("Team X wins!")
6   elif team_y_score > team_x_score:
7       print("Team Y wins!")
8   else:
9       print("It's a draw!")
10
```

Output:

In the first program, **team_y_score** is greater than **team_x_score**, so it prints "Team Y wins".

```
Team Y wins!
```

```
team_x_score = 3
team_y_score = 2

if team_x_score > team_y_score:
    print("Team X wins!")
elif team_y_score > team_x_score:
    print("Team Y wins!")
else:
    print("It's a draw!")

```

In the next example, **team_x_score** is greater than **team_y_score**, so it prints “Team X wins”.

Output:

```
Team X wins!
```

Team Winner

whowon.py

```
team_x_score = 1
team_y_score = 1

if team_x_score > team_y_score:
    print("Team X wins!")
elif team_y_score > team_x_score:
    print("Team Y wins!")
else:
    print("It's a draw!")

```

In the next example, team_x_score is equal to team_y_score, so it prints “It’s a draw”.

Output:

```
It's a draw!
```

Exercises to Practice

1. Write a program that stores the number of substitutions in a variable and checks if it is less or more than 5. If the number is more than 5, print out that there are no more substitutions allowed. If it's less than 5, print out how many substitutions are left in the game.
2. Create two variables that contain the points received so far in the league for two teams that are playing a game. Write a conditional that checks the result of the game. If the game is a draw, both teams receive a point. If a team wins, the winner receives three points. Increase the value of the variables based on the result of the game.
3. Create two variables for goals scored and goals conceded for a team in the league. Calculate the goal difference for the team:
   goal difference = goals scored – goals conceded
   If the goal difference is above 0, print out that the team is performing below par, and if it's above 0, print out that the team is doing well.

User Input in Python

An important aspect of any programming language is the ability to accept data from the user while the program is running. This is called user input and is one of the most useful features of programming. With user input data, there is no need to change the data every time the variable value needs to be changed. Python is no different. In Python, we accept user input through the **input()** function, as shown below:

ui=input("Enter Anything:")

The words within the brackets on the input function are printed on the screen. So, **"Enter Anything"** is printed on the screen. The user now has the option to type something on the screen. Whatever the user types on the screen is stored in the variable **ui**.

Now, let's look at an example. In the program below, we ask the user to input their favorite soccer player, and print that on the screen. In line 1, the user inputs their favorite soccer player and it is stored in string variable **favp**. The default data type for a user input variable is a string.

In line 2, this is printed on the screen.

```
1  favp = input ("Who is your favorite soccer player?");
2  print("Your favorite soccer player is "+favp);
```

Output:

```
Who is your favorite soccer player?
```

```
Who is your favorite soccer player?Ronaldo
```

```
Who is your favorite soccer player?Ronaldo
Your favorite soccer player is Ronaldo
```

In the next example, the user inputs 2 separate values for goals scored and goals against and prints out the goal difference on the screen. The variables **goals1** and **goals2** store the user input variables for goals scored and goals conceded respectively. Since the default data type is string, both variables are converted to int before being stored. This is done so they can be used in line 3 as integers.

The goal difference is calculated in line 3 and stored in variable **goaldiff**.

In line 4, the value of **goaldiff** is printed on the screen. The required output for the print function is string, so the integer is converted to a string using **str(goaldiff)**.

```
1   goals1 = int(input ("Enter total goals scored: "))
2   goals2 = int(input ("Enter total goals conceded: "))
3   goaldiff=goals1-goals2
4   print("Team's Goal difference "+str(goaldiff))
```

Output:

```
Enter total goals scored: 15
Enter total goals conceded: 13
Team's Goal difference 2
```

```
Enter total goals scored: 12
Enter total goals conceded: 15
Team's Goal difference -3
```

```
Enter total goals scored: 10
Enter total goals conceded: 2
Team's Goal difference 8
```

Exercises to Practice

1. Write a program that takes in the value of your favorite soccer team and prints it on the screen.
2. Write a program that takes in the value of 15 players in your team and stores it in 15 different variables. Print out the names of only the starting 11 players at the end of the program.

Learn Loops Using Soccer

A loop in programming is a set of instructions that is repeated a fixed number of times.

In Python, a loop is declared as follows:

for x in range(a,b)

The above line has **x** as the counter of the loop, and it starts off with the value of **a**. The loop ends as soon as the counter x hits the value **b**.

In the first example below, the program prints out each penalty kick in a 30-kick penalty training session using a for loop.

The counter is the variable **kicks**. It starts with the number 1 and ends before it hits the number 31.

The penalty kick number is printed in each iteration of the loop, and the end of the session is printed after the loop is over in line 4.

Loop 1 Example: Penalty Kicks

```
for kicks in range(1, 31):
    print("Finished Kick Number ",kicks)
print (" ")
print("End of penalty kick session")
```

Output:

```
Finished Kick Number  1
Finished Kick Number  2
Finished Kick Number  3
Finished Kick Number  4
Finished Kick Number  5
Finished Kick Number  6
Finished Kick Number  7
Finished Kick Number  8
Finished Kick Number  9
Finished Kick Number  10
Finished Kick Number  11
Finished Kick Number  12
Finished Kick Number  13
Finished Kick Number  14
Finished Kick Number  15
Finished Kick Number  16
Finished Kick Number  17
Finished Kick Number  18
Finished Kick Number  19
Finished Kick Number  20
Finished Kick Number  21
Finished Kick Number  22
Finished Kick Number  23
Finished Kick Number  24
Finished Kick Number  25
Finished Kick Number  26
Finished Kick Number  27
Finished Kick Number  28
Finished Kick Number  29
Finished Kick Number  30

End of penalty kick session
```

Loop 2 Example

The next program has a for loop that counts 5 substitutions for a team in a game.

```
1 for subs in range(1, 6):
2     print("Completed sub number ",subs)
3 print (" ")
4 print("No more substitutions left")
5
```

The for loop counter variable called **subs** takes on values from 1 to 5. The range(1, 6) function generates a sequence of numbers starting from 1 and ending at 5 (not including 6). So, **subs** will take on values 1, 2, 3, 4, and 5 in each iteration of the loop.

In each iteration of the loop, this line prints a message to the console. The message is a combination of a string ("Completed sub number ") and the current value of the subs variable, which represents the current iteration of the loop. This line will print messages like "Completed sub number 1," "Completed sub number 2," and so on, for each iteration of the loop.

After the loop is over in line 4, the programs prints that there are no more substitutions left for the team. This is seen in the output below.

Output:

```
Completed sub number  1
Completed sub number  2
Completed sub number  3
Completed sub number  4
Completed sub number  5

No more substitutions left
```

Example Loop 3: Fitness Training Session

In the next example, we create a loop that calculates the number of laps around a running track that a player does during a fitness training session.

In line 1, we create a variable **runningloops** that runs from 1 to 10 in a for loop. In each iteration of the loop, the program prints the lap number.

Once the loop is completed in line 4, the program prints that the running session is over for the player. This is seen in the output below.

```
1 for runningloops in range(1, 11):
2     print("Completed lap number ",runningloops)
3 print (" ")
4 print("Finishing running session")
```

Output:

```
Completed lap number  1
Completed lap number  2
Completed lap number  3
Completed lap number  4
Completed lap number  5
Completed lap number  6
Completed lap number  7
Completed lap number  8
Completed lap number  9
Completed lap number  10

Finishing running session
```

Loop Example: Nested Loops to count free kicks per training week.

In the next example, we explain the concept of a nested loop. A nested loop is just one loop within another.

A team has 3 training sessions per week, and 10 free kicks within each training session. To track and print each free kick in a training session, we create a loop with counter **weeklysessions** from 1 to 3. This is called the outer loop.

Each time the outer loop starts, we print the weekly session number in line 2.

Then, we create another loop within with the counter freekicks from 1 to 10. This is the inner loop. Within the inner loop, we print out the freekicks number, which helps keep track of the free kicks within each training session.

Once 10 freekicks are over, then the outer loop **weeklysessions** increases by 1 and we move back to line 2 to repeat the outer loop. And the process repeats till all weekly sessions are over. Once all weekly sessions are over, the outer loop is over, and we print out that we have finished the weekly training session in line 6.

```
1 for weeklysessions in range(1, 4):
2     print("Weekly session: ", weeklysessions)
3     for freekicks in range(1, 11):
4         print("Completed free kick number ", freekicks)
5 print(" ")
6 print("Finishing weekly free kick training")
7
```

Output:

As seen in the output below, we print out 10 free kicks in each weekly session and then move on to next one. This continues till all 3 weekly sessions are over.

```
Weekly session:  1
Completed free kick number  1
Completed free kick number  2
Completed free kick number  3
Completed free kick number  4
Completed free kick number  5
Completed free kick number  6
Completed free kick number  7
Completed free kick number  8
Completed free kick number  9
Completed free kick number  10
Weekly session:  2
Completed free kick number  1
Completed free kick number  2
Completed free kick number  3
Completed free kick number  4
Completed free kick number  5
Completed free kick number  6
Completed free kick number  7
Completed free kick number  8
Completed free kick number  9
Completed free kick number  10
Weekly session:  3
Completed free kick number  1
Completed free kick number  2
Completed free kick number  3
Completed free kick number  4
Completed free kick number  5
Completed free kick number  6
Completed free kick number  7
Completed free kick number  8
Completed free kick number  9
Completed free kick number  10

Finishing weekly free kick training
```

Exercises to Practice

1. Build a Python program that simulates a workout session for a player with only 20 push ups. Print out the completion of each push up using a for loop.
2. Write a Python program that simulates 3 soccer training sessions. Each soccer training session has 20 free kicks, 10 penalty kicks, and 20 laps round the field.
   Hint: Use a nested loop with the outer loop that counts the number of training sessions. There are 3 inner loops that track free kicks, penalty kicks and laps.

Basic Math in Python using Soccer

Python is a great program to do basic math calculations. In this chapter, we'll look at basic programs that perform these operations.

Addition

Python does simple addition using the '+' sign. To illustrate with an example, we add the goals scored in 5 games and add them together.

Below program has 5 variables that holds the goals in 5 games. A 6th variable holds the sum of these 5 variables and prints it on the screen.

The 5 variables are **game1goals**, **game2goals**, **game3goals**, **game4goals** and **game5goals**. The variable **sumofgoals** in line 7 calculates the sum of these 5 variables and prints it on the screen.

The sum of all 5 variables in lines 1-5 is **8**, and this value is printed as an output on the screen.

```
game1goals = 1
game2goals = 0
game3goals = 2
game4goals = 0
game5goals = 5

sumofgoals = game1goals + game2goals + game3goals + game4goals + game5goals
print("Number of goals scored in 5 games")
print(sumofgoals)
```

Output:

```
Number of goals scored in 5 games
8
```

Subtraction

Python does simple subtraction using the '-' sign.

Below program has 2 variables that holds the total goals scored in a season, and total goals scored by Ronaldo. The program calculates the goals scored without Ronaldo. This is an important variable as Ronaldo is leaving at the end of the season. The variable **totalseasongoals** holds the total team goals, **ronaldogoals** holds total goals scored by Ronaldo.

A 3rd variable **estimated_goals_without_ronaldo** is the difference between the first 2 variables, and estimates the goals scored by the team without Ronaldo.

The difference of the two variables in lines 1-2 is **53** (85-32), and this value is printed as an output on the screen.

whowon.py sumofgoals.py season-goals.py

```
totalseasongoals = 85
ronaldogoals = 32

estimated_goals_without_ronaldo = totalseasongoals - ronaldogoals
print("Estimated Goals Without Ronaldo")
print(estimated_goals_without_ronaldo)
```

Output:

```
Estimated Goals Without Ronaldo
53
```

Multiplication:

Python does simple multiplication using the '*' sign.

In below program, we are trying to calculate the total penalty kicks taken by a team per week in practice. We have 3 variables that can help with this data. The integer variable **weeklypracticesessions** holds the number of team practice sessions per week, **playerstotal** is total number of players taking penalty kicks, and **penaltypicksperplayer** is the number of penalty kicks taken per player per session

These 2 numbers are multiplied and stored in the variable **totalpenaltypicksperweek**, and this value is output on the screen.

```
weeklypracticesessions=2
playerstotal=15
penaltykicksperplayer=20
totalpenaltykicksperweek = weeklypracticesessions*playerstotal*penaltykicksperplayer

print("Total Team Penalty Kicks Per Week")
print(totalpenaltykicksperweek)
```

Output:

In the code, we multiply the 3 integer variables to get an output of **600** (2 x 15 x 20)

```
Total Team Penalty Kicks Per Week
600
```

Division and Remainder

Python does simple division using the '/' sign.

Python calculates remainder using the modulus or percentage '%' sign.

In the next program, we are given the total budget for a team this season and this is stored in the variable **totalseasonbudget**. We are only given the cost per game, and this is stored in the variable **costspergame**. We need to find the number of games that this team can afford, and the money left over after these games.

In line 4, we calculate the number of games that the team can afford. This is converted to an int variable (as the number of games cannot be a decimal). The value is stored in the integer variable **numberofgames**.

Money left over is calculated in line 5 as a remainder and is stored in integer value of **moneyleft**.

With a total season budget of 50000, and expenses of 8000 per game, the team can afford 6 games and 2000 is left over as seen in the output.

```
1  totalseasonbudget = 50000
2  costspergame = 8000
3
4  numberofgames = int(totalseasonbudget/costspergame)
5  moneyleft = totalseasonbudget%costspergame
6
7  print("No. of games team can afford to play")
8  print(numberofgames)
9  print("Money left at end of season")
10 print(moneyleft)
```

Output:

```
No. of games team can afford to play
6
Money left at end of season
2000
```

A Soccer Statistics Calculator

To demonstrate the concepts, we're going to create a program that calculates different basic statistics in soccer. The program takes in wins, losses, draws, goals scored and goals conceded by a team in a season. The program calculates total games played, total points, goal difference and average goals per game.

In lines 1-5, we declare integer variables **wins**, **losses**, **draws**, **goals_for** and **goals_against**. The user inputs integer values for each of them.

In line 7, variable **gamesplayed** calculates the sum of wins, losses and draws to get the number of games played.

In line 8, variable **points** stores the total number of points obtained by the team. 3 points for each win and 1 point for a draw.

In line 9, variable **goal_difference** is calculated as the difference between the goals scored and goals conceded.

In line 10, **goals_per_game** is the goals scored divided by total games played.

In lines 12-14, these statistics are printed using **fprint**.

```
1  wins = int(input("Enter the number of wins: "))
2  losses = int(input("Enter the number of losses: "))
3  draws= int(input("Enter the number of losses: "))
4  goals_for = int(input("Enter the number of goals scored this season: "))
5  goals_against = int(input("Enter the number of goals conceded this season: "))
6
7  gamesplayed=wins+losses+draws
8  points = wins*3+draws*1
9  goal_difference = goals_for - goals_against
10 goals_per_game = goals_for/gamesplayed
11
12 print(f"Total Points: {points} in {gamesplayed} games")
13 print(f"Goal Difference: {goal_difference}")
14 print(f"Average Goals Per Game: {goals_per_game} goals per game")
15
```

Output:

```
Enter the number of wins: 25
Enter the number of losses: 5
Enter the number of losses: 8
Enter the number of goals scored this season: 76
Enter the number of goals conceded this season: 65
Total Points: 83 in 38 games
Goal Difference: 11
Average Goals Per Game: 2.0 goals per game
```

Random numbers

In Python, we can generate random numbers and use it to create randomized output. In the code below, we use a random number to check if the goalkeeper dives the same side as the penalty taker shoots. We assume that the goalkeeper saves the goal if he dives to the correct side. This is done for 10 shots, and the number of goals scored is printed out at the end.

In line 1, we import Python library **random** which allows us to create and manipulate random variables.

In line 4-5, we declare **penalty_shots** and **goals** as variables for the total penalty shots taken and goals scored respectively. There are 10 penalty shots to be taken, and 0 goals initially.

In line 7, a for loop from 1 to 10(penalty_shots) is set up.

In line 8, a random variable **goalkeeper_side_dive** is set up. Random.random() is a function within the random library that creates a decimal number between 0 and 1. We multiply that by 2 to get a number between 0 and 2. If **goalkeeper_side_dive** is less than 1, then the goalkeeper dives the wrong way, and it is a goal. We increase the number of goals by 1.

If **goalkeeper_side_dive** is greater than 1, the goalkeeper dives the right way and saves the goal. After the loop ends, we print the number of goals scored.

```
import random

# Simulate a penalty shootout
penalty_shots = 10
goals = 0

for penalty in range(penalty_shots):
    goalkeeper_side_dive = random.random()*2

    if goalkeeper_side_dive < 1:
        print("The goalkeeper dived the wrong way. Goal!!")
        goals = goals + 1
    else:
        print("Saved! The goalkeeper made the right move. No Goal!!")

print(" ")
print("Total goals scored in 10 shots:", goals)
```

Output:

In below output, the goalkeeper dives the right way only 3 times. So, 7 goals out of 10 are scored. The result of the shot is seen after each of the 10 shots as either a goal or no goal. Run the program a couple of times to ensure that a different answer (random answer) is created each time.

```
The goalkeeper dived the wrong way. Goal!!
Saved! The goalkeeper made the right move. No Goal!!
The goalkeeper dived the wrong way. Goal!!
The goalkeeper dived the wrong way. Goal!!
Saved! The goalkeeper made the right move. No Goal!!
The goalkeeper dived the wrong way. Goal!!
The goalkeeper dived the wrong way. Goal!!
The goalkeeper dived the wrong way. Goal!!
Saved! The goalkeeper made the right move. No Goal!!
The goalkeeper dived the wrong way. Goal!!

Total goals scored in 10 shots: 7
```

Random Variable Example 2

In the next example, a team's manager wants to give a player a gift. He labels all 20 players in the squad 1-20 and puts the number into a hat. He pulls out a number randomly to pick the lucky winner. Now, let's do this with a Python program. In Line 1, we import the random library.

In line 2, we create the random variable **random_player** as a random number between 1 and 20. It is converted to integer to make sure that it is a whole number.

In line 5, the lucky player number is output on the screen.

```
1  import random
2  random_player = int(random.random()*20)
3
4  print(" ")
5  print("Lucky soccer player is Player Number ", random_player)
```

Output:

Run the program a few times to ensure that we get a different player every time.

```
Lucky soccer player is Player Number  5
```

```
Lucky soccer player is Player Number  16
```

```
Lucky soccer player is Player Number  4
```

The next few examples are great ways to show the use of Python as a calculator, but it requires knowledge of exponents, logarithms and square root which are normally only taught after year 8 in school. So, the rest of this chapter is great for kids over the age of 12.

Exponents

In the next problem, we have a soccer fan who just started a club last year. He's starting off with a very small base of 100 people, but he's confident that he can double his fan base every year. He's trying to figure out how many fans he'll have after 10 years.

```
new_club_fanbase = 100
growth_exp = 2
years = 10

fanbase_10years = new_club_fanbase * (growth_exp ** years)
print(f"After {years} years, the fanbase will be {fanbase_10years} fans.")
```

In line 1-3, we declare variables **new_club_fanbase, growth_exp** and **years** as for the current fan base number, growth rate and years to be taken into account for calculation respectively. **Growth_exp** is 2 since we expect the fanbase to double each year. Exponents are a great way to solve this. The formula is shown below:

$$fanbase\_10years = new\_club\_fanbase * (grwoth\_exp^{years})$$

In Python, we use the double star symbol for exponentiation (**) and the single star for multiplication (*).

This is shown in line 5 when the equation is written.

The output from the equation is printed on the screen in line 6.

Output:

As seen in the output, the club will have 102400 fans in 10 years.

```
After 10 years, the fanbase will be 102400 fans.
```

Logarithms

Logarithms are basically the reverse of exponents, and can be used to solve problems that are the inverse of the previous ones. For example, what if the revenue of a club increases by 50% per year, and we want to figure out how many years it takes to get to $1 million. Logarithms are the best way to do so.

Logarithms are included in the math library in Python so we import the Math library in line 1.

The variables for initial revenue, target revenue and growth rate are declared in lines 3-5. A growth rate of 50% is indicated by a **growth_rate** of 0.5 below.

The formula to calculate number of years based on declared variables is:

$$years = \frac{\log \frac{target\_revenue}{initial\_revenue}}{\log(1 + growth\_rate)}$$

This is calculated in line 6 and converted into an integer variable (as we are looking for an approximate number of years).

```
1  import math
2
3  initial_revenue = 1000
4  target_revenue = 1000000
5  growth_rate = 0.5
6
7  years = int(math.log(target_revenue / initial_revenue) / math.log(1 + growth_rate))
8  print(f"It will take {years} years for the club to reach an annual revenue of $1 million.")
9
```

Output:

Based on the numbers and the formula, it takes this club 17 years to reach its goal.

```
It will take 17 years for the club to reach an annual revenue of $1 million.
```

Square root

Square roots in Python can be done using the **sqrt()** function in the Math library.

The problem we're trying to solve is that a soccer team has a square space of 2000 square meters to practice soccer. The team needs to calculate the length of each side, and that will help determine number of cones needed for each side of the square. Each cone covers 1 meter length of the side.

The math library in Python is used to calculate a lot of the basic and advanced math functionality.

So, it's good practice to import the Math library into Python when doing calculation. This is done in line 1 below.

In line 3, the variable **square_field** has an area of 2000.

In line 4, square root is calculated using **math.sqrt** of **square_field**. It is converted into int as we cannot have fractional cones to put on each side.

In line 6, we print out the number of cones needed.

```
1 import math
2
3 square_field = 2000;
4 length = int(math.sqrt(square_field))
5 number_cones = length;
6 print(f"It will take approximately {number_cones} cones per side to get a field of {square_field} square meters.")
```

Output:

Each side is 44 meters, which means 44 cones are needed for each side.

```
It will take approximately 44 cones per side to get a field of 2000 square meters.
```

Trigonometry

Basic trigonometry can be done in Python using the sin(), cos(), tan() functions in the Math library.

In the below program, the ball is 10 meters high, and at an angle of 30 degrees to the foot of the player. How far is the ball from the player's foot? To solve this problem, we use trigonometry.

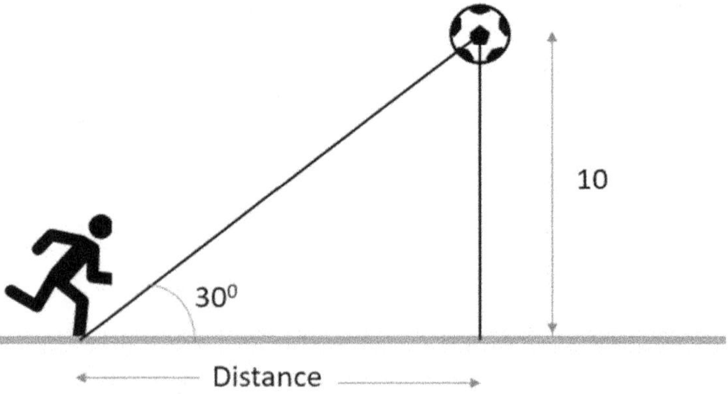

$$\tan(30) = \frac{10}{Distance}$$

$$Distance = \frac{10}{\tan(30)}$$

We use the tan function which is part of the Python math library.

The functions work on angles in radian units.

The angle needs to be converted into radian using **math.radians** in line 3.

The distance is then calculated using the formula in line 5. The distance is a float variable with 10 decimal places. To make it more readable, we round it to two decimal places using the **round()** function in line 7.

The output is then printed on the screen in line 7.

```
1  import math
2  angle = 30
3  ang_rad=math.radians(angle)
4  v_dist = 10
5  h_dist=10/math.tan(ang_rad)
6  rounded_height=round(h_dist, 2)
7  print(f"The player is {rounded_height}m away from the player.")
```

Output:

```
The player is 17.32m away from the player
```

Exercises to practice

1. Create 10 variables to store the goals scored by a team in ten different games. Then calculate and print the total number of goals scored and average goals per game for those games.
2. Create a program that calculates the goal difference for a team given the goals scored and goals conceded which are stored in two different variables.
3. Calculate the average salary for a player per season given the salary per game and total number of games per season.
4. Create a Python program to determine how many players a soccer team can buy in the off season given its total player budget and the average cost per player. Use variables to store the total off season budget and the cost per player, and then calculate and print the number of players the team can afford, along with the money left over.
5. Pick a random player in a team of 11 to take a penalty shoot out and print out the player number on screen (eg. "Player 1 takes the shot", "Player 2 takes the shot" etc. etc.)
6. Create a Python program that simulates the growth of the Sydney League over the next 10 years, considering it has a fan base of 15000 and a growth rate of 20% per year. How many fans will it have after 10 years? Then, calculate how many years it will take to reach 1 million fans?

7. A square practice soccer field is 15 meters on each side. How much does it cost the team to water the field if it costs $100 per square meter to do so?
8. A soccer ball is 20 meters away from the goal and on the ground. The goal post bar is 10 meters high. What is the maximum angle a player can shoot at to ensure that it doesn't go over the bar?

Arrays in Python

An array is a group of variables of the same data type and with the same name. It helps with better organizing the code.
To demonstrate this, let's look at a simple example. If you want to store 10 numbers in 10 integer variables, we need to create 10 different integer variables as below.

```
num1=5
num2=6
num3=7
num4=9
num5=34
num6=9
num7=99
num8=67
num9=4
num10=3
```

With arrays, we can create the variable like this:

```
num = [5,6,7,9,34,9,99,67,4,3]
```

num is an array of size 10.
If we want to print the numbers, just print out the numbers using the index. The first index starts at 0. So, if we want to print out the first number, then:

print (num[0]) prints out 5.

Print (num[1]) prints out 6 and so on.

Arrays use less computer memory and make programs run faster. They also help to organize code better and make code more understandable.

Now, let's look at an example where we input the names of 10 Premier League clubs into an array.

In line 1, we create an empty array called **soccer_clubs** that we can enter data into.

Lines 3-5 have a 10 item for-loop where we enter the names of the Premier League clubs.

In line 4, the user enters the name of the Premier League clubs and stores it in string **club_name**.

In line 5, **club_name** is added to array **soccer_clubs** using **append()** function. The **append** function is used to add items to the end of an array.

In line 8-9, we have another for loop that prints the items in the array.

```
1    soccer_clubs = []
2
3    for i in range(10):
4        club_name = input(f"Enter the name of soccer club {i + 1}: ")
5        soccer_clubs.append(club_name)
6
7    print("List of Premier League Soccer Clubs:")
8    for club in soccer_clubs:
9        print(club)
```

Output:

```
Enter the name of soccer club 1: Manchester United
Enter the name of soccer club 2: Manchester City
Enter the name of soccer club 3: Arsenal
Enter the name of soccer club 4: Tottenham Hotspurs
Enter the name of soccer club 5: Bolton Wanderers
Enter the name of soccer club 6: West Ham United
Enter the name of soccer club 7: Chelsea
Enter the name of soccer club 8: Liverpool
Enter the name of soccer club 9: Leicester City
Enter the name of soccer club 10: Ipswich City
List of Premier League Soccer Clubs:
Manchester United
Manchester City
Arsenal
Tottenham Hotspurs
Bolton Wanderers
West Ham United
Chelsea
Liverpool
Leicester City
Ipswich City
```

Adding and Removing Items from an Array

We can also add and remove elements in an array. To remove elements, we use the function remove() and to add elements we use the function **append()**.

In the number array at the start of the chapter, we can use **num.remove(67)** to remove the number 67 from the array. And we can add a new number (let's say 100) by using **num.append(100).**

In the next example, let's create an array of Premier League clubs and remove one club at the end of the season. And then, we add a newly promoted club to the array.

In line 1, we declare array **club_name** which contains names of 10 clubs in the premier league. In lines 4-5 we print the club names, so the user knows which clubs are there before any changes are made.

In line 6, the user inputs the club the user wants to remove, and it is stored in variable **relegatedclub**. In line 7, the user inputs the club the user wants to add and stores it in variable **promotedclub**.

And then, in lines 10-11, we print out all the list of club names with the new club.

```
club_name = ["Manchester United", "Manchester City", "Arsenal", "Tottenham Hotspur", "Bolton Wanderers", "West Ham United",
"Chelsea", "Liverpool", "Leicester City", "Ipswich City" ]
print("The Premier League clubs are: ")
for club in club_name:
    print(club)
relegatedclub = input("Which club performed the worst last season?")
promotedclub = input("Which club was promoted last season?")
club_name.remove(relegatedclub)
club_name.append(promotedclub)
print("The new Premier League clubs are: ")
for club in club_name:
    print(club)
```

Output:

In this example, the **relegatedclub** is Chelsea and the **promotedclub** is Blackburn Rovers. This is the seen in the second list where Chelsea is remove and Blackburn Rovers is added.

```
The Premier League clubs are:
Manchester United
Manchester City
Arsenal
Tottenham Hotspur
Bolton Wanderers
West Ham United
Chelsea
Liverpool
Leicester City
Ipswich City
Which club performed the worst last season?Chelsea
Which club was promoted last season?Blackburn Robers
The new Premier League clubs are:
Manchester United
Manchester City
Arsenal
Tottenham Hotspur
Bolton Wanderers
West Ham United
Liverpool
Leicester City
Ipswich City
Blackburn Robers
```

Premier League teams with wins, losses and draws

We can also use elements in multiple arrays and create a third one that's a product of the two. For example, if num1 and num2 are two arrays such that:

num1 = [1,2,3]

num2 = [10,9,8]

Then we can create num3 which is a product of num1 and num2 using the zip function below:

num3 = [num1*num2 for num1, num2 in zip(num1,num2)]

zip is a function used to access data in multiple arrays at the same time. It can also be used in for loops.

Now, we get the result below:

num3 = [1*10,2*9,3*8]

num3 = [10, 18, 24]

In the next example, we create three arrays for the wins, losses and draws for three premier league teams. We then calculate the total points scored for each club and store it in a fourth array. Each team gets 3 points for a win and 1 for a draw.

In line 1, we declare array **club_name** which contains names of 10 clubs in the premier league. In lines 3-5, we create three arrays **club_wins**, **club_losses** and **club_draws** that contain the number of wins, losses and draws for the teams in array **club_name**.

In lines 7-8, we print the names of the clubs with the number of wins, losses and draws in a for loop. We need to use the zip function as it accesses data from multiple arrays.

In line 9, we use the zip function again to calculate the number of points for each team and store it in an array called **club_points**.

In line 12-13, we print out the names of the clubs with the number of points scored.

```
1  club_name = ["Manchester United", "Manchester City", "Arsenal", "Tottenham Hotspur", "Bolton Wanderers", "West Ham United",
2  "Chelsea", "Liverpool", "Leicester City", "Ipswich City" ]
3  club_wins = [10,9,10,7,8,6,5,3,4,5]
4  club_losses = [4,3,5,3,2,2,2,4,2,1]
5  club_draws = [4,6,3,8,8,9,11,11,12,12]
6  print("The Premier League clubs are: ")
7  for club,wins,losses,draws in zip(club_name, club_wins, club_losses,club_draws):
8      print("Club " + club + "= "+ str(wins) + " Wins "+ str(losses) + " Losses " + str(draws) + " Drawn ")
9  club_points = [club_wins*3+club_draws*1 for club_wins, club_draws in zip(club_wins, club_draws)]
10 print("")
11 print("Points")
12 for club,wins,losses, draws, points in zip(club_name, club_wins, club_losses,club_draws, club_points):
13     print("Club " + club + "= "+ str(points)+" Points")
14
```

Output:

```
The Premier League clubs are:
Club Manchester United= 10 Wins 4 Losses 4 Draws
Club Manchester City= 9 Wins 3 Losses 6 Draws
Club Arsenal= 10 Wins 5 Losses 3 Draws
Club Tottenham Hotspur= 7 Wins 3 Losses 8 Draws
Club Bolton Wanderers= 8 Wins 2 Losses 8 Draws
Club West Ham United= 6 Wins 2 Losses 9 Draws
Club Chelsea= 5 Wins 2 Losses 11 Draws
Club Liverpool= 3 Wins 4 Losses 11 Draws
Club Leicester City= 4 Wins 2 Losses 12 Draws
Club Ipswich City= 5 Wins 1 Losses 12 Draws

Points
Club Manchester United= 34 Points
Club Manchester City= 33 Points
Club Arsenal= 33 Points
Club Tottenham Hotspur= 29 Points
Club Bolton Wanderers= 32 Points
Club West Ham United= 27 Points
Club Chelsea= 26 Points
Club Liverpool= 20 Points
Club Leicester City= 24 Points
Club Ipswich City= 27 Points
```

Exercises to Practice

1. Create an array of 5 soccer players with another array containing number of goals scored by each player during the season. Print out the names of all players with the number of goals scored.
2. Create an array of 10 soccer teams with arrays containing the number of red cards and yellow cards each team had. Calculate a negative sportsmanship score. A higher score is worse. There are 10 points for each red card, and 3 points for a yellow. Print out the team names with their sportsmanship score.
3. Create an array of 8 soccer stadiums with arrays containing their capacity. Print out the values for each stadium.
4. Create an array of 6 soccer teams with arrays containing the number of goals scored and the number of goals conceded by each team in the current season. Calculate and print the goal difference (goals scored minus goals conceded) for each team.
5. Create an array of 10 soccer players with arrays containing the number of assists and the number of goals they've scored in the current season. Calculate and print the goal-to-assist ratio for each player.

Lists in Python

What is a List?

Another programming data structure that is very useful is a list. It also stores multiple elements like arrays, but it can store items of different data types. A single list can store both integer and string variables. For example, let's create a list below called **lista**.

Lista = ['a','Tom',5,6.5,False]

lista contains 5 elements. 'a' and 'Tom' are string variables; 5 is an integer variable, 6.5 is a float variable and False is a Boolean. A list is great for organizing data of different data types.

We can access different elements of a list using an index. The index of the first element is 0.

So, **print(lista[0])** prints 'a' on the screen.

Print(lista[01]) prints 'Tom' on the screen.

We can add elements to a list using append function and remove elements from a list using the remove function.

Lista.append(9) adds 9 to the end of the list. The list now becomes

lista = ['a','Tom',5, 6.5, False,9]

lista.remove(6.5) removes the first occurrence of 6.5 in lista. So, the list now becomes:

lista = ['a','Tom',5, False,9]

Lists with Multiple elements

If we create a list with multiple elements with the same data type, we need to create a reference to access the data.

In the example below, we want to create a list of 5 soccer players with player name, games played, and goals scored. So, we create a reference for each data value that is the same across the list. We create a reference "**name**" for all soccer names in the list; a reference **"games_played"** for games played and a reference **"goals_scored"** for number of goals scored. This is seen when creating the list **soccer_players** in lines 1-6.

When we access the data for printing, we use the reference name to access the data. In the for loop in line 10, player is a counter that iterates through **soccer_players**. We use **player['name']** to access name data, **player['games_played']** to access games played data, and **player['goals_scored']** to access goals scored data. This is seen when printing the output below.

```python
soccer_players = [
    {"name": "Lionel Messi", "games_played": 800, "goals_scored": 700},
    {"name": "Cristiano Ronaldo", "games_played": 850, "goals_scored": 750},
    {"name": "Neymar Jr.", "games_played": 600, "goals_scored": 300},
    {"name": "Kylian Mbappé", "games_played": 250, "goals_scored": 150},
    {"name": "Robert Lewandowski", "games_played": 400, "goals_scored": 380},
]

print("List of Soccer Players:")
for player in soccer_players:
    print(f"Name: {player['name']}")
    print(f"Games Played: {player['games_played']}")
    print(f"Goals Scored: {player['goals_scored']}")
    print()
```

Output:

```
List of Soccer Players:
Name: Lionel Messi
Games Played: 800
Goals Scored: 700

Name: Cristiano Ronaldo
Games Played: 850
Goals Scored: 750

Name: Neymar Jr.
Games Played: 600
Goals Scored: 300

Name: Kylian Mbappé
Games Played: 250
Goals Scored: 150

Name: Robert Lewandowski
Games Played: 400
Goals Scored: 380
```

Sorting data in a list

To sort data in a list, we use a function called **sorted()**. If there are multiple elements in a list, we can sort based on one of the elements of the list. In the above example, we can sort the players based on the number of goals scored. They can be sorted in ascending or descending order. In this case, we will sort it in descending order.

To sort the data, we add line 9 in program below. We create a new list called **sorted_players** which contains the list sorted in descending order of goals scored.

Here's the elements of the sorted() function with their explanations:

soccer_players is the list of players we want to sort that is an input into sorted()

key = lambda x: x["goals scored"] :This is a key function that tells sorted() how to extract the sorting key from each element in **soccer_players**. In this case, it's a lambda function that takes an element x and returns the element with a reference name of goals scored. This means you are sorting the elements in **club_info** based on the values in **goals_scored** in the list.

Reverse=True means that you are sorting in descending order of value. Reverse=False would sort in ascending order of value.

In the output below, we see that the list is now sorted with the highest goal scorer at the top of the list, and the lowest at the bottom.

```
soccer_players = [
    {"name": "Lionel Messi", "games_played": 800, "goals_scored": 700},
    {"name": "Cristiano Ronaldo", "games_played": 850, "goals_scored": 750},
    {"name": "Neymar Jr.", "games_played": 600, "goals_scored": 300},
    {"name": "Kylian Mbappé", "games_played": 250, "goals_scored": 150},
    {"name": "Robert Lewandowski", "games_played": 400, "goals_scored": 380},
]

sorted_players = sorted(soccer_players, key=lambda x: x["goals_scored"], reverse=True)

print("Soccer Players Sorted by Goals Scored:")
for player in sorted_players:
    print(f"Name: {player['name']}")
    print(f"Games Played: {player['games_played']}")
    print(f"Goals Scored: {player['goals_scored']}")
    print()
```

Output:

```
Soccer Players Sorted by Goals Scored:
Name: Cristiano Ronaldo
Games Played: 850
Goals Scored: 750

Name: Lionel Messi
Games Played: 800
Goals Scored: 700

Name: Robert Lewandowski
Games Played: 400
Goals Scored: 380

Name: Neymar Jr.
Games Played: 600
Goals Scored: 300

Name: Kylian Mbappé
Games Played: 250
Goals Scored: 150
```

Now, we do the same sorting operation for the Premier league table created in the previous chapter on arrays.

We create a list **club_info** of club names and points scored in line 8.

We then use the **sorted()** function in line 10 to create a sorted array called **sorted_clubs**. It sorts **club_info** in descending order based on the values in **club_points**. **X[1]** indicates that the sorting is done based on the 2nd element of the list(which is **club_points**). So, this means that the Premier league clubs are being sorted based on total number of points in descending order.

```
1  club_name = ["Manchester United", "Manchester City", "Arsenal", "Tottenham Hotspur", "Bolton Wanderers", "West Ham United",
2               "Chelsea", "Liverpool", "Leicester City", "Ipswich City"]
3  club_wins = [10, 9, 10, 7, 8, 6, 5, 3, 4, 5]
4  club_losses = [4, 3, 5, 3, 2, 2, 2, 4, 2, 1]
5  club_draws = [4, 6, 3, 8, 8, 9, 11, 11, 12, 12]
6  club_points = [club_wins * 3 + club_draws * 1 for club_wins, club_draws in zip(club_wins, club_draws)]
7
8  club_info = list(zip(club_name, club_points))
9
10 sorted_clubs = sorted(club_info, key=lambda x: x[1], reverse=True)
11
12 print("Premier League clubs sorted by points (descending order):")
13 for club, points in sorted_clubs:
14     print(f"Club {club} = {points} Points")
15
```

```
Premier League clubs sorted by points (descending order):
Club Manchester United = 34 Points
Club Manchester City = 33 Points
Club Arsenal = 33 Points
Club Bolton Wanderers = 32 Points
Club Tottenham Hotspur = 29 Points
Club West Ham United = 27 Points
Club Ipswich City = 27 Points
Club Chelsea = 26 Points
Club Leicester City = 24 Points
Club Liverpool = 20 Points
```

Accessing and Modifying elements in a list

We already know we can access elements of a list using an index value. We can also figure where an element occurs in the list using a function called index.

In the below example, we modify the Premier league table based on the results of a match. We add 3 points to the winner's total; or 1 point to both teams playing if it's a draw.

In lines 8-9, we accept user input for names of teams playing, and store the team names in variables **team1** and **team2**.

In line 11, we accept the result of the match. The user inputs 1 for team1 win, 2 for team2 win and 3 for a draw.

The value is stored in a integer variable called **result**.

We then use the index function to figure out where in the list each team is located.

Team1_index is an integer variable that stores the list index value of team1. It basically searches through the list for occurrence of team1 value and stores it. If the value does not occur, it stores a value of -1.

Team2_index does the same for the index value of team2.

Based on the index value, the result value is added to **team2_index**.

If result is 1, the value of **club_points** at **team1index** are increased by 3; meaning that team 1 gets 3 points added. (line 16-17)

If result is 2, the value of **club_points** at **team2index** are increased by 3; meaning that team 2 gets 3 points added. (line 18-19)

If result is 3, the value of **club_points** at both **team1index** and **team2index** are increased by 1; meaning that both team 1 and team 2 gets 1 point added. (line 20-22).

The clubs are then sorted based on points; and the Premier League points table is printed out.

This is shown in output below the code.

```
1  club_name = ["Manchester United", "Manchester City", "Arsenal", "Tottenham Hotspur", "Bolton Wanderers", "West Ham United",
2               "Chelsea", "Liverpool", "Leicester City", "Ipswich City"]
3  club_wins = [10, 9, 10, 7, 8, 6, 5, 3, 4, 5]
4  club_losses = [4, 3, 5, 3, 2, 2, 2, 4, 2, 1]
5  club_draws = [4, 6, 3, 8, 8, 9, 11, 11, 12, 12]
6  club_points = [club_wins * 3 + club_draws * 1 for club_wins, club_draws in zip(club_wins, club_draws)]
7
8  team1 = input("Enter the name of the home team: ")
9  team2 = input("Enter the name of the away team: ")
10
11 result = input("Enter the result of the match (1 for home team win, 2 for away team win, 0 for a draw): ")
12
13 team1_index = club_name.index(team1)
14 team2_index = club_name.index(team2)
15
16 if result == "1":
17     club_points[team1_index] += 3
18 elif result == "2":
19     club_points[team2_index] += 3
20 elif result == "0":
21     club_points[team1_index] += 1
22     club_points[team2_index] += 1
23
24 print("\nUpdated Premier League clubs sorted by points (descending order):")
25 club_info = list(zip(club_name, club_points))
26
27 sorted_clubs = sorted(club_info, key=lambda x: x[1], reverse=True)
28 for club, points in sorted_clubs:
29     print(f"Club {club} = {points} Points")
30
```

Output:

```
Enter the name of the home team: Manchester United
Enter the name of the away team: Arsenal
Enter the result of the match (1 for home team win, 2 for away team win, 0 for a draw): 0

Updated Premier League clubs sorted by points (descending order):
Club Manchester United = 35 Points
Club Arsenal = 34 Points
Club Manchester City = 33 Points
Club Bolton Wanderers = 32 Points
Club Tottenham Hotspur = 29 Points
Club West Ham United = 27 Points
Club Ipswich City = 27 Points
Club Chelsea = 26 Points
Club Leicester City = 24 Points
Club Liverpool = 20 Points
```

Exercises to Practice

1. Create a list of 10 soccer stadiums with stadium name, stadium city and stadium capacity. Sort the stadiums based on stadium capacity and print them out.
2. Create a list of 5 soccer players with player name, champions league medals won, world cup medals won; and sort them based on total medals won.
3. Create a list of 10 soccer clubs with club name, club city, and the year the club was founded. Sort the clubs based on the founding year in ascending order and print them out.
4. Create a list of 8 national soccer teams with team name, FIFA World Rankings, and the number of World Cup titles won. Sort the national teams based on their FIFA World Rankings in ascending order and print them out.

Drawing in Python

Now, let's get to the really fun part. Drawing, Art, Animation, whatever you like to call it. Python can do it too. Drawing soccer objects and images is a great way to learn Python.

In Python, we're going to draw using the turtle library. The turtle library is a graphics library. It lets user draw on the screen as if one were using a pen. We invoke the use of the turtle library using the line:

import turtle

The turtle library has several functions that one can use to draw objects such as lines, squares, rectangles, circles etc.

We're going to learn these functions through the use of 5 examples in this chapter. First, we're going to learn how to draw a line. Using that knowledge, we're going to learn how to draw a rectangle. Then we're going to draw a circle. Using the knowledge from drawings we just completed, we're going to now draw a green soccer field with all the relevant lines in it. And then add a soccer ball to the center of the field.

Before we get started, let's go over the different steps involved in drawing something:

1. Create a screen object. This causes turtle to open a new screen.
2. Create a turtle object that can be used as a pen.
3. Assign a pen speed. This is the speed that the program would draw at.
4. Determine the coordinates of the item you want to draw.
5. Figure out the starting point. This is where the pen starts.
6. Determine the pen color. This is the color that the object is drawn in, and the color the shape is filled in with.

Now, let's get started.

Drawing a Line

In the program below, we're going to draw three lines of 3 different colors and 3 different thicknesses at 3 different locations on the screen.

In line 1, we import the **turtle** library so we can use the drawing functions.

In line 3, we create a screen object, to draw items on it.

In line 5, we create a turtle object called **pen**. This object will be used to draw on the screen object. Think of it as holding a pen and drawing on a screen.

In line 7, we set the speed for the object. A faster speed is good for drawing larger items, while a slower speed works for small items like lines, circles etc. We recommend a smaller speed while doing your first programs.

Lines 9-14: The first line is created. It is a red line with size 2. In line 10, we start the drawing at (-150,0) which is the location on the screen. In line 11, we use the **pendown()** function to start drawing. Think of it as putting the pen down on a blank piece of paper. After **pendown()** function is invoked, all marks will be seen on the screen. In line 12, we set the pen size as 2 using the **pensize()** function. In line 13, we set the color as red using the **pencolor()** function. In line 14, we create a line of 200 pixels moving the pen to the right using the **forward()** function. The default direction for the forward function is to the right. We can change the default direction if we need to by using the rotate() function.

In lines 16-21, we create a line of size 4 that is blue in color. It is double in thickness of the first line and starts at (0,-50). The starting point is 150 pixels higher than the first line, and 50 pixels to the right.

In lines 23-28, we create the final line of size 6 that is green in color. It is three times the thickness of the first line and starts at (100,50). The starting point is 200 pixels higher than the first line and 100 pixels to the right.

Finally, in line 30, the programs stops with a **screen.exitonclick()** function. When this function is called, the screen closes when the user anywhere on the screen.

All three lines are seen in the output below the code.

```
1  import turtle
2
3  screen = turtle.Screen()
4
5  pen = turtle.Turtle()
6
7  pen.speed(1)
8
9  pen.penup()
10 pen.goto(-150, 0)
11 pen.pendown()
12 pen.pensize(2)
13 pen.pencolor("red")
14 pen.forward(200)
15
16 pen.penup()
17 pen.goto(0, -50)
18 pen.pendown()
19 pen.pensize(4)
20 pen.pencolor("blue")
21 pen.forward(150)
22
23 pen.penup()
24 pen.goto(100, 50)
25 pen.pendown()
26 pen.pensize(6)
27 pen.pencolor("green")
28 pen.forward(100)
29
30 screen.exitonclick()
```

Output:

Drawing a Rectangle

In the next example, we create a rectangle in Python by drawing 4 red lines. Then we fill the rectangle with red color.

In lines 1-7, we create the screen and pen objects and set the speed as in the previous program.

In line 9, we set a **begin_fill()** function as it is required to start filling of an object in turtle. We set the color as red in line 10.

In line 12-14, we start the program by getting the pen to coordinates **(-350,-300)** which is the bottom left of the screen.

In line 16, we draw a line of length 600 by moving the pen to the right with the **forward()** function. This draws the first line of the rectangle.

For the second line, we need to move up instead of right. We must change the direction the **forward()** function moves by rotating the direction.

In line 17, we rotate the pen to the left by 90 degrees using the function **left(90)**. Then, in line 18, we move the pen up a length of 200. In line 19, we rotate the pen to the left another 90 degrees for the third line of the rectangle.

In line 20-23, we repeat above steps by drawing a line of length 600 to the left, rotating 90 degrees. And we finally complete the rectangle by drawing a length of length 200 down.

In line 25, we fill the rectangle with **end_fill()** function.

The red rectangle is seen in the output below the code.

```
import turtle

screen = turtle.Screen()

pen = turtle.Turtle()

pen.speed(1)

pen.begin_fill()
pen.fillcolor("red")

pen.penup()
pen.goto(-350, -300)
pen.pendown()

pen.forward(600)
pen.left(90)
pen.forward(200)
pen.left(90)
pen.forward(600)
pen.left(90)
pen.forward(200)
pen.left(90)

pen.end_fill()
screen.exitonclick()
```

Output:

Drawing a Circle

In the next example, we draw a blue circle with a diameter of 200. It is done using the **circle(200)** function in line 16.

In lines 1-10, the process is similar to the previous problems where a screen object and pen object are created. The speed is set to 1, and the color is set to blue.

We start the drawing at (-100,-100) using the **goto(-100,-100)** function. These are the coordinates of the bottom of the circle (and not the center).

In line 18, we use the **end_fill()** to complete filling the circle.

We see the blue circle on the screen in the output below the code.

```
import turtle

screen = turtle.Screen()

pen = turtle.Turtle()

pen.speed(1)

pen.begin_fill()
pen.fillcolor("blue")

pen.penup()
pen.goto(-100, -100)
pen.pendown()

pen.circle(200)

pen.end_fill()

screen.exitonclick()
```

Output:

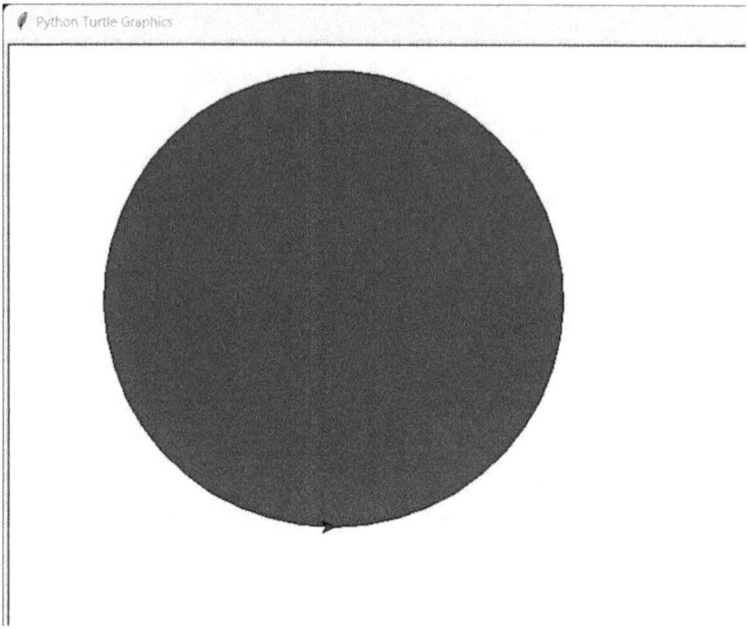

Drawing a Soccer Field

Now for the soccer part. Let's use the knowledge we have from the previous drawings and draw a full soccer field. That's right!! We're going to draw a green rectangle which represents the soccer field grass. Then we're going to draw a line that goes through the center of the screen. This is the halfway line.

In the next step, we draw the center circle in the center of the field.

Then, we draw the left penalty box which is a white rectangle at the left-hand corner of the field. We do the same for the right penalty box which is on the right-hand corner of the field.

Finally, we draw a white spot at the center of the field, which is the kick off spot.

So, let's start off with the field.

Drawing the Green Rectangle (Lines 9-21)

The rectangle starts from the bottom left of the screen at (-300, -200) and is set up for a length of 600 and width of 400. It is filled with green which simulates the grass in the soccer field.

Drawing the Center Line (Lines 23-29)

The center line is drawn from the bottom center of the rectangle at (0,-200). The pensize is increased to 4 to increase visibility, and it set to color white.
Since the last direction for the forward() function in the program was to move down (last line in the rectangle), we need to add an extra 180 degree rotation in line 28 to make it move up. After the rotation, it moves up for a distance of 400, so that the center line width of the field.

Drawing the Center Circle (Lines 32-35)

The center circle is set to a width of 50. So, it starts at (50,0) which is the bottom of the circle.

Left Penalty Area (Lines 37-47)

The left penalty area is a rectangle in white. We start at the top left corner and start moving right. However, in the last line, we moved up while drawing the center line. So, we rotate the pen to the right by 90 degrees in line 40. The rectangle has a width of 50 and a length of 100.

Right Penalty Area (Lines 49-59)

Now, we do the same for the right-hand side. We start at the top right corner and create a rectangle again with a width of 50 and length of 100.

Center Dot (Lines 61-64)

Finally, we create a dot at the center of the center circle. This is the kickoff spot. It is set to a thickness of 10 and a location of (0,0).

We see the green soccer field drawn below the output code.

```
import turtle

screen = turtle.Screen()

pen = turtle.Turtle()

pen.speed(2)

pen.penup()
pen.goto(-300, -200)
pen.pendown()
pen.begin_fill()
pen.fillcolor("green")
pen.forward(600)
pen.left(90)
pen.forward(400)
pen.left(90)
pen.forward(600)
pen.left(90)
pen.forward(400)
pen.end_fill()

pen.penup()
pen.goto(0, -200)
pen.pendown()
pen.pensize(4)
pen.pencolor("white")
pen.left(180)
pen.forward(400)
```

```
pen.penup()
pen.goto(50, 0)
pen.pendown()
pen.circle(50)

pen.penup()
pen.goto(-300, 50)
pen.pendown()
pen.right(90)
pen.forward(50)
pen.right(90)
pen.forward(100)
pen.right(90)
pen.forward(100)
pen.right(90)
pen.forward(50)

pen.penup()
pen.goto(300, 50)
pen.pendown()
pen.left(90)
pen.forward(50)
pen.left(90)
pen.forward(100)
pen.left(90)
pen.forward(50)
pen.left(90)
pen.forward(100)

pen.penup()
pen.goto(0, 0)
pen.pendown()
pen.dot(10)

screen.exitonclick()
```

Output:

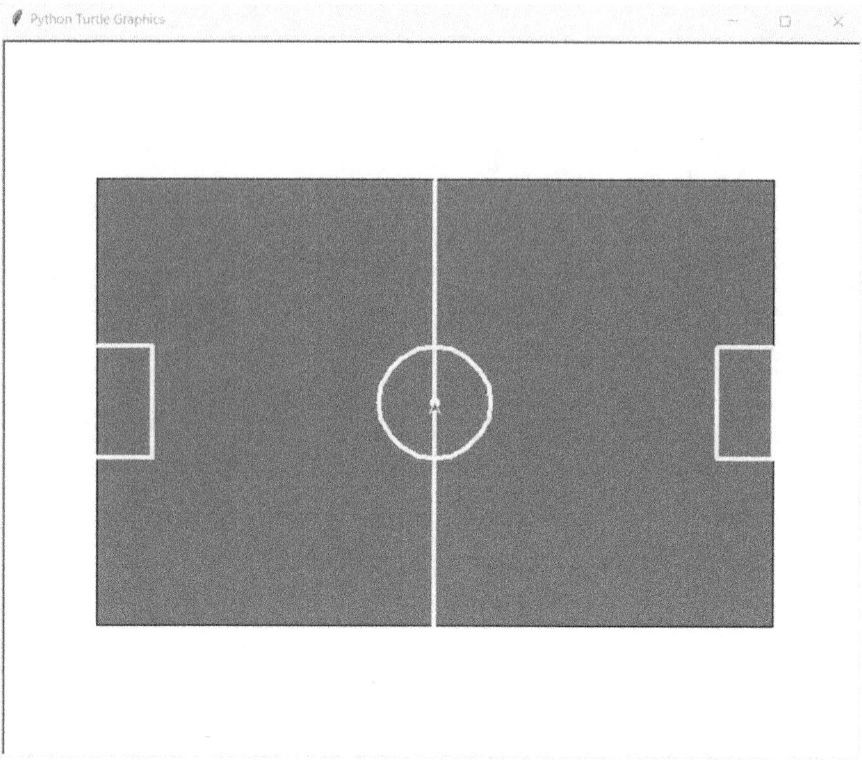

Drawing a Soccer Ball on a Soccer Field

In this example, we take the soccer field from the previous program and draw a black soccer ball in the middle of the field. So, we basically use the same program as in the previous example and add lines 66-73 to the program. The soccer ball is a circle of size 5 and filled with black color. In line 69, the color of the circle outline is set as black. And, in line 71, the color of the circle interior is set to black as well. This needs to be done as the interior of the ball needs to be filled.

In line 67, the pen is set to start at bottom corner of the circle at (5,0). And in line 72, the circle is drawn with a radius set as a size 5.

```
import turtle

screen = turtle.Screen()

pen = turtle.Turtle()

pen.speed(2)

pen.penup()
pen.goto(-300, -200)
pen.pendown()
pen.begin_fill()
pen.fillcolor("green")
pen.forward(600)
pen.left(90)
pen.forward(400)
pen.left(90)
pen.forward(600)
pen.left(90)
pen.forward(400)
pen.end_fill()

pen.penup()
pen.goto(0, -200)
pen.pendown()
pen.pensize(4)
pen.pencolor("white")
pen.left(180)
pen.forward(400)
```

```
pen.penup()
pen.goto(50, 0)
pen.pendown()
pen.circle(50)

pen.penup()
pen.goto(-300, 50)
pen.pendown()
pen.right(90)
pen.forward(50)
pen.right(90)
pen.forward(100)
pen.right(90)
pen.forward(100)
pen.right(90)
pen.forward(50)

pen.penup()
pen.goto(300, 50)
pen.pendown()
pen.left(90)
pen.forward(50)
pen.left(90)
pen.forward(100)
pen.left(90)
pen.forward(50)
pen.left(90)
pen.forward(100)

pen.penup()
pen.goto(0, 0)
pen.pendown()
pen.dot(10)
```

```
pen.penup()
pen.goto(5, 0)
pen.begin_fill()
pen.pencolor("black")
pen.pendown()
pen.fillcolor("black")
pen.circle(5)
pen.end_fill()

screen.exitonclick()
```

Output:

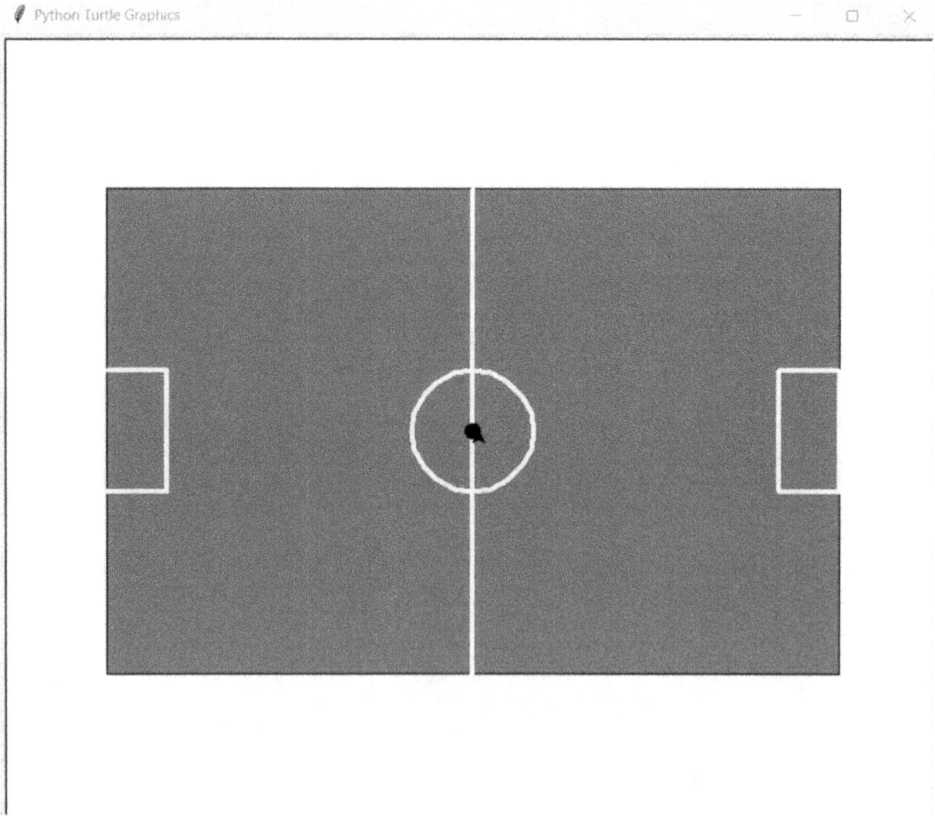

Exercises to Practice

1. Draw the following lines on a Python screen:
    a. A purple horizontal line of a certain thickness at the bottom left of the screen.
    b. A green vertical line of double the thickness of the previous line, in the center of the screen.
    c. A red vertical line of double the thickness of the previous line anywhere on the screen.
2. Draw a rectangle filled with green and fit 4 soccer balls on the 4 corners of the screen which have 4 different colors.
3. Draw a soccer ball with a cross in the middle. The cross is basically two diametric lines at 90 degrees to each other.
4. Draw a square green practice soccer field. This soccer field has:
    a. 4 orange dots at the 4 corners, which represent 4 soccer cones.
    b. One black circle in the center which represents a dummy.
    c. 2 blue soccer balls near the ends of the soccer cones. You can pick any two soccer cones.

    This simulates a practice session where players try to pass the ball to each other trying to avoid the dummy in the middle.

Moving a Soccer Ball on the Screen

Now, let's have some more fun.

We can actually move items on the turtle screen. We're going to create a soccer field and a ball that can move on the soccer field. The ball moves in the direction that the user presses the arrow keys on the keyboard.

The first step we do is to create a screen. Then, we create a vertical line that goes through the center of the screen. This is the center line that cuts the soccer field in half.

Then, we create a circle at the center of the screen which is the center circle of the field.

Next, we create a black soccer ball which starts at the center of the field.

For the soccer ball, we create functions that move the soccer ball up, down, right and left. These functions determine how far the soccer ball coordinates move each time we want it to move in that direction.

And finally, we determine which of the above functions are activated when certain keys on the keyboard are pressed. For example, if the right direction key on the keyboard is pressed, we'd ask the program to run the function that moves the soccer ball to the right.

Now that we have an outline, let's look at the actual program below.

In Lines 1-5 of the program, we create a turtle screen object and set it to a green color.

Then, in lines 7-12, we create the center line. The center line is created as the center of the entire screen. So, it doesn't matter if we change the screen size. The line will always be in the center. (Remember, in the last program, we made the line the center of a green rectangle). To do so, we create a turtle object called **line**. The line is set to **white** color and is set to go from (0, -**screen.window_height**/2) to (0, **screen.window_height**/2). **Screen.window_height** is the vertical height of the window. This makes the center line stretch to the size of the window while remaining in the center.

In lines 14-19, we create the center circle of the field to a radius of 100. A turtle object called **midcircle** is created to achieve this. This is done in exactly the same way as the previous program. It is set to **white** color and starts at **(0,-100)** which is the bottom of the circle.

```
1   import turtle
2
3   screen = turtle.Screen()
4   screen.title("Moving Circle with Center Line")
5   screen.bgcolor("green")
6
7   line = turtle.Turtle()
8   line.penup()
9   line.color("white")
10  line.goto(0, -screen.window_height() // 2)
11  line.pendown()
12  line.goto(0, screen.window_height() // 2)
13
14  midcircle = turtle.Turtle()
15  midcircle.penup()
16  midcircle.color("white")
17  midcircle.goto(0, -100)
18  midcircle.pendown()
19  midcircle.circle(100)
```

In lines 21-27, we create the drawing of the soccer ball. We create an object called **soccerball** which is right at the center of the screen and is filled with black color.

In lines 29-46, we create the functions that move the ball in the direction we want. The code in lines 29-30 create the function **moveto(x,y)** that move the ball to location with x-coordinate x and y-coordinate y.

We create the functions **move_left(), move_right(), move_up()** and **move_down()** which move the soccer ball left, right, up and down respectively.

To explain how these functions work, let's look at one of these functions **move_left()**. In **move_left()** in line 32, we set the values x and y as the current x and y co-ordinates of the **soccerball** object. Then, in line 33, we subtract the x value by 20. This simulates the motion of the ball to the left by 20. If we want the ball to move faster, we increase this from 20 to 30/40/50 etc. If we want the ball to move slower, we reduce the value. And then, in line 34, we call the function **move_to(x,y)** with the new values of x and y. This moves the soccer ball to the new x and y locations.

The function **move_right()** similarly adds 20 to x, the **soccerball** right by 20. The function **move_up()** adds 20 to y, and moves **soccerball** up. The function **move_down()** reduces y by 20 to move **soccerball** down by 20.

In lines 48-53, we check if the user clicks on the arrow buttons. For example, in line 48, the program checks if the user has clicked on the **"Left"** button. If this has happened, then it runs the function **move_left()** and the ball moves left. The same check is done for the user clicking the **"Right", "Up" and "Down"** button.

The **screen.listen()** function in line 52 makes sure that the screen is checking if the user touches keys on the keyboard.

The **screen.mailoop()** function in line 53 makes sure that the program keeps running after the user has typed in one of the buttons.

```python

soccerball = turtle.Turtle()
soccerball.shape("circle")
soccerball.color("black")
soccerball.penup()
soccerball.speed(1)

soccerball.goto(0, 0)

def move_to(x, y):
    soccerball.goto(x, y)
def move_left():
    x, y = soccerball.xcor(), soccerball.ycor()
    x -= 20
    move_to(x, y)
def move_right():
    x, y = soccerball.xcor(), soccerball.ycor()
    x += 20
    move_to(x, y)
def move_up():
    x, y = soccerball.xcor(), soccerball.ycor()
    y += 20
    move_to(x, y)
def move_down():
    x, y = soccerball.xcor(), soccerball.ycor()
    y -= 20
    move_to(x, y)

screen.onkey(move_left, "Left")
screen.onkey(move_right, "Right")
screen.onkey(move_up, "Up")
screen.onkey(move_down, "Down")
screen.listen()
screen.mainloop()
```

Output:

At Start:

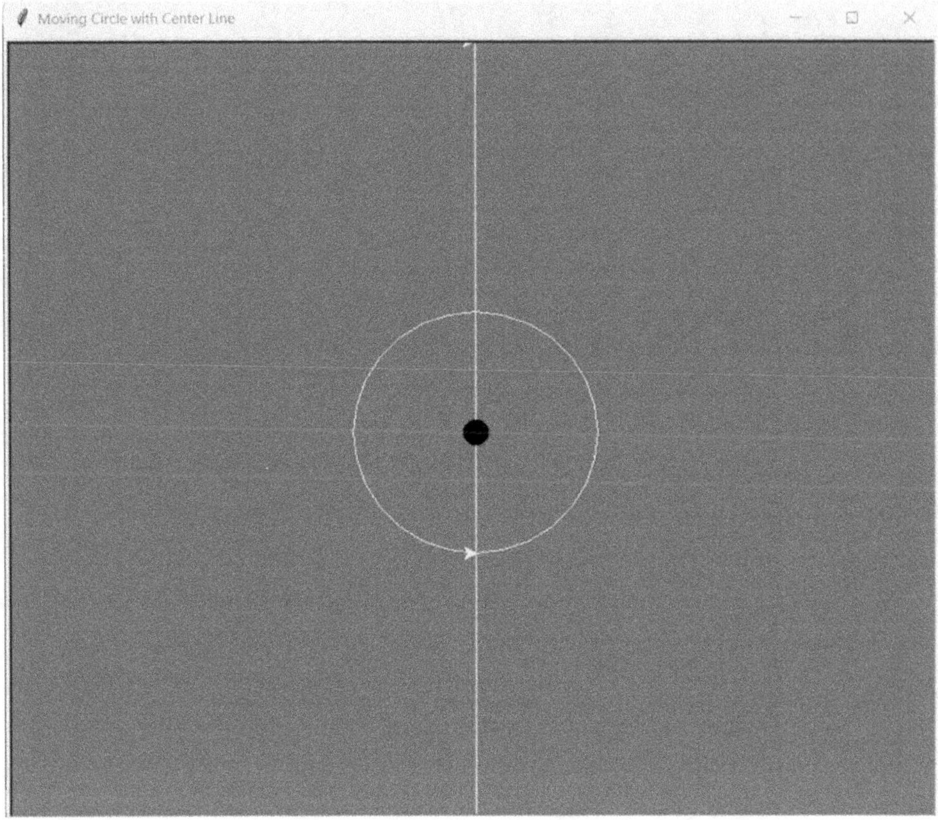

After Moving Ball Right Twice (Right by 40):

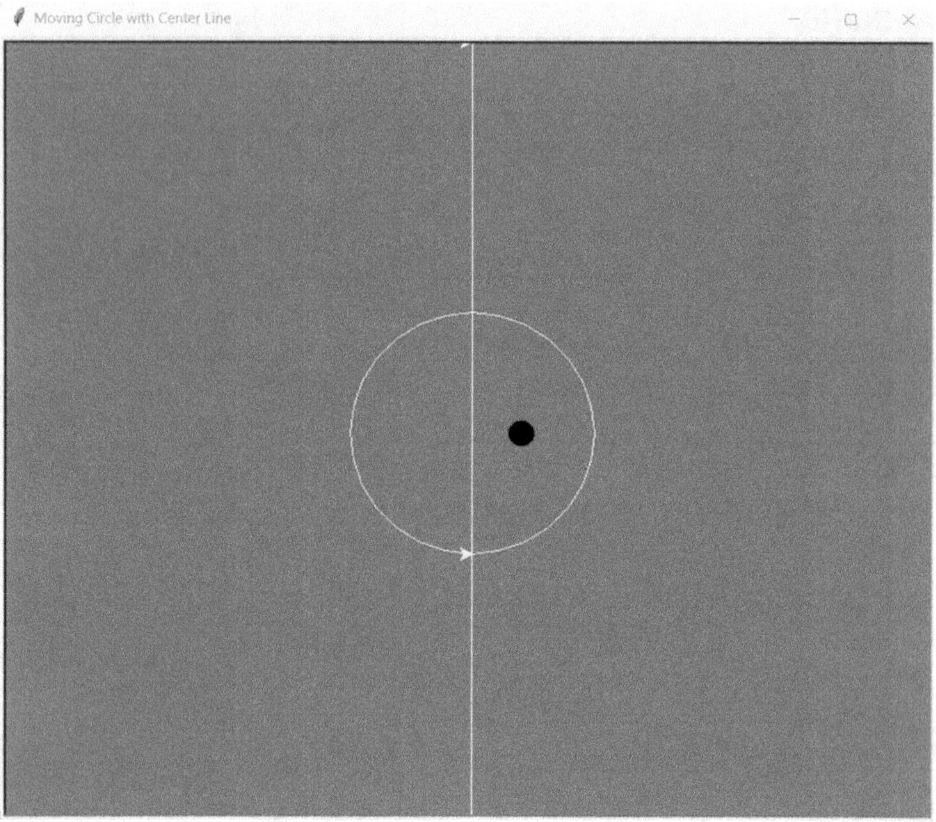

Moving Ball Down Four Times (Down by 80):

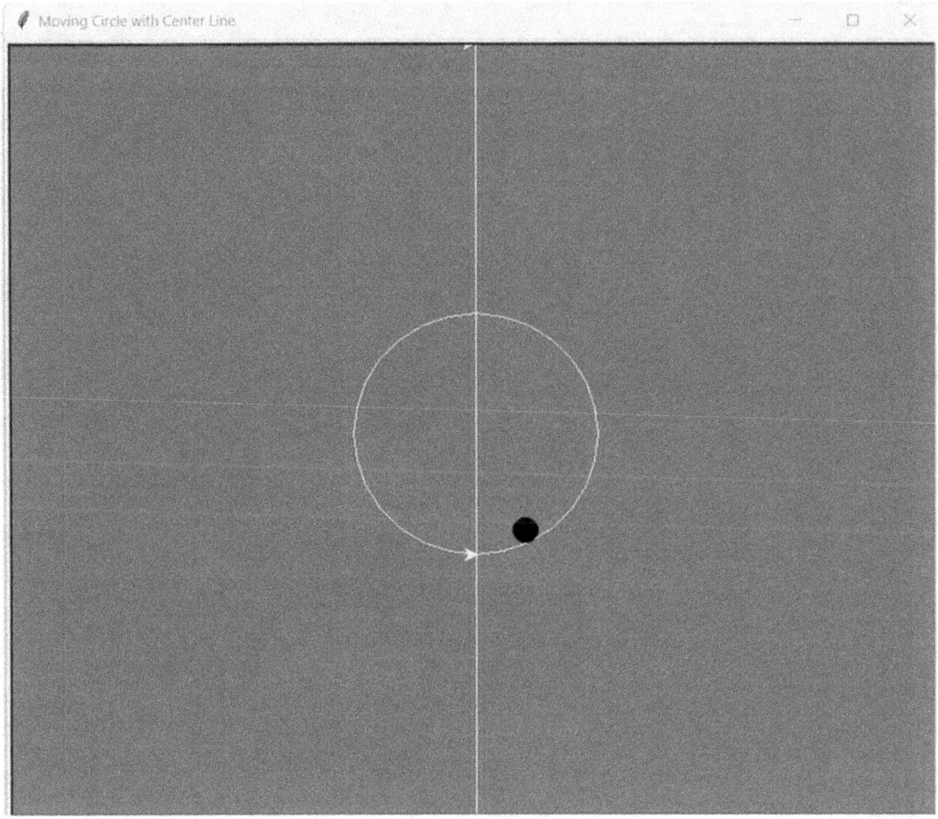

Moving Ball Left Six Times (Left by 120):

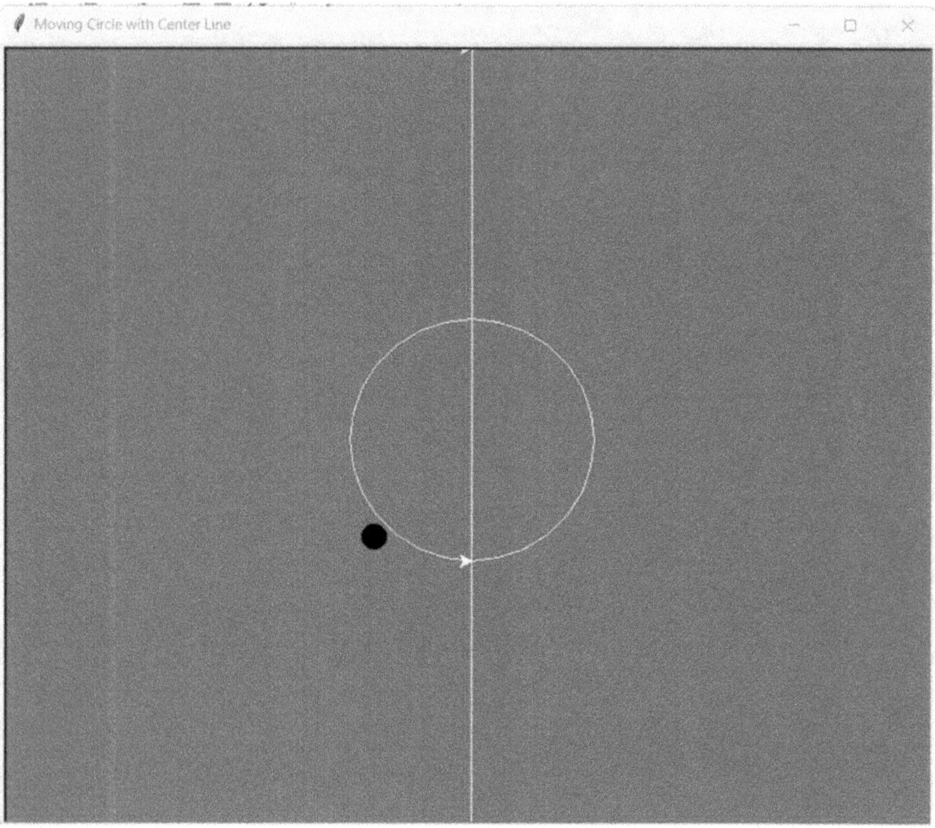

Moving Ball Up Twice (Up by 40):

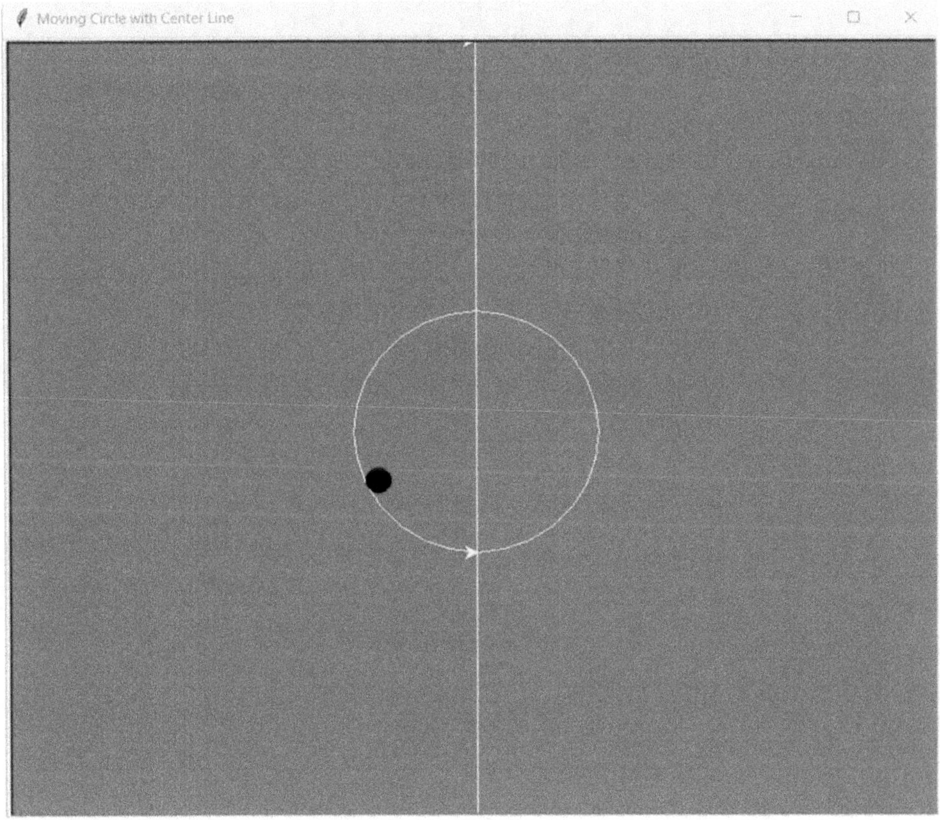

Exercises to Practice

1. Using the same code for soccer field above:
    a. Add two rectangles to the right and left that simulate soccer goal position.
    b. Check if the ball has reached the right goal. Increase the number of goals by 1 for team 1 if that happens, and restart location to center.
    c. Check if the ball has reached the left goal. Increase the number of goals by 1 for team 2 if that happens, and restart location to center.
    d. Double the speed of motion of the ball and see what happens.

Practice Test

All right. We've reached the end of the theory section of the book. It's time to test your skills. We have a 25 question quiz now so you have the chance to apply all that you've learnt so far.

Question 1

Why is Python a great language to start programming with?

a. It is a simple and easy to read open-source language, with a large community.
b. It is the most powerful computing language.
c. It has the best graphics.
d. It is the best for programming websites.

Question 2

Which website do you download python from?

a. www.facebook.com
b. www.youtube.com
c. www.python.org/downloads/
d. www.python.com

Question 3

What is a variable?

a. An item that stores a value in the program.
b. An item that can change in value during the program.
c. This item is referenced by a certain name all throughout the program.
d. All of the above

Question 4

How do I create a random variable in Python?

a. Write numbers on a card and have your mom pick a card. Use that card to determine random value.
b. Use the rand() function in the random library in Python.
c. Toss a coin to add randomness to your program.
d. Take a shower before programming to inspire random thoughts.

Question 5

How do you calculate remainder in Python?

a. Use the modulus sign %
b. Use the division sign /
c. Use the plus sign +
d. Use the minus sign –

Question 6

What is an array in Python?

a. An array is a group of variables.

b. The variables are of the same data type.
c. Each item in an array is referenced using an index.
d. The first index in an array is 0.
e. All of the above.

Question 7

What is a list in Python?

a. An list is a group of variables.
b. The variables can be of different data types.
c. Each item in a list is referenced using an index.
d. The reference index can be a string or number.
e. All of the above.

Question 8

What is the difference between a list and an array?

a. You have to write down a list on paper but can program an array.
b. A list has a maximum number of items, but an array has unlimited number of items
c. The reference index in an array is a number starting at 0, while the reference in a list can be a string or number.
d. A list can have different data types while an array has items of the same data type.
e. c and d above.

Question 9

Which Python is the best for creating drawings and animations?

a. Math library

b. Numpy library

c. Turtle library

d. Random library

Question 10

How do drawings work on Python library?

a. Uses your dreams and imagination to locate a point and draw what you feel like is best.

b. Draw an item on paper and take a picture. Then upload the picture, and Python will create a replica of it.

c. Create a separate screen for the drawing.

d. Uses a pen object that starts at a certain point and moves in a certain direction to a certain length.

e. c and d above

Question 11

Create two integer variables called teamA and teamB and assign integer values to them representing the number of goals each team scored in a soccer game. Print out the values of each variable on the screen. Then, create a Boolean variable teamAWon to determine if Team A won the game, and print out the result using the Boolean value. Then, create a second Boolean called draw and check if the result is a draw.

Question 12

Create two variables to store the heights of two soccer players, named heightFriend1 and heightFriend2, respectively. Print their heights on the screen. Then, create a Boolean variable tallerFriend1 to figure out which player is taller, and print out the result using the Boolean value.

Question 13

Create two variables, player1 and player2, to store the names of two famous soccer stars. Create two integer variables, goals1 and goals2, to represent the number of goals they've scored. Print on the screen "Player 1 has x goals" and "Player 2 has y goals" using the four methods you've learned in the chapter "Printing Data onto a Screen in Python". Of course, you'd replace

"Player 1" and "Player 2" with the actual names entered, and x and y with the actual number of goals scored.

Question 14

Write a program that takes in the value of your favorite stadium and prints it on the screen.

Question 15

Write a program that takes in the value of 10 soccer teams in your league and stores it in 10 different variables. Print out the teams at the end of the program.

Question 16

Create an array of 12 soccer teams with arrays containing the number of goals scored and goals conceded in a season. Calculate and print the team name and goal difference for the team.

Question 17

Create an array of 6 soccer stadiums with arrays containing the seating capacity and the city where each stadium is located. Print out the names of the stadiums along with their seating capacity and city.

Question 18

Create an array of 9 soccer players with distance covered in the season, and total number of games played. Calculate and print the distance covered per game for each player and also store the data in a third array.

Question 19

Create an array of 7 soccer players with their heights (in inches) and another array with their weights (in pounds). Print out the names of all players along with their height and weight.

Question 20

Create a Python program that draws the following shapes on the screen:

a. A horizonal blue line of size 3 in the top corner.

b. A vertical green line in the center of the screen of size 1.

c. A horizontal blue line in the bottom-right corner.

Question 21

Develop a Python script to draw 10 soccer balls in a horizontal row. The soccer balls are all of different colors.

Question 22

Create a Python program that draws a simple house on the screen. The house should have a brown rectangular base, a red triangular roof, and a yellow square window.

Question 23

Create a simple Python program that creates a circular soccer practice field with 10 soccer cones located anywhere on the circle. (Use dots for circles)

Question 24

Create a soccer ball animation where it checks if it hits the ground and stops the motion of the ball. (Check if the y-coordinate of the ball is below a horizontal line y-coordinate. You need to create a line for the ground, in addition to the ball)

Question 25

Using the code in the final chapter 'Moving a Soccer Ball on the Screen', create a second ball that moves using the keys **a,s,d** and **w**. This simulates a second player with a second ball. The key **a** is left, **d** is right, **w** is up and **s** is down. Make the ball color '**white'** so it stands out from the player one ball color.

Answers:

Answer 1 a)

Answer 2 c)

Answer 3 d)

Answer 4 b)

Answer 5 a)

Answer 6 e)

Question 7 e)

Question 8 e)

Question 9 c)

Question 10 e)

Conclusion / Next Steps

Thank you for taking the team to read this book.

I hope you had lots of fun and found it useful. If you've been through the exercises, you now understand the basics of Python, and able to program much more advanced applications in the future.

If you liked my book and you'd like to learn more, check out my Author page below. I'll have another book out soon that shows how to create a shopping cart from scratch using html, css and JavaScript.

https://www.amazon.com/Bob-Mather/e/B07HHQZC4Y

I'd also recommend looking at the other books in the section, especially the ones on how Artificial Intelligence will take over the world.

If you'd like any clarification regarding the topics; or any suggestions; please email me at: abiprod.pty.ltd@gmail.com

I also do one-one coaching online if you are interested in personalized help.

The end... almost!

Reviews are not easy to come by.

As an independent author with a tiny marketing budget, I rely on readers, like you, to leave a short review on Amazon.

Even if it's just a sentence or two!

So if you enjoyed the book, please click below and leave a review...

I am very appreciative for your review as it truly makes a difference.

Thank you from the bottom of my heart for purchasing this book and reading it.

Book 4:
Python Programming Projects Workbook for Kids

Introduction

"How is he going to cope?". It was a cold, snowy November afternoon in New York. Wyatt's parents were really worried about their son's future prospects. He was a shy and reserved 10-year-old who struggled with self-esteem and academic challenges. They had just removed him from public school, where he was bullied for being slow in class, and for looking different. They spent a substantial percentage of their savings to get him enrolled in a good private school in their area. However, Wyatt was struggling with low confidence and was intimidated by the students in his class.

They decided to enrol him in a coding class after school to improve his focus and engage him in a fun pursuit. Over the next few months, they saw Wyatt struggle a little. However, it was clear that he was enjoying it and learning something creative. Wyatt seemed to enjoy the struggle and also enjoyed putting programs together. One thing he complained about was that regular coding textbooks were too abstract and didn't have enough examples. They didn't really make sense for someone who just started coding.

Then, his mom came across a few coding workbooks that were full of examples. These books had examples such as fill in the blanks coding, predicting code output and other fun exercises. Once Wyatt started working on these, that took his learning to a new level. He started making advanced Python programs within weeks. As he improved, his confidence soared, and he started doing well at coding competitions in school. The success from his coding achievements positively affected his overall attitude towards learning, and this led to a strong improvement in his overall grade in school. Programming became a tool for Wyatt to express himself and discover his capabilities, transforming his academic journey. This eventually led to a new career as an engineer later in life.

This Python workbook has been created to ensure that you and your kid will learn and learn quickly. A lot of students have read our books and benefitted greatly from the content. However, they have asked us for more examples, workbooks that focus on practice that will get them moving forward. There are programming exercises, fill in the code, predict the code output and correct code error exercises which very much represent the real world. This will make your kid a programming whiz within a few months. Each chapter has a few basics that we will cover, and then hit you with tons of outrageously fun exercises.

If you want to get a head start before this book, I recommend our Coding for Kids in Python book here as a guide. Scan the barcode below to get your gift.

Why Python?

You may be wondering why we chose Python of all programming languages for this book. To be completely honest, we have books in C++, JavaScript and Python.

Python is among the best languages for beginners. It is the most versatile of the languages. It can be used for a wide range of applications, with widespread adoption in AI and machine language. So, if you start off with Python, you don't need to learn another language to do more advanced training. You can go ahead and build on your Python language.

Python has a clear syntax that is very similar to the English language. It's a lot easier to learn than other programming languages that may have tons of complex jargon.

Python has a strong community of developers who you can work with if you get stuck on a problem or want to learn more. There are thousands of Facebook groups, Redditt groups, Quora forums where millions of developers help each other get to the next level. There's also a lot of documentation and Python libraries built that one can use to build on.

Python can be run on various operating systems and is a cross-platform language.

And most importantly, Python is a free and open-source language which is free to use and modify. It is great for those who are on a budget starting off.
Python's wide variety of applications and easy integration with machine learning and data science make it a great way to start a career in technology.

Why a Coding Workbook Instead of a Textbook?

The vast majority of coding reference books on the market today are coding textbooks. These have been written by professionals in the field and are used to teach students in universities and colleges across the world. However, they are not very engaging and don't cater to people who prefer hands-on learning. The sheer volume of information may be very intimidating to beginners. Without proper guidance, it is very easy for beginner programmers to give up or move to other pursuits.
A lot of those who are starting off with coding, and especially those who are learning on their own, really enjoy hands-on, practical learning in a coding workbook. Workbooks are filled with exercises and challenges that require you to apply the concepts that you learn.
Workbooks also follow a certain curriculum, with a step-by-step process involving increasingly difficult exercises. This helps you

build a solid foundation, before you do harder programs, or larger coding projects. Workbooks also give you more immediate feedback, with the answer keys right at the back of the book; and also has code that you can instantly implement on your computer. It helps you quickly identify and correct errors, speeding up the learning process. The interactive nature of the workbook can be more motivating than simply reading a textbook.

Installing Python

Your first step to starting your Python journey is to download Python from the website, and then install it onto your computer. Go to the website https://www.python.org/downloads/ and download the latest version of Python.

Windows Download

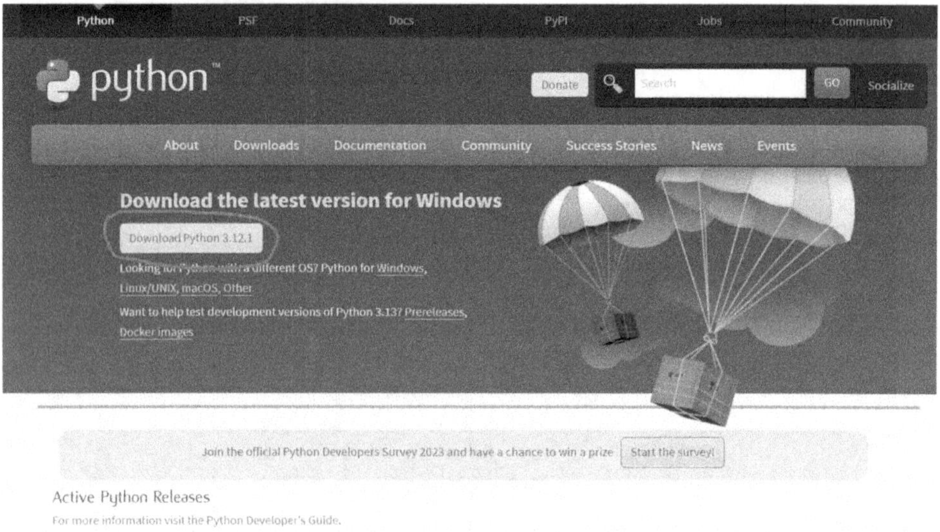

MAC Download

If you own a MAC, browse to https://www.python.org/downloads/macos/, and download the latest version.

After downloading Python, install it on your computer as shown below. To ensure Python runs smoothly on your computer, ensure that you "Add Python.exe to PATH" as shown below.

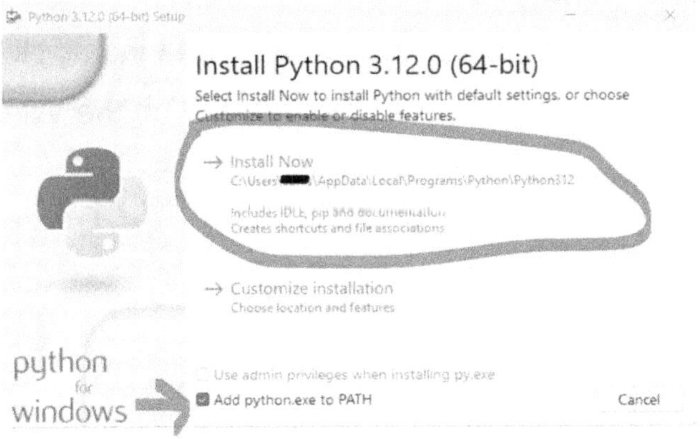

Text Editor

For the purposes of this book, we will run Python on a text editor. A text editor is a place where we write/edit/debug our code. We save the text file in as a Python file, and then run it. Our preferred text editor is NotePad++.

Download the latest version of NotePad Plus at: https://notepad-plus-plus.org/downloads/.

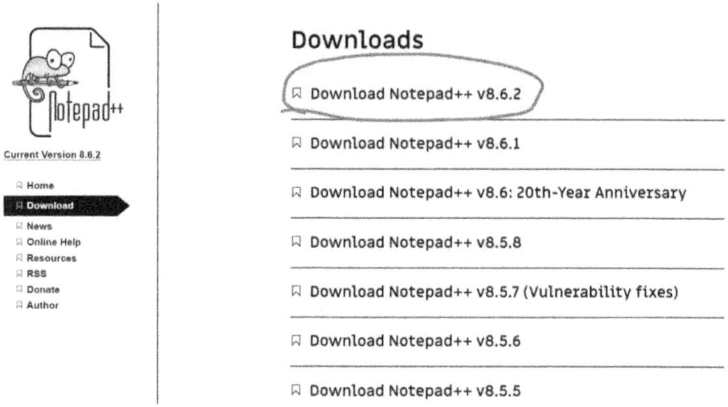

After you download it, follow the prompts and install NotePad++. Once Installed, you can type in "Notepad++" in the Windows TaskBar and open up NotePad++ as below:

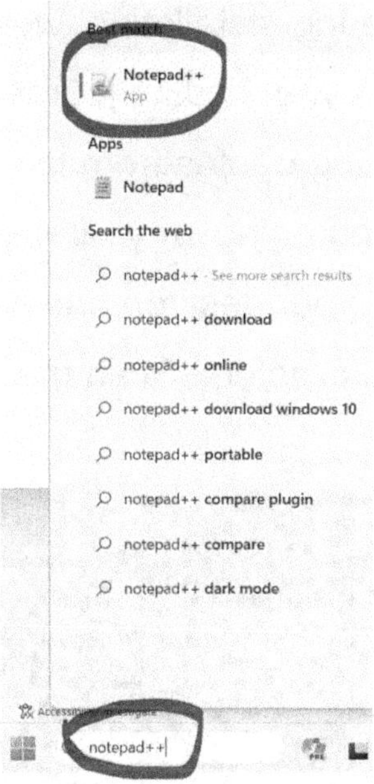

A blank notepad opens up as shown below. You are now ready to write your first program.

As a reward for completing installation, we're going to give you a gift that'll inspire you on your coding journey. This is a list of 15 inspirational programming quotes from famous programmers and scientists that'll keep you going on your programming journey. You can stick these on your desktop and look to them when you're struggling with a problem. Scan the barcode below to get your gift.

Your First Program in Python

Now, that you've got Python installed, you must be excited to get started.

Now, hold on.

First step you've got to do is create a folder where you're doing to store all your python programs.

We're going to Right-click > Create a new folder and name it "python-coding". We're going to save and run all the Python programs in this book from this folder.

Copy the path that the file is located and store it as we're going to use it while running programs.

Now, we're going to start:

Step 1: Search for NotePad++ in the Windows taskbar below and open Notepad++.

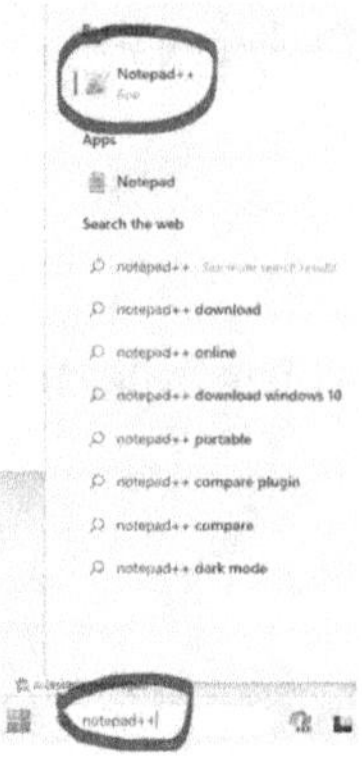

Step 2: We're going to start off with one line of code in NotePad++. We're going to print the words **"This is my first program".** To do so, we use a Python function called **print**. The print function works with brackets and quotes. Whatever needs to be printed is put in between the brackets. And if you are printing text, it should be within double quotes as well.

So, the line

print("This is my first program")

prints the words "This is my first program" on the screen.

This is shown in the Python program below.

```
print("This is my first Python program")
```

Step 3: Now, we're going to save the file.

Click, **File > Save As**

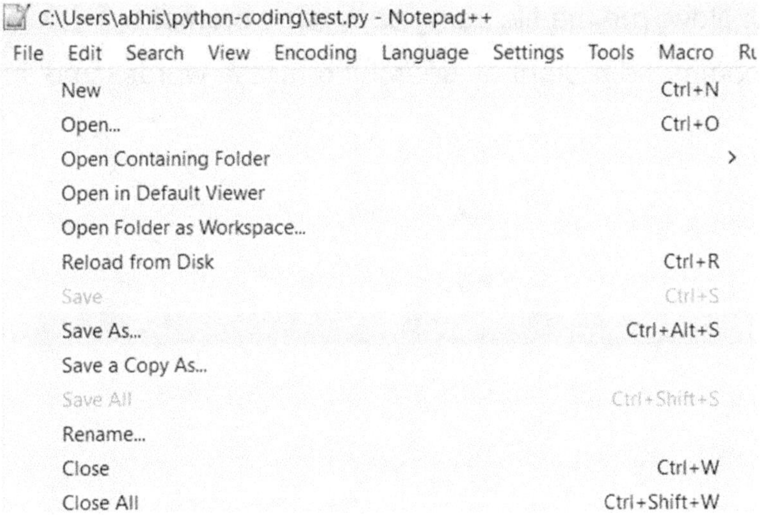

Save the file as shown below.

Browse to the python-coding folder and name the file “test”. Save it as a Python file.

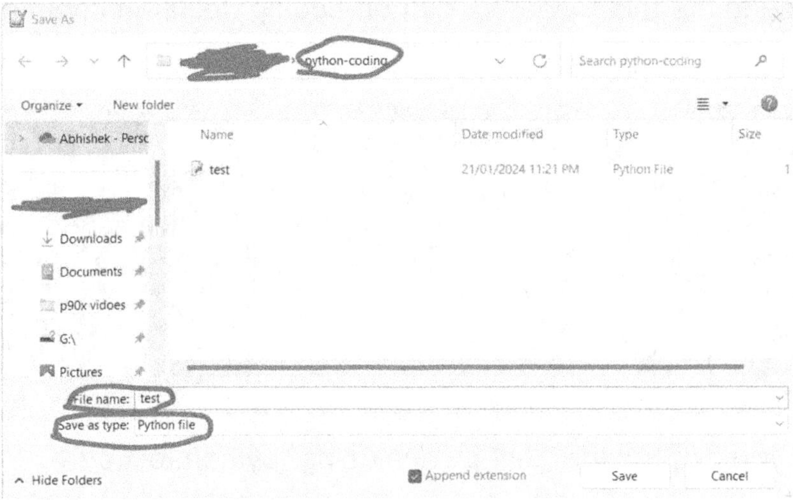

Step 4: Now, run the file using command prompt.

Open command prompt by searching for the words 'cmd' in the taskbar.

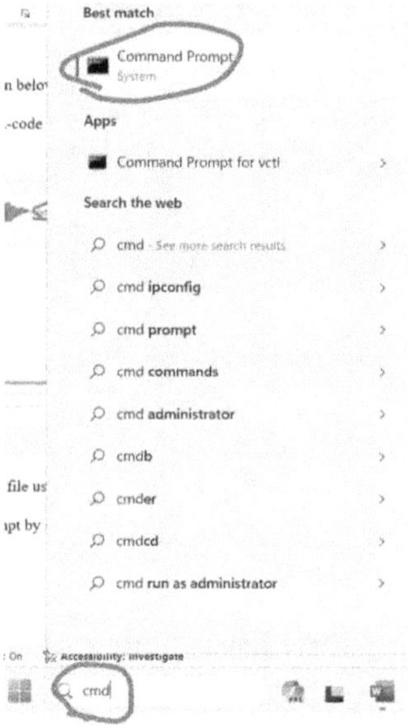

Browse to the folder named "python-coding" folder in command prompt as shown below.

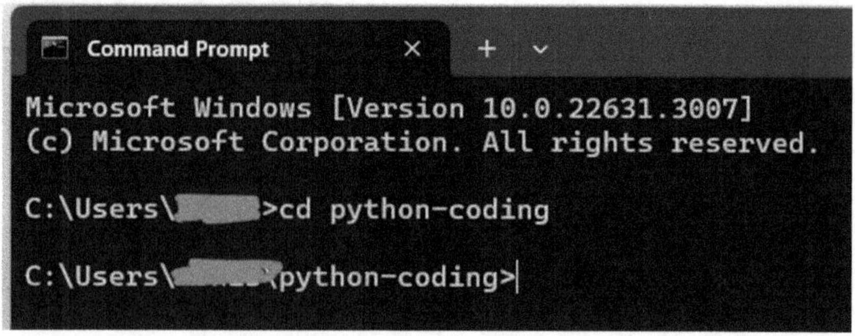

Now, you can run the "test.py" file using "python test.py"

```
C:\Users\[redacted]\python-coding>python test.py
This is my first Python program

C:\Users\[redacted]\python-coding>
```

As you can see, this prints the words “This is my first Python program.”

Now, let’s make a change to the program.

Let’s change the program to make a different output. Open test.py in Notepad++. We’re going to add another line to the program. You’re going to introduce yourself just as I did in the program.

```
test.py
print("This is my first Python program")
print("My name is Bob")
```

This is going to change the output. So, let’s save it as a different file called test2.

Now, let’s run the file using command prompt and let’s see what we get.

```
C:\Users\[redacted]\python-coding>python test2.py
This is my first Python program
My name is Bob
```

As you can see, when we run “test2.py” we get an extra line of code as output.

Now, we’re going to do a few simple exercises to make sure you are on top of this.

Correct the Error

The first 3 exercises are mistakes that I intentionally put into the program, and you have to correct them.

What is wrong with the line below?

```
print("I have 1 dog)
```

What is wrong with line below?

```
print(I drove to Mexico)
```

What is wrong with line below?

```
C:\Users\[redacted]>cd python-code
```

Answer 1: The line is missing the double quotation on the right of the string. It is likely to produce an unterminated string error when you run the program. The correct code is below.

```
print("I have 1 dog")
```

Answer 2: The line is missing the double quotation on the left of the string. It is likely to produce an unterminated string error when you run the program. The correct code is below.

```
print("I drove to Mexico")
```

Answer 3: The folder "python-code" is the incorrect folder, so it is going to produce wrong directory error.

So, we correct the error using the proper folder name 'python-coding' as shown below.

```
C:\Users\[redacted]>cd python-coding

C:\Users\[redacted]\python-coding>
```

The final 3 exercises are exercises that we can use to practice.

Exercises to Practice

1. Print out the name of your pet on the screen using a simple Python program with the print function.
2. Use the print function to print out the name of your favorite sports team on the screen.

Variables

What is a variable?

A variable is a location on the computer program where a value is stored. It is stored using a certain name. And the value of the variable can change during the computer program.

To explain this, let's imagine you have a magic box. The box can hold different things at different times. It can store snacks, toys, books, balls etc. It can hold a lot of different things.

Now, let's say you want to use the box to store balls of wool. You want to count how many balls of wool are in the box each time you add a ball.

A variable is like a sticker that you put on the box to hold the information. Each time you add a ball, you can increase the number on the sticker by 1.

The name of the sticker is the variable name. The number of balls is the value of the variable, and the type of item in the box is the data type.

Now, let's code this example.

```
1   woolbox=10
2   print(woolbox)
3   woolbox=woolbox+1
4   print(woolbox)
```

Output:

```
C:\Users\[redacted]s\python-coding>python variable.py
10
11
```

In code below in line 1, we declare a variable named **woolbox** and set it to a value of 10. The name of the variable is **woolbox** and the variable value is 10.

We print out the value of woolbox in line 2. There's no need for quotation marks inside the brackets if you're using a variable. We can use the output as 10.

In line 3, we increase the value of woolbox by 1 since another woolen ball has been added to the box.

In line 4, we print out the new value of woolbox. We see that the variable value has increased by 1 to 11.

This is a good simple example to demonstrate how variables work.

As we mentioned, in this workbook, we're going to put a lot of emphasis on worksheets and examples. That's what we're going to do in this chapter. In the first few exercises, we're going to give you some code and you're going to predict the output for each of them.

Predict Output

In the first set of exercises, you're going to predict the output of the code. The answers are at the end of the chapter.

Exercise 4

```
x=5
x=x+2
print(x)
```

Exercise 5

```
chocolates =7
chocolates = chocolates-1
chocolates=chocolates*2
print(chocolates)
```

Exercise 6

```
cats=9
cats=cats*2
print(cats)
```

Exercise 7

```
apartments=34
print(apartments)
apartments=apartments/2
print(apartments)
```

Exercise 8

```
var1=7
var2=8
var3=var1+var2
print(var1)
print(var2)
print(var3)
```

Complete the code (Obtain the Output).

In the next few exercises, figure out what is missing in the blank to get the output that is provided.

Exercise 9 (Output=5)

```
x=_+2
```

Exercise 10 (Output=4)

```
cakes = 5
cakes = cakes-1
_____________
```

Exercise 11 (Output=8)

```
x=_
x=x*2
print(x)
```

Exercise 12 (Output=0)

```
var1=3
var2=3
var3=var1-___
print(var3)
```

Find the error in the code.

In the following exercises, the code does not work due to an error by the programmer. Fix the error so the code works.

Exercise 13

```
x=3
y=y+2
print(y)
```

Exercise 14

```
cakes =7
cakes = cakes-1
print cakes
```

Exercise 15

```
c=9
c=c*2
print(d)
```

Answers

Exercise 4: 7

Exercise 5: 12

Exercise 6: 18

Exercise 7: 17

Exercise 8: 7,8,15

Exercise 9: x

Exercise 10: print(cakes)

Exercise 11: 4

Exercise 12: var2

Exercise 13:

```
1 y=3
2 y=y+2
3 print(y)
```

The error was that y was not defined and you are adding 2 to a variable that does not exist. We replace ‘x=3’ in line 1 with ‘y=3’ to ensure that y is defined. Variable x is not used anywhere in the program so it’s good to remove x.

Exercise 14:

```
1 cakes =7
2 cakes = cakes-1
3 print (cakes)
```

The error was that there were no brackets used during printing in line 3. We add brackets and that prints the output with no error.

Exercise 15:

```
c=9
c=c*2
print(c)
```

The error was that variable d that we were trying to print was not defined anywhere. We just replace variable d with variable c in line 3 and that removes the error. Variable c is defined in line 1, so there is no error.

Exercises to Practice

1. Create two integer variables called **num1** and **num2** and assign two numerical values to them. Print out the values of each variable on the screen.
2. Write a program that creates two variables and prints out the sum and difference between the two numbers.

Conditionals

What are Conditionals?

A conditional in programming is a statement that chooses what actions the program must take. The choice of action the program takes is dependent on whether certain conditions are true/false. The basic objective is to control the flow of the program.

Fun Example with Code

Now, let's take a simple example. Let's say a robot friend of yours is walking from his house to yours. He must choose between two paths, Path A or Path B. He calculates the distance to your house through each path, and calls the variables **distanceA** and **distanceB**. If **distanceA** is smaller, he goes through Path A, else he goes through Path b

```
if distanceA<distanceB
    Robot goes through Path A
Else:
   Robot goes through Path B
```

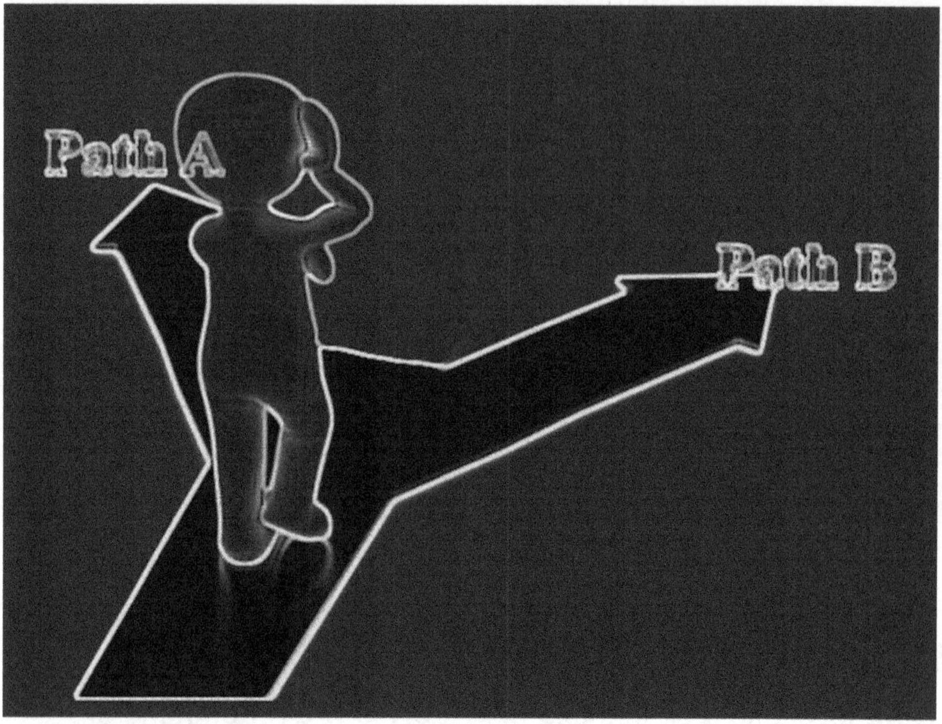

Now, let's do this with simple Python code.

In Python code, make sure that you use a colon after each if statement or else statement, or it will produce an error. So, do "if:" instead of "if".

In Scenario 1, we see that the program prints "Robot goes through Path A" as distanceA is smaller than distanceB. In Scenario 2, we see that the program prints out "Robot goes through Path B" as distanceB is smaller.

Scenario 1: Distance A is smaller

```
distanceA=5
distanceB=10
if(distanceA<distanceB):
    print("Robot goes through Path A")
else:
    print("Robot goes through Path B")
```

Output:

```
Robot goes through Path A
```

Scenario 2: Distance B is smaller

```
distanceA=6
distanceB=4
if(distanceA<distanceB):
    print("Robot goes through Path A")
else:
    print("Robot goes through Path B")
```

```
Robot goes through Path B
```

Now, let's do some worksheets.

Predict Output

In the first set of exercises, you're going to predict the output of the code. The answers are at the end of the chapter.

Exercise 16: Umbrella

```
raining = 1
if (raining==1):
    print("Take umbrella with you")
else:
    print("No need to take umbrella with you")
```

Exercise 17: Umbrella 2

```
raining = 0
if (raining==1):
    print("Take umbrella with you")
else:
    print("No need to take umbrella with you")
```

Exercise 18: Vehicle choice 1

```
budget = 3000
if (budget<=5000):
    print("Buy a used car")
elif (budget<=25000):
    print("Your car is a Toyota Corolla")
else:
    print("You can buy a Ford F150")
```

Exercise 19: Vehicle choice 2

```
budget = 15000
if (budget<=5000):
    print("Buy a used car")
elif (budget<=25000):
    print("Your car is a Toyota Corolla")
else:
    print("You can buy a Ford F150")
```

Exercise 20: Vehicle choice 3

```
budget = 40000
if (budget<=5000):
    print("Buy a used car")
elif (budget<=25000):
    print("Your car is a Toyota Corolla")
else:
    print("You can buy a Ford F150")
```

Complete the Code (Obtain the Output)

In the next few exercises, figure out what is missing in the blank to get the output that is provided.

Exercise 21 (Output="Robot goes through Path B")

```
distanceA=_
distanceB=4
if(distanceA<distanceB):
    print("Robot goes through Path A")
else:
    print("Robot goes through Path B")
```

Exercise 22 (Output = "Robot goes through Path A")

```
distanceA=6
distanceB=_
if(distanceA<distanceB):
    print("Robot goes through Path A")
else:
    print("Robot goes through Path B")
```

Exercise 23 (Output = "Toast Bread")

```
choice = _
if (choice==1):
    print("Cook rice")
elif (choice==2):
    print("Cook pasta")
else:
    print("Toast bread")
```

Exercise 24 (Output = “Cook pasta”)

```
choice = 3
if (choice==1):
    print("Cook rice")
elif (choice==_):
    print("Cook pasta")
else:
    print("Toast bread")
```

Find the Error in the Code

The programs below all produce an error while running. Can you spot the error in the code?

Exercise 25:

```
raining = 0
if (raining==1):
    print("Take umbrella with you")
else
    print("No need to take umbrella with you")
```

Exercise 26:

```
distanceA=6
distanceB=4
if(distanceA<distanceB)
    print("Robot goes through Path A")
else:
    print("Robot goes through Path B")
```

Exercise 27:

```
raining = 0
if (raining==1):
    print("Take umbrella with you)
else:
    print("No need to take umbrella with you")
```

Exercise 28:

```
budget = 40000
if (budget<=5000):
    print("Buy a used car")
else if (budget<=25000):
    print("Your car is a Toyota Corolla")
else:
    print("You can buy a Ford F150")
```

Answers

Exercise 16:

```
Take umbrella with you
```

Exercise 17:

```
No need to take umbrella with you
```

Exercise 18:

```
Buy a used car
```

Exercise 19:

```
Your car is a Toyota Corolla
```

Exercise 20:

```
You can buy a Ford F150
```

Exercise 21: Answer is any value 5 or over

Exercise 22: Answer is any value 7 or over

Exercise 23: Answer is any value other than 1 or 2

Exercise 24: Answer is 3

Exercise 25:

The error in the code is in line 4. The else statement needs to have the ":" operator. See correct code below.

```
1 raining = 0
2 if (raining==1):
3     print("Take umbrella with you")
4 else:
5     print("No need to take umbrella with you")
```

Exercise 26:

The error in the code is in line 3. The statement needs to end with a “:” operator. See correct code below.

```
1 distanceA=6
2 distanceB=4
3 if(distanceA<distanceB):
4     print("Robot goes through Path A")
5 else:
6     print("Robot goes through Path B")
7
```

Exercise 27:

The error in the code is in line 3. The statement inside print is missing a right double quotation mark ”. See correct code below.

```
1 raining = 0
2 if (raining==1):
3     print("Take umbrella with you")
4 else:
5     print("No need to take umbrella with you")
```

Exercise 28:

The error in the code is in line 4. The statement “else if” produces an error as it does not exist in Python. You need to use “elif” in Python. See correct code below.

```
budget = 40000
if (budget<=5000):
    print("Buy a used car")
elif (budget<=25000):
    print("Your car is a Toyota Corolla")
else:
    print("You can buy a Ford F150")
```

Exercises to Practice

1. Write a program that prints out a student's Math grades based on his score. Any score over 90 is an A, between 80-90 is a B, between 70-80 is a C and anything below 60 is an F.
2. Write a program that classifies a student as high school, middle school or primary school based on age. A student between 14-18 years is in the high school, between 9-13 is in middle school and children below 9 are in primary school.

User Inputs

Why User Input?

So far, in this book, we have assigned values to variables at the start of the code. However, what if this is not possible? What if it's a program that needs data from a different user each time it is run. For example, if you need to write a program that takes in a person's height and prints it out. Then, we need to print out a different height each time the program is run. This is not possible if we assign a variable value each time we run the program.
We need to accept values from the user. We need user input.

Simple Example with Code

So now, let's write a program that takes in user values and prints the value out each time.

```
1  user_height = input("What is your height (in inches)
2  print("Hello, your height is "+user_height+ " inches
```

In line 1, we accept the person's height using the **input()** function. The input() function is used in Python to accept user input. The string that the user sees before typing in the screen in this case is **"What is your height (in inches)?"**. This string needs to be in quotes and within the input() function brackets.

In line 2, we print the number input by the user. In this case, we combine the string **"your height is"** and **"inches"** with the variable **user_height**. We can do this in Python using the + sign inside the print function.

In the output, we see that the height printed varies depending on what the user inputs, which is the objective of this program.

Output:

```
What is your height (in inches)? 69
Hello, your height is 69 inches
```

```
What is your height (in inches)? 72
Hello, your height is 72 inches
```

Predict Output

For the below three programs, read the program and the user input entered, and predict what is printed on the screen.

Exercise 29:

```
name = input("What's your name? ")
age = input("What's your age? ")
print("Hello, your name is "+ name + " and your age is "+age)
```

When the program is run, the user enters below data:

```
What's your name? Bob
What's your age? 37
```

Exercise 30:

```
name = input("What's your name? ")
age = input("What's your age? ")
print("Hello, your name is "+ name + " and your age is "+age)
```

```
What's your name? Steve
What's your age? 23
```

Exercise 31:

```
name = input("What's your name? ")
age = input("What's your age? ")
print("Hello, your name is "+ name + " and your age is "+age)
```

```
What's your name? Jessica
What's your age? 33
```

Exercise 32:

```
name = input("What's your name? ")
age = input("What's your favorite color? ")
print("Hello, your name is "+ name + " and your favorite color is "+age)
```

```
What's your name? Matt
What's your favorite color? blue
```

Find the Error in the Code

For the next few exercises, read the code and spot the mistake. Correct the mistake in the notes section and check if your answer is correct at the end of the chapter.

Exercise 33:

```
name = input("What's your name? ")
age = input("What's your favorite color? ")
print("Hello, your name is "name + " and your favorite color is "+age)
```

Exercise 34:

```
name = input("What's your name? ")
age = input("What's your favorite color? "
print("Hello, your name is "+name + " and your favorite color is "+age)
```

Exercise 35:

```
name = input("What's your name? ")
age = input("What's your favorite color? )
print("Hello, your name is "+name + " and your favorite color is "+age)
```

Answers

Exercise 29

```
Hello, your name is Bob and your age is 37
```

Exercise 30

```
Hello, your name is Steve and your age is 23
```

Exercise 31

```
Hello, your name is Jessica and your age is 33
```

Exercise 32

```
Hello, your name is Matt and your favorite color is blue
```

Exercise 33

The error in this program is in line 3. There is a "+" sign missing at the left of the variable name. This is needed to combine the variable and string text inside the print statement. See correct code below.

```
1 name = input("What's your name? ")
2 age = input("What's your favorite color? ")
3 print("Hello, your name is "+ name + " and your favorite color is "+age)
```

Exercise 34

The error in this program is in line 2. The input statement is missing a close bracket ")" at the end of the line. See correct code below.

```
1 name = input("What's your name? ")
2 age = input("What's your favorite color? ")
3 print("Hello, your name is "+ name + " and your favorite color is "+age)
```

Exercise 35

The error in this program is in line 2. The input statement is missing a double quote at the end of the word 'color?'. See correct code below.

```
1 name = input("What's your name? ")
2 age = input("What's your favorite color? ")
3 print("Hello, your name is "+ name + " and your favorite color is "+age)
```

Exercises to Practice

1. Write a program that accepts your name and names of your family members as user input and prints them on the screen.
2. Write a program that accepts your favorite team's name and prints them on the screen.
3. Write a program that accepts your name and telephone number and prints them on the screen.

Basic Math in Python

Math in Python

Basic Math in Python is simple and straightforward and is just the same as you would do it on a piece of paper. You can complete the operations in the program itself, but it is recommended to store each number used in a separate variable (that are input by the user), and the result in another variable. This is recommended so that you can use different numbers each time the program runs. These simple operations include addition (+), subtraction (-), multiplication (X), division(/) and remainder(%). We're going to do a couple of simple examples to demonstrate this. In the first example, we're going to have the user input 2 numbers and then find the sum, difference, product and quotient for the two numbers.

```
var1 = input("Enter first number:")
var2 = input("Enter second number:")
num1=int(var1)
num2=int(var2)
sum1=num1+num2;
diff=num1-num2;
prod=num1*num2;
quotient = num1/num2;
print("The sum of the two numbers is: "+str(sum1))
print("The difference of the two numbers is: "+str(diff))
print("The product of the two numbers is: "+str(prod))
print("The quotient of the two numbers is: "+str(quotient))
```

We can see the results from the program in the output below:

Output:

```
Enter first number:7
Enter second number:3
The sum of the two numbers is: 10
The difference of the two numbers is: 4
The product of the two numbers is: 21
The quotient of the two numbers is: 2.3333333333333335
```

```
Enter first number:4
Enter second number:5
The sum of the two numbers is: 9
The difference of the two numbers is: -1
The product of the two numbers is: 20
The quotient of the two numbers is: 0.8
```

In the program above, the user inputs two numbers and stores it in variables **var1** and **var2**. However, the **input()** function stores the data as strings. These need to be converted into numbers before any operations can be done on it.

In lines 3 and 4, we convert strings **var1** and **var2** into numbers using the **int()** function.

In lines 5-8, we use '+', '-' , '*' and '/' to do addition, subtraction, multiplication and division operations respectively. These results are stored in variables sum1, diff, prod and quotient.

In lines 9-12, the results are printed on the screen. We use the **str()** function to convert result integer variables into strings. This is because the statement inside the print() function needs to be either a string or an integer. It cannot be a combination of both.

In the next program, we calculate the reminder for two numbers using the modulus symbol **'%'**. See program below.

```
1 var1 = input("Enter first number:")
2 var2 = input("Enter second number:")
3 num1=int(var1)
4 num2=int(var2)
5 rem=num1%num2;
6 print("The remainder when "+str(num1)+" is divided by "+str(num2)+ " is: "+str(rem))
```

Here's the output for the code below:

```
Enter first number:45
Enter second number:6
The remainder when 45 is divided by 6 is: 3
```

```
Enter first number:13
Enter second number:4
The remainder when 13 is divided by 4 is: 1
```

In line 5, the remainder is calculated using **'num1%num2'** where **num1** is divided by **num2**; and the remainder is stored in variable **rem**.

In line 6, we print the output using the **print()** function and the variables num1, num2 and rem are converted to strings using the **str()** function.

Predict Output

For the following exercises, read the code and the user input and predict the output. Check your answer at the end of the chapter.

Exercise 36

```
a = input("Enter first number:")
b = input("Enter second number:")
a=int(a)
b=int(b)
result1=2*a+b
print("The answer is: "+str(result1))
```

```
Enter first number:4
Enter second number:5
```

Exercise 37

```
a = input("Enter first number:")
b = input("Enter second number:")
c = input("Enter third number:")
a=int(a)
b=int(b)
c=int(c)
result1=a-b-c
print("The answer is: "+str(result1))
```

```
Enter first number:3
Enter second number:4
Enter third number:5
```

Exercise 38

```
a = input("Enter first number:")
b = input("Enter second number:")
c = input("Enter third number:")
a=int(a)
b=int(b)
c=int(c)
result1=a*b*c
print("The answer is: "+str(result1))
```

```
Enter first number:3
Enter second number:4
Enter third number:5
```

Exercise 39

```
a = input("Enter first number:")
b = input("Enter second number:")
a=int(a)
b=int(b)
result1=a/b
result2=a%b
print("The quotient of the two numbers is: "+str(result1))
print("The remainder is: "+str(result2))
```

```
Enter first number:45
Enter second number:4
```

Exercise 40

```
a = input("Enter first number:")
b = input("Enter second number:")
a=int(a)
b=int(b)
result1=a/b
result2=a%b
print("The quotient of the two numbers is: "+str(result1))
print("The remainder is: "+str(result2))
```

```
Enter first number:34
Enter second number:4
```

Complete the code (Obtain the Output).

In the next few exercises, figure out what is missing in the blank to get the output that is provided.

Exercise 41 (Output is 3)

```
a = input("Enter first number:")
b = input("Enter second number:")
a=int(a)
b=int(b)
result1=a_b
print("The answer is: "+str(result1))
```

```
Enter first number:7
Enter second number:4
```

Exercise 42 (Output is 0)

```
a = input("Enter first number:")
b = input("Enter second number:")
a=int(a)
b=int(b)
result1=a_b
print("The answer is: "+str(result1))
```

```
Enter first number:20
Enter second number:4
```

Exercise 43 (Output is 7)

```
a = input("Enter first number:")
b = input("Enter second number:")
a=int(a)
b=int(b)
result1=a_b
print("The answer is: "+str(result1))
```

```
Enter first number:7
Enter second number:1
```

Find the Error in the Code

For the next few exercises, read the code and spot the mistake. Correct the mistake and check if your answer is correct at the end of the chapter.

Exercise 44

```
a = input("Enter first number:")
b = input("Enter second number:")
c = input("Enter third number:")
result1=a*b*c
print("The answer is: "+str(result1))
```

Exercise 45

```
a = input("Enter first number:")
b = input("Enter second number:")
a=int(a)
b=int(b)
result1=a+b*b
print("The answer is: "+result1)
```

Exercise 46

```
a = input("Enter first number:")
b = input("Enter second number:")
a=int(a)
b=int(b)
result1=a+b*c
print("The answer is: "+result1)
```

Answers

Exercise 36

```
The answer is: 13
```

Exercise 37

```
The answer is: -6
```

Exercise 38

```
The answer is: 60
```

Exercise 39

```
The quotient of the two numbers is: 11.25
The remainder is: 1
```

Exercise 40

```
The quotient of the two numbers is: 8.5
The remainder is: 2
```

Exercise 41 (Answer is -)

```
a = input("Enter first number:")
b = input("Enter second number:")
a=int(a)
b=int(b)
result1=a-b
print("The answer is: "+str(result1))
```

Exercise 42 (Answer is %)

```
a = input("Enter first number:")
b = input("Enter second number:")
a=int(a)
b=int(b)
result1=a%b
print("The answer is: "+str(result1))
```

Exercise 43 (Answer is *)

```
a = input("Enter first number:")
b = input("Enter second number:")
a=int(a)
b=int(b)
result1=a*b
print("The answer is: "+str(result1))
```

Exercise 44

In this program, the variables a,b and c are strings since the **input()** function is used.

This is going to produce an error in line 7 as we are trying to multiply three strings as if they were numbers. We need to convert all of them to integers using **int()** function as shown in correct code below.

```
a = input("Enter first number:")
b = input("Enter second number:")
c = input("Enter third number:")
a=int(a)
b=int(b)
c=int(c)
result1=a*b*c
print("The answer is: "+str(result1))
```

Exercise 45

In this program, result1 is an integer and the print() function in line 6 combines it with a string “The answer is”. So result1 needs to be converted to a string using the str() function as shown in the code below.

```
1 a = input("Enter first number:")
2 b = input("Enter second number:")
3 a=int(a)
4 b=int(b)
5 result1=a*b*b
6 print("The answer is: "+str(result1))
```

Exercise 46

The operation in line 5 references a variable c when it does result1=a*b*c, but c is not declared and does not have any value. So, we need to declare variable c in line 3 as shown in program below.

```
a = input("Enter first number:")
b = input("Enter second number:")
c = input("Enter third number:")
result1=a*b*c
print("The answer is: "+str(result1))
```

Exercises to Practice

1. Write a program that takes in values of two variables for weights of your 2 bags. Calculate the total weight of your cabin luggage and check if it is larger than 23 kg. If it is larger then calculate how overweight it is and print it on the screen. If it is smaller, then print that the weight is good.
2. Write a program that takes in values of two variables for number of people and number of apartments per person. Calculate and print the total number of apartments needed.

Loops

What is a Loop?

A loop is just a set of instructions that are repeated in a program a fixed number of times. Let's say you want to repeat a particular task multiple times, like solving a puzzle, printing an item or drawing a pattern. Instead of repeating the same instruction multiple times, you can just write the instructions once, and use a loop.

If you want to print "Bob" on the screen 1000 times, you would need to write:

print("Bob")

on your NotePad++ a 1000 times. This is a waste of your time, a waste of computer memory and a waste of space on your NotePad++.

Instead, you can do the program below:

```
for i in range(1000):
    print("Bob")
```

We get output below. It prints "Bob" a 1000 times on the screen. We're not going to show all the 1000 times as we don't want to waste space in the book. However, you can try out the program and see it.

The above loop is called a **FOR Loop** in Python. We use this kind of loop when we know how many times, we need to run the program. Line 1 in above program shows the loop structure. The variable i is the counter. It starts at a value of 0 and increments by 1 a thousand times. The for loop ends with a colon operator “:”.

The next few lines are indented to indicate that these are the lines inside the loop.

Output:

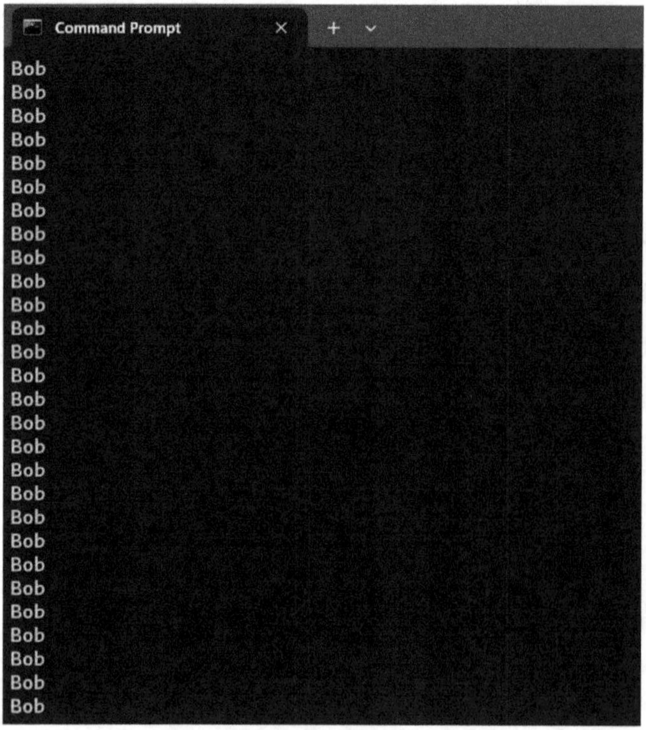

However, sometimes we don't know how many times the program is run. In such a case, we cannot use a FOR Loop. Instead, we use what is known as a WHILE Loop.

In the below program, we print Bob's name on the screen as long as a user input says "yes". Every time we print Bob's name, we ask the user if he wants to keep printing. If he says yes, then the program prints "Bob" 1 more time. If not, the program ends.

```
1 user_response="yes"
2 while user_response=="yes":
3     print("Bob")
4     user_response = input("Do you still want to print Bob's name? (yes/no): ")
5     if user_response.lower() != "yes":
6         break
7
```

In line 1, we declare **user_response** to a value of yes so that the program enters the while loop. The while loop is between line 2 and line 6.

Inside the while loop, we print "Bob" in line 3.

In line 4, we get a user response using the **input()** function.

In lines 5-6, we set an exit condition. We can exit a loop using a function called **break()**. The break function is in line 6. If user response is not a value of **"yes"**, the program enters line 6 and we end the program.

Below is an output for the program where the user enters "yes" 3 times, and then enters a "no".

Output:

```
Bob
Do you still want to print Bob's name? (yes/no): yes
Bob
Do you still want to print Bob's name? (yes/no): yes
Bob
Do you still want to print Bob's name? (yes/no): no
```

Predict Output

For the following exercises, read the code and the user input and predict the output. Check your answer at the end of the chapter.

Exercise 47

```
for i in range(10):
    print(i)
```

Exercise 48

```
for i in range(10):
    print(i+1)
```

Exercise 49

```
for i in range(3):
    name = input("Your name? ")
    print("Student "+str(i+1)+" = "+name)
```

Exercise 50

```
for i in range(5):
    print(i*3)
```

Exercise 51

```
name="Sam"
while name!="stop":
    print(name)
    name = input("What's your name? (Enter 'stop' if out of names): ")
    if name.lower() == "stop":
        break
```

Complete the code (Obtain the Output).

In the next few exercises, figure out what is missing from the program in the blanks to obtain output. Answers are the end of the chapter.

Exercise 52

```
for i in range(5):
    print (___)
```

Output:

```
0
2
4
6
8
```

Exercise 53

```
for i in range(_)
    print (i*3)
```

Output:

```
0
3
6
```

Exercise 54

```
for i in range(10):
    print ("Print Number: "+____)
```

Output:

```
Print Number: 1
Print Number: 2
Print Number: 3
Print Number: 4
Print Number: 5
Print Number: 6
Print Number: 7
Print Number: 8
Print Number: 9
Print Number: 10
```

Exercise 55

```
for i in range(_):
    print ("Steve")
```

Output:

```
Steve
Steve
Steve
Steve
Steve
Steve
Steve
```

Find the Error in the Code

For the next few exercises, read the code and spot the mistake. Correct the mistake and check if your answer is correct at the end of the chapter.

Exercise 56

```
for i in range(5)
    print (i*3)
```

Exercise 57

```
for i in range(10):
    print i
```

Exercise 58

```
name="Sam"
while name!="stop":
    print(name)
    name = input("What's your name? (Enter 'stop' if out of names): ")
    if name.lower() == "stop"
        break
```

Answers

Exercise 47

```
0
1
2
3
4
5
6
7
8
9
```

Exercise 48

```
1
2
3
4
5
6
7
8
9
10
```

Exercise 49

```
Your name? Steve
Student 1 = Steve
Your name? Robery
Student 2 = Robery
Your name? Jose
Student 3 = Jose
```

Exercise 50

```
0
3
6
9
12
```

Exercise 51

```
Sam
What's your name? (Enter 'stop' if out of names): Tim
Tim
What's your name? (Enter 'stop' if out of names): Bob
Bob
What's your name? (Enter 'stop' if out of names): Feather
Feather
What's your name? (Enter 'stop' if out of names): stop
```

Exercise 52 (Answer is i*2)

Exercise 53 (Answer is 3)

Exercise 54 (Answer is str(i+1))

Exercise 55 (Answer is 7)

Exercise 56

There's a missing colon at the end of the For loop in line 1. Just add a colon as below:

```
1  for i in range(5):
2      print(i*3)
```

Exercise 57

There's a missing bracket in the print function in line 2. Just add opening and closing brackets around the i in line 2.

```
for i in range(10):
    print (i)
```

1.

Exercise 58

There's a missing colon at the end of the if conditional in line 5. Just add a colon as below:

```
1 name="Sam"
2 while name!="stop":
3     print(name)
4     name = input("What's your name? (Enter 'stop' if out of names): ")
5     if name.lower() == "stop":
6         break
```

Exercises to Practice

1. Create a loop that takes in names of 5 people and their ages and prints them each on the screen.
2. Create a loop that takes in names of 10 dog names with their weights and prints them all on the screen.

If you liked the book so far, you'll find our next gift very useful for your programming journey. It's a list of 10 most common programming errors, and how to solve them. Just scan the barcode below to obtain it.

Nested Loops

What are Nested Loops?

Nested Loops are basically loops within loops. So, in a regular loop you complete a task a fixed number of times. However, what if each time you complete a task, you want to perform another task or check to ensure that the task is completed.

In the previous chapter, we wanted to print Bob a thousand times. What if each time you want to print Bob on the screen, you want to print Lisa on the screen three times. So, you want to maintain a ratio of 1:3 of Bob:Lisa printed on the screen.

In this case, you'd need another For Loop where you print Lisa each time you print Bob. So, let's have a look at the code.

```
1 for i in range(1000):
2     print("Bob")
3     for i in range(3):
4         print("Lisa")
```

As you can see in Lines 3-4, we add another for loop that prints "Lisa" on the screen 3 times.

We can see this in the output below, where Lisa is printed every 3 times Bob is printed.

So, in this program, Bob is printed 1000 times and Lisa is printed 3000 times.

Output:

```
Bob
Lisa
Lisa
Lisa
Bob
Lisa
Lisa
Lisa
Bob
Lisa
Lisa
Lisa
Bob
Lisa
Lisa
Lisa
Bob
Lisa
Lisa
Lisa
Bob
Lisa
Lisa
Lisa
Bob
Lisa
Lisa
Lisa
```

The above loop is called a Nested **For Loop** in Python.

Predict Output

For the following exercises, read the code and the user input and predict the output. Check your answer at the end of the chapter.

Exercise 59

```
for a in range(1, 4):
    for b in range(1, 4):
        result = a * b
        print(str(a)+" * "+ str(b) + " = " + str(result))
```

Exercise 60

```
for row in range(1, 6):
    for col in range(1, row + 1):
        print("*", end=" ")
    print()
```

Exercise 61

```
matrix = [
        [1, 4, 7],
        [2, 5, 8],
        [3, 6, 9]
  ]

for row in matrix:
    for element in row:
        print(element, end=" ")
    print()
```

Complete the code (Obtain the Output).

In the next few exercises, figure out what is missing from the program in the blanks to obtain output. Answers are the end of the chapter.

Exercise 62

```
for a in range(1, _):
    for b in range(1, _):
        result = a + b
        print(str(a)+" + "+ str(b) + " = " + str(result))
```

Output:

```
1 + 1 = 2
1 + 2 = 3
1 + 3 = 4
1 + 4 = 5
2 + 1 = 3
2 + 2 = 4
2 + 3 = 5
2 + 4 = 6
3 + 1 = 4
3 + 2 = 5
3 + 3 = 6
3 + 4 = 7
4 + 1 = 5
4 + 2 = 6
4 + 3 = 7
4 + 4 = 8
```

Exercise 63

```
for row in range(1, 6):
    for col in range(1, row + 1):
        print(__, end=" ")
    print()
```

Output:

```
1
1 2
1 2 3
1 2 3 4
1 2 3 4 5
```

Exercise 64

```
for row in range(5, _, -1):
    for col in range(1, row + 1):
        print("*", end=" ")
    print()
```

Output:

```
* * * * *
* * * *
* * *
* *
*
```

Find the Error in the Code

For the next few exercises, read the code and spot the mistake. Correct the mistake and check if your answer is correct at the end of the chapter.

Exercise 65

```
for row in range(1, 6):
    for col in range(1, row + 1)
        print(col, end=" ")
    print()
```

Exercise 66

```
for a in range(1, 4):
    for b in range(1, 4):
        result = a * b
        print(a+" * "+ b + " = " + result)
```

Exercise 67

```
for row in (1, 6):
    for col in (1, row + 1):
        print(col, end=' ')
    print()
```

Answers

Exercise 59

```
1 * 1 = 1
1 * 2 = 2
1 * 3 = 3
2 * 1 = 2
2 * 2 = 4
2 * 3 = 6
3 * 1 = 3
3 * 2 = 6
3 * 3 = 9
```

Exercise 60

```
*
* *
* * *
* * * *
* * * * *
```

Exercise 61

```
1 4 7
2 5 8
3 6 9
```

Exercise 62 (Answer is 5)

Exercise 63 (Answer is col)

Exercise 64 (Answer is 0)

Exercise 65

There's a colon missing at the end of the for loop in line 2. You can add that in as below.

```
1 for row in range(1, 6):
2     for col in range(1, row + 1):
3         print(col, end=" ")
4     print()
5
```

Exercise 66

The variables a and b in line 3 are integers. The print function would throw up an error as it requires string variables inside. So, we can convert the integers to strings using str() function as shown below:

```
1 for a in range(1, 4):
2     for b in range(1, 4):
3         result = a * b
4         print(str(a)+" * "+ str(b) + " = " + str(result))
```

Exercise 67

The for loop in lines 1 and 2 is missing a range. The range is the number that it starts and ends. We see that below, where range is added. A range of (1,6) means that it goes from 1 to 6 in an increment of 1.

```
for row in range(1, 6):
    for col in range(1, row + 1):
        print(col, end=' ')
    print()
```

Exercises to Practice

1. Write a program that creates two loops. Both loops are loops that start at 1 and end at 10. Print out the difference between the two numbers in a nested loop. So, the first output would be "1-1=0", second would be "1-2=-1" etc. etc.
2. Create a loop that prints the character "&" on the screen in the following manner:

   &&

   &&&&

   &&&&&&

   &&&&&&&&

   &&&&&&&&&&

   &&&&&&&&&&&&

   &&&&&&&&&&&&&&

Arrays

What are Arrays?

An array is just a group of variables of the same data type. Each variable can be accessed by an index number or key. Arrays are an efficient way to organize and access data in a program.

If we need to create a program that needs 10 different numbers, we can instead create an integer array of size 10.

An array is like a row of boxes that hold a particular item. Let's say each box holds a ball. Each box has a number on it. The first box is 0, the second is 1, the third is 2 and so on. The nice thing is that you can easily find a particular ball by referencing it's box number. So, if 10 people are storing their sports balls in each box, each number would reference a person; and they can access their ball by checking their box number. The number of boxes is the size of the array; the number on the box is the index of the array. The name in each box is the value of the array at that index location.

The picture below shows 10 boxes labelled 0-9

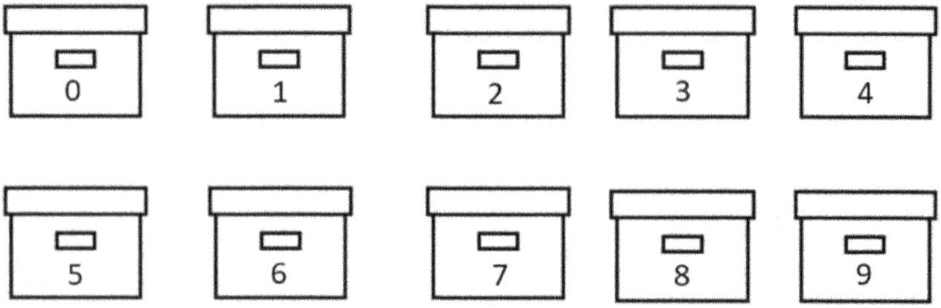

In Python, this would be defined as below. We put the box owner name as the value of the array.

```
1 box_array = ["Alice", "Bob", "Charlie", "David", "Eva", "Frank", "Grace", "Henry", "Ivy", "Jack"]
2 print(box_array)
```

When we print the output in line 2, we get array below.

Output:

```
['Alice', 'Bob', 'Charlie', 'David', 'Eva', 'Frank', 'Grace', 'Henry', 'Ivy', 'Jack']
```

Array Operations

Referencing an item

We can reference any item in an array by using the index number as shown below. The first element of an array in Python is indexed at 0.

```
box_array = ["Alice", "Bob", "Charlie", "David", "Eva", "Frank", "Grace", "Henry", "Ivy", "Jack"]
print("The first box is owned by:"+box_array[0])
print("The fifth box is owned by:"+box_array[4])
```

box_array[0] references the first person in the array, and box_array[4] references the fifth person in the array, as shown in output below:

Output:

```
The first box is owned by:Alice
The fifth box is owned by:Eva
```

Changing an item

Any item can be replaced with another item by referencing its index and assigned the index to a different value. This is shown in code below, where the 1st box owner is changed to Matt.

```
1 box_array = ["Alice", "Bob", "Charlie", "David", "Eva", "Frank", "Grace", "Henry", "Ivy", "Jack"]
2 print("The first box is owned by:"+box_array[0])
3 box_array[0]="Matt"
4 print("The first box is now owned by:"+box_array[0])
```

We can see in the output below where the box owner is printed before and after the item change in line 3.

Output:

```
The first box is owned by:Alice
The first box is now owned by:Matt
```

Adding an item

We can add items to an array by using the **append()** function. The item is added to the end of the array as shown below. The item "Jeff" is added in line 2 and the printed out shows "Jeff" as the owner of the 11th box.

```
1 box_array = ["Alice", "Bob", "Charlie", "David", "Eva", "Frank", "Grace", "Henry", "Ivy", "Jack"]
2 box_array.append("Jeff")
3 print(box_array)
```

Output:

```
['Alice', 'Bob', 'Charlie', 'David', 'Eva', 'Frank', 'Grace', 'Henry', 'Ivy',
```

Removing an item

We can remove an item by using the remove() function. The name of the item to be removed is put within brackets in the remove function. In the program below, “Bob” is removed in line 2, and the printed array in line 3 shows one less element of the array and without the name “Bob”.

```
1 box_array = ["Alice", "Bob", "Charlie", "David", "Eva", "Frank", "Grace", "Henry", "Ivy", "Jack"]
2 box_array.remove("Bob")
3 print(box_array)
```

Output:

```
['Alice', 'Charlie', 'David', 'Eva', 'Frank', 'Grace', 'Henry', 'Ivy', 'Jack']
```

Finding Elements in an Array

We can also find the index location of a certain item in an array using the index() function. In below code, we try to find location of “Eva” in the array.

In the output we see that Eva is at index 4, which is the 5th name in the array.

```
box_array = ["Alice", "Bob", "Charlie", "David", "Eva", "Frank", "Grace", "Henry", "Ivy", "Jack"]
a=box_array.index("Eva")
print("Eva is at index: "+str(a)+ " in the array")
```

Output:

```
Eva is at index: 4 in the array
```

Length of the Array

We can also find the length of an array using the len() function as seen in code below.

```
box_array = ["Alice", "Bob", "Charlie", "David", "Eva", "Frank", "Grace", "Henry", "Ivy", "Jack"]
l=len(box_array)
print("Length of array: "+str(l))
```

Output:

```
Length of array: 10
```

Predict Output

For the following exercises, read the code and the user input and predict the output. Check your answer at the end of the chapter.

Exercise 68

```
ht_array = [151, 176, 181, 133, 143, 171, 177, 164, 192]
l=len(ht_array)
fel=ht_array[0]
fel2=ht_array[2]
print(l)
print(fel)
print(fel2)
```

Exercise 69

```
ht_array = [151, 176, 181, 133, 143, 171, 177, 164, 192]
l=len(ht_array)
ht_array[3] = 170
print(ht_array)
```

Exercise 70

```
ht_array = [151, 176, 181, 133, 143, 171, 177, 164, 192]
ht_array.append(180)
l=len(ht_array)
print(l)
print(ht_array)
```

Exercise 71

```
ht_array = [151, 176, 181, 133, 143, 171, 177, 164, 192]
ht_array.append(132)
ht_array.remove(151)
ht_array.remove(181)
l=len(ht_array)
print(l)
print(ht_array)
```

Exercise 72

```
ht_array = [151, 176, 181, 133, 143, 171, 177, 164, 192]
i1=ht_array.index(151)
i2=ht_array.index(192)
print(i1)
print(i2)
```

Complete the code (Obtain the Output).

In the next few exercises, figure out what is missing from the program in the blank area to obtain output. Answers are the end of the chapter.

Exercise 73 (Output is 88)

```
math_grades = (85, 92, 78, 95, 88, 90, 83, 91, 87, 89)
fifth_student_grade = math_grades[_]
print("Fifth Student's Math Grade:", fifth_student_grade)
```

Exercise 74 (Output is 85)

```
math_grades = (85, 92, 78, 95, 88, 90, 83, 91, 87, 89)
first_student_grade = math_grades[_]
print("First Student's Math Grade:", first_student_grade)
```

Exercise 75 (Output is 5)

```
math_grades = (85, 92, 78, 95, 88, 90, 83, 91, 87, 89)
student_90 = math_grades.index(_)
print("Index of student who got 90: ", student 90)
```

Exercise 76 (Output is 79)

```
math_grades = (85, 92, 78, 80, 88, 90, 83, 91, 87, 89)
average_2 = (math_grades[2]+math_grades[3])/_
print("Average of 2 students ", average_2)
```

Exercise 77 (Output is 78)

```
math_grades = [85, 92, 78, 80, 88, 90, 83, 91, 87, 89]
math_grades.append(100)
math_grades.remove(85)
math_grades.remove(__)
print("The first element is ", math_grades[0])
```

Find the Error in the Code

For the next few exercises, read the code and spot the mistake. Correct the mistake and check if your answer is correct at the end of the chapter.

Exercise 78

```
running_times = (360, 420, 390, 410, 380, 430, 400, 415, 370, 395)
l = len(running_times)
print("Number of students:", l)
```

Exercise 79

```
running_times = (360, 420, 390, 410, 380, 430, 400, 415, 370, 395)
a=running_times[10]
print("Last Student time:", a)
```

Exercise 80

```
running_times = (360, 420, 390, 410, 380, 430 400, 415, 370, 395)
a=running_times[-1]
print("Last Student time:", a)
```

Exercise 81

```
running_times = (360, 420, 390, 410, 380, 430, 400, 415, 370, 395)
a=running_times(8)
print("Last Student time:", a)
```

Answers

Exercise 68

```
9
151
181
```

Exercise 69

```
[151, 176, 181, 170, 143, 171, 177, 164, 192]
```

Exercise 70

```
10
[151, 176, 181, 133, 143, 171, 177, 164, 192, 180]
```

Exercise 71

8

```
[176, 133, 143, 171, 177, 164, 192, 132]
```

Exercise 72

```
0
8
```

Exercise 73 (Answer is 4)

Exercise 74 (Answer is 0)

Exercise 75(Answer is 90)

Exercise 76(Answer is 2)

Exercise 77(Answer is 92)

Exercise 78

The len function in line 2 needs square brackets ("[ ]") around it inside of curved brackets "( )". See correct code below.

```
1  running_times = (360, 420, 390, 410, 380, 430, 400, 415, 370, 395)
2  l = len[running_times]
3  print("Number of students:", l)
```

Exercise 79

Running_times[10] references an item that does not exist. The last item in the array is referenced by **running_times[9].** For an array of 10 running times, the first index is 0 and last index is 9. This is shown in correct code below.

```
1  running_times = (360, 420, 390, 410, 380, 430, 400, 415, 370, 395)
2  a=running_times[9]
3  print("Last Student time:", a)
```

We can also reference the last item of any array by using the index -1. So **running_times[-1]** references the last item of the **running_times[]** regardless of the length of the array. See correct code below.

```
1  running_times = (360, 420, 390, 410, 380, 430, 400, 415, 370, 395)
2  a=running_times[-1]
3  print("Last Student time:", a)
4
```

Exercise 80

There is a comma missing between the array elements 430 and 400 in line 1. This is added in correct code below.

```
1  running_times = (360, 420, 390, 410, 380, 430, 400, 415, 370, 395)
2  a=running_times[-1]
3  print("Last Student time:", a)
```

Exercise 81

In line 2, we need to square brackets around 8 to properly reference items in an array. So, we need to do **running_times[8]** to properly reference the 7th item in the array.

Exercises to Practice

1. Create an array of geography scores of 10 students. Print the score of the first student, last student and the average of the scores of all the students.
2. Create an array of 10 students and their names. Create another array that contains their favorite sport. Print out both the names of the students and their favorite sport.
3. Create an array that takes in names of 10 students through a user input and stores it in an array. (Hint: Use a for-loop and the index of the for-loop is the index of the array.)
4. You are conducting a survey to understand students' favorite subjects and preferences. Here's what you need to do:
    a. Create an array containing the names of 10 students.
    b. Create another array containing each student's favorite subject.
    c. Print out the names of the students along with their favorite subject.

d. Determine and print out the most popular subject among the students.

5. You are organizing a program for students of different age groups. Here's what you need to do:

   a. Create an array representing the ages of 10 students.
   b. Divide the students into two groups: those aged below 12 and those aged 12 or above. Create separate arrays for both groups.
   c. Print out the number of students in each group.
   d. Calculate and print out the average age of each group.

Advanced Math

More Math Operations in Python

In this chapter, we're going to go over a few more advanced Math operations in Python. These Math operations are within year 7 level (or age 12) in the United States. So, some of the topics may be a bit advanced for those who are in the younger age group below 10.

We're going to go over the following Math operations: Average, Standard Deviation, Minimum, Maximum, Area of a Circle and Circumference of a Circle.

Python Library NumPy

In Python, a lot of advanced and intermediate Math functions are stored in a Python library called Numpy. We need to install this first using Command Prompt.

So, first browse to the folder on Command Prompt where you want to run programs, and then type in "pip install numpy". This installs numpy library, and you are ready to get started.

```
C:\Users\[redacted]\python-coding>pip install numpy
```

```
C:\Users\[redacted]\python-coding>pip install numpy
Collecting numpy
  Obtaining dependency information for numpy from https://files.pythonhosted.org/packages/16/2e/86f24451c2d530c88daf997c
b8d6ac622c1d40d19f5a031ed68a4b73a374/numpy-1.26.4-cp312-cp312-win_amd64.whl.metadata
  Downloading numpy-1.26.4-cp312-cp312-win_amd64.whl.metadata (61 kB)
     ---------------------------------------- 61.0/61.0 kB 105.0 kB/s eta 0:00:00
Downloading numpy-1.26.4-cp312-cp312-win_amd64.whl (15.5 MB)
   ---------------------------------------- 15.5/15.5 MB 2.1 MB/s eta 0:00:00
Installing collected packages: numpy
Successfully installed numpy-1.26.4
```

First, we're going to create an array of 10 numbers and find the average, standard deviation, minimum and maximum of the numbers in that area.

```
1  import numpy as np
2  array = [77, 45, 12, 56, 89, 22, 56, 8, 90, 10]
3  minimum = np.min(array)
4  maximum = np.max(array)
5  average = np.mean(array)
6  std_deviation = np.std(array)
7  print("Array:", array)
8  print("Minimum:", minimum)
9  print("Maximum:", maximum)
10 print("Average:", average)
11 print("Standard Deviation:", std_deviation)
```

In program above in line 1, we import numpy and store it in a library object called **np**. A library object is used to access all functions inside the particular library.

We create the array of 10 numbers in line 2.

In lines 3-6, we use **np.min()** function, **np.max()** function, **np.mean()** function and **np.std()** function to calculate minimum, maximum, mean and standard deviation respectively.

The values are stored in variables **maximum**, **minimum**, **average** and **std_deviation.** These values are printed in lines 7-11 as seen in output below the code.

Output:

```
Array: [77, 45, 12, 56, 89, 22, 56, 8, 90, 10]
Minimum: 8
Maximum: 90
Average: 46.5
Standard Deviation: 30.686316168611704
```

Circle Area and Circumference

Now, we're going to calculate the area and circumference of a circle using a circle radius that is input by the user.

```
1 import math as m
2 radius = float(input("Enter the radius of the circle: "))
3 area = m.pi * radius ** 2
4 circumference = 2 * m.pi * radius
5 print("Area of the circle: "+str(area))
6 print("Circumference of the circle: "+str(circumference))
```

In line 1, we import the math library and store it as a library object m.

In line 2, we accept the circle radius from the user and convert it to a float variable. The **float()** function allows the variable to be stored as a decimal value. Without **float()**, the number entered would be converted to an integer.

The radius of the circle is stored in variable radius.

In line 3, we calculate area of the circle and store it in a variable area. This value is printed in line 5 using the **print()** function.

Note that we use **m.pi()** function to get the value of π and "**" symbol is used for exponentiation. So radius^2 is radius**2.

In line 4, we calculate circumference of the circle and store it in a variable circumference. This value is printed in line 6 using the **print()** function.

Output:

In the first output, we enter a radius of 4 and in the second output, we enter a radius of 7. We can see the calculated areas and circumferences below.

```
Enter the radius of the circle: 4
Area of the circle: 50.26548245743669
Circumference of the circle: 25.132741228718345
```

```
Enter the radius of the circle: 7
Area of the circle: 153.93804002589985
Circumference of the circle: 43.982297150257104
```

Random Numbers

In Python, we can create a number that is generated randomly by the program. We can specify the lower and upper bound of the random number. This is great for creating quizzes, activities and animations in Python, but in this book, we're going to stick with the basics.

```
1 import random as rn
2 random_number = rn.randint(0, 50)
3 print("Random number:", random_number)
```

In Python, the random function is stored in library called random. We import this in line 1 and store it in library object **rn**.

In line 2, we use the function **randint(0,50)** to create a random number between 0 and 50. It is stored in random variable **random_number**.

This value is printed in line 3 using the **print()** function.

Output:

When we run the program 5 different times, we get 5 different random numbers below between 0 and 50.

```
Random number: 32
```

```
Random number: 23
```

```
Random number: 44
```

```
Random number: 17
```

```
Random number: 47
```

Predict Output

For the following exercises, read the code and the user input and predict the output. Check your answer at the end of the chapter.

Exercise 82

```
import numpy as np
math_grades = [65, 72, 98, 81, 98, 70, 73, 81, 97, 79]
maxi = np.max(math_grades)
mini = np.min(math_grades)
avg = np.average(math_grades)
print("Maximum: ", maxi)
print("Minimum: ", mini)
print("Average: ", avg)
```

Exercise 83

```
import math

for radius in range(5, 11):
    circumference = 2 * math.pi * radius
    print("For radius "+ str(radius) + " the circumference is:" +str(circumference))
```

Exercise 84

```
import math
import random as rn

random_number = rn.randint(0,20)

area = math.pi * random_number ** 2

print("The radius is:",random_number)
print("The area corresponding to the random number is:", area)
```

Complete the code (Obtain the Output).

In the next few exercises, figure out what is missing from the program in the blank area to obtain the output. Answers are the end of the chapter.

Exercise 85 (Output is 113.09733552923255)

```
import math
radius = _
area = math.pi * radius ** 2
print("For radius "+ str(radius) + " the area is: " +str(area))
```

Exercise 86 (Output is 314.1592653589793)

```
import math
radius = _
area = math.pi * radius ** 2
print("For radius "+ str(radius) + " the area is: " +str(area))
```

Exercise 87 (Output is 96,78)

```
import numpy as np

science_grades = [85, 92, 78, 88, __]

maximum_grade = np.max(science_grades)
minimum_grade = np.min(science_grades)

print("Maximum Grade:", maximum_grade)
print("Minimum Grade:", minimum_grade)
```

Exercise 88 (Output is 87.8)

```
import numpy as np

science_grades = [85, 92, 78, 88, 96]

a = np.______(science_grades)

print(a)
```

Find the Error in the Code

For the next few exercises, read the code and spot the mistake. Correct the mistake and check if your answer is correct at the end of the chapter.

Exercise 89

```
radius = 7
circumference = 2 * math.pi * radius
print("For radius " + str(radius) + " the circumference is: " + circumference)
```

Exercise 90

```
import math
radius = 7
area = math.pi * radius ^ 2;
print(area)
```

Exercise 91

```
import numpy as x

science_grades = [85, 92, 78, 88, 95]

maximum_grade = x.maximum(science_grades)
minimum_grade = x.minimum(science_grades)
average_grade = x.mean(science_grades)

print("Maximum Grade:", maximum_grade)
print("Minimum Grade:", minimum_grade)
print("Average Grade:", average_grade)
```

Exercise 92

```
import numpy as x

science_grades = [85, 92 78, 88, 95]

maximum_grade = x.max(science_grades)
minimum_grade = x.min(science_grades)
average_grade = x.mean(science_grades)

print("Maximum Grade:", maximum_grade)
print("Minimum Grade:", minimum_grade)
print("Average Grade:", average_grade)
```

Answers

Exercise 82

```
Maximum:  98
Minimum:  65
Average:  81.4
```

Exercise 83

```
For radius 5 the circumference is:31.41592653589793
For radius 6 the circumference is:37.69911184307752
For radius 7 the circumference is:43.982297150257104
For radius 8 the circumference is:50.26548245743669
For radius 9 the circumference is:56.548667764616276
For radius 10 the circumference is:62.83185307179586
```

Exercise 84

```
The radius is: 11.0
The area corresponding to the random number is: 380.132711084365
```

```
The radius is: 7
The area corresponding to the random number is: 153.93804002589985
```

Exercise 85: Answer is 6

Exercise 86: Answer is 10

Exercise 87: Answer is 96

Exercise 88: Answer is mean

Exercise 89:

There are 2 errors in this program:

a. Math.pi is called in line 2 without using the Math library function. So we need to add a Math library function at the start of the function.

b. In line 3, circumference needs to be converted to a string so that it can be in the same format as the rest of the print function. So, we use str(circumference) to achieve this.

Both changes are shown in code below:

```
1 import math
2 radius = 7
3 circumference = 2 * math.pi * radius
4 print("For radius " + str(radius) + " the circumference is: " + str(circumference))
```

Exercise 90

In line 3, "^" is not a character defined in Python. We need to use "**" for power to represent r^2. This is shown in code below.

```
1 import math
2 radius = 7
3 area = math.pi * radius ** 2;
4 print(area)
```

Exercise 91

In lines 5 and 6, maximum and minimum are not defined functions in numpy. We need to use max() and min() functions as shown below in correct code.

```python
import numpy as x

science_grades = [85, 92, 78, 88, 95]

maximum_grade = x.max(science_grades)
minimum_grade = x.min(science_grades)
average_grade = x.mean(science_grades)

print("Maximum Grade:", maximum_grade)
print("Minimum Grade:", minimum_grade)
print("Average Grade:", average_grade)
```

Exercise 92

There is a comma separator missing in line 3 between 92 and 78.

We add that in correct code below.

```python
1  import numpy as x
2
3  science_grades = [85, 92, 78, 88, 95]
4
5  maximum_grade = x.max(science_grades)
6  minimum_grade = x.min(science_grades)
7  average_grade = x.mean(science_grades)
8
9  print("Maximum Grade:", maximum_grade)
10 print("Minimum Grade:", minimum_grade)
11 print("Average Grade:", average_grade)
```

Exercises to Practice

1. Create an array of 10 students with Chemistry quiz grades between 0 and 10. These are randomly assigned using a random variable and printed on the screen.
2. Create a game where 5 people reveal their names and they are each randomly assigned a number between 1 and 100. These numbers and their names are stored in an array. Find the person

who got the maximum number and print the number as well as their name.

3. A group of 8 friends decided to go hiking. Each friend recorded the distance they hiked in kilometers. Create an array of these distances and calculate the total distance covered by all the friends.
4. In a mathematics competition, 12 students competed and received scores between 0 and 100. Create an array of these scores and find the average score achieved by the students.
5. Create a loop of 10. In each iteration of the loop, a circle radius between 0 and 50 is randomly generated. The area is calculated for each iteration and stored in an array. The array is printed at the end, with the maximum radius and corresponding area.

Strings

What are Strings?

A string is a type of variable that holds a single character or a sequence of characters. The characters are enclosed within single quotes or double quotes. For example, the variable name below holds the value Bob.

```
name="Bob"
print(name)
```

Output:

```
Bob
```

Just like any variable, the value of the variable can change throughout the program. Here we change the value of the variable from Bob to Steve.

```
name="Bob"
print(name)
name="Steve"
print(name)
```

Output:

```
Bob
Steve
```

String Operations

Strings can be a lot of fun to play with. Check out all that we can do below.

Adding Strings

We can add two strings together into one using the "+" operator below.

In below code, we add the strings "Bob" and "is great" together.

```
name="Bob"
string2=" is great."
result = name + string2
print(result)
```

Output:

```
Bob is great.
```

Indexing

Each string is automatically indexed in Python with the first index at 0. We can access the elements of a string as shown below.

In code below, we print first element of the string "Bob is great" using result[0] below. This is the letter "B" as shown in the output.

```
name="Bob"
string2=" is great."
result = name + string2
print(result[0])
```

Output:

```
B
```

Substring

We can get different parts of a string using a start index and an end index. In below code, we get a substring which is between 3rd and 9th element of the result string. This is done using result[4:10].

```
name="Bob"
string2=" is great."
result = name + string2
print(result[4:10])
```

Output:

```
is gre
```

Length

We can get the length of a string using the len() function. In below code, we get the length of both the name and the result string and print them out.

```
name="Bob"
string2=" is great."
result = name + string2
lengthname=len(name)
lengthresult=len(result)
print(lengthname)
print(lengthresult)
```

Output:

```
3
13
```

Upper/Lower Case

We can change any string to a lower case using the lower() function; and to upper case using the upper() function. In below code, we find both the upper and lower case of the result string and print them out.

```
name="Bob"
string2=" is great."
result = name + string2
uresult=result.upper()
lresult=result.lower()
print(uresult)
print(lresult)
```

Output:

```
BOB IS GREAT.
bob is great.
```

Split a String

If a string has a character (such as a comma or semicolon or space) that separates items in it, we can split the string into substrings with the character as the separator. In below code, we get all words of the result string by splitting the string based on a space operator (" ").

```
name="Bob"
string2=" is great."
result = name + string2
splitr=result.split(" ")
print(splitr)
```

Output:

```
['Bob', 'is', 'great.']
```

Predict Output

For the following exercises, read the code and the user input and predict the output. Check your answer at the end of the chapter.

Exercise 93

```
string1 = "Hello"
string2 = "Sam"
result = string1 + " " + string2
print("New String:", result)
```

Exercise 94

```
strings = "My name is Steve and I am 25 years old"
print(len(strings))
print(strings.upper())
print(strings.lower())
```

Exercise 95

```
strings = "My name is Steve and I am 25 years old"
print(strings[5])
print(strings[15])
print(strings[11:16])
```

Exercise 96

```
stringb = "red;blue;green"
print(stringb.split(";"))
```

Exercise 97

```
name = input("What is your name?")
age=input("What is your age?")
stringcomb = "My name is "+ name+ " and my age is " +age
print(stringcomb)
```

```
What is your name?Warren
What is your age?94
```

Complete the code (Obtain the Output).

In the next few exercises, figure out what is missing from the program to obtain the output. Answers are the end of the chapter.

Exercise 98 (Output = "We will win")

```
string1="We will"
string2= ____
sumstr = string1 + string2
print(sumstr)
```

Exercise 99 (Output = ['We', 'will', 'run', 'today'])

```
string1="We will"
string2= " run today"
sumstr = string1 + string2
print(sumstr.split(    ))
```

Exercise 100 (Output = “W”)

```
string1="We will"
string2= " run today"
sumstr = string1 + string2
print(sumstr[ ])
```

Exercise 101 (Output = “run”)

```
string1="We will"
string2= " run today"
sumstr = string1 + string2
print(sumstr[___])
```

Exercise 102 (Output = “toda”)

```
string1="We will"
string2= " run today"
sumstr = string1 + string2
print(sumstr[___])
```

Find the Error in the Code

For the next few exercises, read the code and spot the mistake. Correct the mistake and check if your answer is correct at the end of the chapter.

Exercise 103

```
name = input("What is your name?")
age=input("What is your age?")
stringcomb = "My name is " name+ " and my age is " +age
print(stringcomb)
```

Exercise 104

```
name="Bob"
string2=" is great."
result = name + string2
splitr=split.result(" ")
print(splitr)
```

Exercise 105

```
string1="We will"
string2= " run today"
sumstr = string1 + string2
print(sumstr(0))
```

Exercise 106

```
string1="We will'
string2= " run today"
sumstr = string1 + string2
print(sumstr(0))
```

Exercise 107

```
string1="We will"
string2= " run today"
sumstr = string + string2
print(sumstr[0])
```

Answers

Exercise 93

```
Combined String: Hello Sam
```

Exercise 94

```
38
MY NAME IS STEVE AND I AM 25 YEARS OLD
my name is steve and i am 25 years old
```

Exercise 95

```
m
e
Steve
```

Exercise 96

```
['red', 'blue', 'green']
```

Exercise 97

```
My name is Warren and my age is 94
```

Exercise 98 (" win.")

Exercise 99 (" ")

Exercise 100 ([0])

Exercise 101 ([8:11])

Exercise 102 ([12:16])

Exercise 103

There is a "+" sign missing in line 3 between string "is" and variable name. This produces an error as the strings are not properly added together. The correct code is below.

```
1  name = input("What is your name?")
2  age=input("What is your age?")
3  stringcomb = "My name is "+ name+ " and my age is " +age
4  print(stringcomb)
```

Exercise 104

In line 4, split.result is used instead of result.split. The correct code is below.

```
1  name="Bob"
2  string2=" is great."
3  result = name + string2
4  splitr=result.split(" ")
5  print(splitr)
```

Exercise 105

In line 3, sumstr(0) is used instead of sumstr[0]. Need to use square brackets instead of round brackets. The correct code is below.

```
1  string1="We will"
2  string2= " run today"
3  sumstr = string1 + string2
4  print(sumstr[0])
```

Exercise 106

In line 1, a single quote (‘) is used instead of a double quote at the end of the line. The correct code is below.

```
1  string1="We will"
2  string2= " run today"
3  sumstr = string1 + string2
4  print(sumstr[0])
```

Exercise 107

In line 3, incorrect variable string is used instead of string1 while adding the strings together. The correct code is below.

```
string1="We will"
string2= " run today"
sumstr = string1 + string2
print(sumstr[0])
```

Exercises to Practice

1. Write a program that takes in a person's name, age, favorite color and favorite animal; and stores all of them in a string. Print out the entire string, and also print out the length of the string.
2. Write a program that takes in a string from the user, and prints out all the words in the string.
3. Write a program that creates a string. The string contains a list of animals separated by a colon. Now print out all the animals in the string.
4. Write a program that takes a paragraph or sentence as input from the user and counts the number of words in it. Words are separated by spaces. Print the total count of words in the input sentence or paragraph.

Lists

What is a List?

A list is a group of variables that can be the same or different data types. Each variable can be accessed by an index number of key. A list is a way to organize data in a program, with the flexibility of using different types of variables. A list is basically an array that can hold different types of variables.

For example, if we want to create a variable that holds data about a single person, including his name, age and favorite color, we can create a variable sam_list below:

```
sam_list = ["Sam", 34, "green"]
print(sam_list)
```

And we get the output below that prints out sam_list.

Output:

```
['Sam', 34, 'green']
```

A list is like a group of boxes that hold different items. Let's say one box holds a ball, the next box can hold a number, the third can hold a name and so on. Each box has a number on it. The first box is labelled 0, the second is 1, the third is 2 and so on. The nice thing is that you can easily find a particular item by referencing its box number. So, if 10 people are storing their items in each box, each number would reference a person; and they can access their item by checking their box number. The number of boxes is the size of the array; the number on the box is the index of the array. The item in each box is the value of the array at that index location.

The picture below shows 10 boxes labelled 0-9

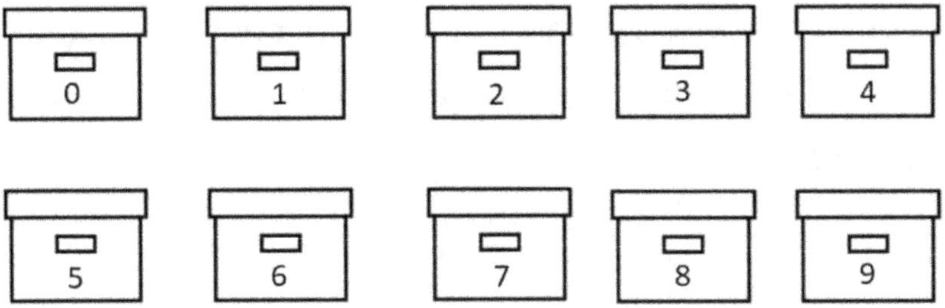


```
box = ["red ball", 34, "Bob", "Sand", "water", "Watson",234,456,"Sam","Barbie" ]
print(box)
```

Output:

```
['red ball', 34, 'Bob', 'Sand', 'water', 'Watson', 234, 456, 'Sam', 'Barbie']
```

List Operations

Accessing Elements

We can access any item in a list by using the index number as shown below. The first element of a list in Python is indexed at 0.

```
box = ["red ball", 34, "Bob", "Sand", "water", "Watson",234,456,"Sam","Barbie" ]
print("The first box contains: "+str(box[0]))
print("The second box contains: "+str(box[1]))
```

box [0] references the first item in the list, and box [1] references the second item in the list, as shown in output below:

Output:

```
The first box contains red ball
The second box contains 34
```

Adding Elements

We can add items to a list by using the **append()** function. The item is added to the end of the list as shown below. The item "Laura" is added in line 2 and the printed out shows "Laura" as the item in the 11th box.

```
1 box = ["red ball", 34, "Bob", "Sand", "water", "Watson",234,456,"Sam","Barbie" ]
2 box.append("Laura")
3 print(box)
```

Output:

```
['red ball', 34, 'Bob', 'Sand', 'water', 'Watson', 234, 456, 'Sam', 'Barbie', 'Laura'
```

Removing Elements

We can remove an item in a list by using the remove() function. The item to be removed is put within brackets in the remove function. In the program below, "Bob" is removed in line 2, and the printed list in line 3 shows one less element of the list and without the name "Bob". The list now only contains 9 elements.

```
1 box = ["red ball", 34, "Bob", "Sand", "water", "Watson",234,456,"Sam","Barbie" ]
2 box.remove("Bob")
3 print(box)
```

Output:

```
['red ball', 34, 'Sand', 'water', 'Watson', 234, 456, 'Sam', 'Barbie']
```

Inserting Elements into a List

We can also add items to the middle of a list using the insert function below. In program below in line 2, the number 45 is inserted at index position 4 (or 5th item).

In the output, we see the number 45 instead of "water" printed out in the list.

```
1 box = ["red ball", 34, "Bob", "Sand", "water", "Watson",234,456,"Sam","Barbie" ]
2 box.insert(4,45)
3 print(box)
```

Output:

```
['red ball', 34, 'Bob', 'Sand', 45, 'water', 'Watson', 234, 456, 'Sam', 'Barbie']
```

Length of List

We can also find the length of a list using the len() function as seen in code below.

```
box = ["red ball", 34, "Bob", "Sand", "water", "Watson",234,456,"Sam","Barbie" ]
l=len(box)
print("The length of the list is: "+str(l))
```

Output:

```
Length of array: 10
```

Sub-List

We can also create a new list that is a subset of the main list using the values at the indexes. In program below, we create a new list called new_box_list that contains items in box between index 1 and index 4 (not including 4). So it includes items at index 1,2,3 as shown in output below.

```
box = ["red ball", 34, "Bob", "Sand", "water", "Watson",234,456,"Sam","Barbie" ]
new_box_list=box[1:4]
print(new box list)
```

Output:

```
[34, 'Bob', 'Sand']
```

Predict Output

For the following exercises, read the code and the user input and predict the output. Check your answer at the end of the chapter.

Exercise 108

```
employee1 = ["Matt", 34, "Minneapolis", 9.5]
employee2 = ["Steve", 45, "Houston", 9.3]
print(employee1[0])
```

Exercise 109

```
employee1 = ["Matt", 34, "Minneapolis", 9.5]
employee2 = ["Steve", 45, "Houston", 9.3]
print("The second employee is "+str(employee2[0])+" and his age is "+str(employee2[1]))
```

Exercise 110

```
employee1 = ["Matt", 34, "Minneapolis", 9.5]
employee2 = ["Steve", 45, "Houston", 9.3]
print("The two employees are "+str(employee1[0])+" and "+str(employee2[0]))
```

Exercise 111

```
employee1 = ["Matt", 34, "Minneapolis", 9.5]
employee2 = ["Steve", 45, "Houston", 9.3]
print(str(employee1[0])+ " is "+str(employee1[1])+" years old and from "+str(employee1[2]) + " and has a rating of " + str(employee1[3]))
```

Exercise 112

```
employee1 = ["Matt", 34, "Minneapolis", 9.5]
employee2 = ["Steve", 45, "Houston", 9.3]
employee3 = ["Andy", 25, "Miami", 7.3]
print(str(employee3[0])+ " has a rating of " + str(employee3[3]))
```

Complete the code (Obtain the Output).

In the next few exercises, figure out what is missing from the program to obtain the output. Answers are the end of the chapter.

Exercise 113 (Output is 75)

```
math1 = ["Andy", 75]
math2 = ["Bob", 83]
math3 = ["Steve", 80]
math4 = ["Billy", 66]
math5 = ["Zach", 94]
math6 = ["Carl", 75]
math7 = ["Dave", 71]
math8 = ["Ed", 92]
math9 = ["Will", 52]
math10 = ["Tate", 66]
print(_____)
```

Exercise 114 (Output is 158)

```
math1 = ["Andy", 75]
math2 = ["Bob", 83]
math3 = ["Steve", 80]
math4 = ["Billy", 66]
math5 = ["Zach", 94]
math6 = ["Carl", 75]
math7 = ["Dave", 71]
math8 = ["Ed", 92]
math9 = ["Will", 52]
math10 = ["Tate", 66]
print(_____)
```

Exercise 115 (Output="Billy's Math Score is 66")

```
math1 = ["Andy", 75]
math2 = ["Bob", 83]
math3 = ["Steve", 80]
math4 = ["Billy", 66]
math5 = ["Zach", 94]
math6 = ["Carl", 75]
math7 = ["Dave", 71]
math8 = ["Ed", 92]
math9 = ["Will", 52]
math10 = ["Tate", 66]
print(_____)
```

Exercise 116 (Output = 73.0)

```
math1 = ["Andy", 75]
math2 = ["Bob", 83]
math3 = ["Steve", 80]
math4 = ["Billy", 66]
math5 = ["Zach", 94]
math6 = ["Carl", 75]
math7 = ["Dave", 71]
math8 = ["Ed", 92]
math9 = ["Will", 52]
math10 = ["Tate", 66]
print(_____)
```

Exercise 117 (Output = "CarlDave")

```
math1 = ["Andy", 75]
math2 = ["Bob", 83]
math3 = ["Steve", 80]
math4 = ["Billy", 66]
math5 = ["Zach", 94]
math6 = ["Carl", 75]
math7 = ["Dave", 71]
math8 = ["Ed", 92]
math9 = ["Will", 52]
math10 = ["Tate", 66]
print(_____)
```

Find the Error in the Code

For the next few exercises, read the code and spot the mistake. Correct the mistake and check if your answer is correct at the end of the chapter.

Exercise 118

```
student1 = ["Grace", 76, 56, 67]
student2 = ["Archer", 93, 89, 99]
student3 = ["Judy", 100, 80, 97]
print("First student name is "+student1[0])
print("First student math score is "+student1[1])
```

Exercise 119

```
student1 = ["Grace", 76, 56, 67]
student2 = ["Archer", 93, 89, 99]
student3 = ["Judy", 100, 80, 97]
average1 = (student1[1]+student1[2]+student1[3])/3
print("First student average score is "+str(average1[0]))
```

Exercise 120

```
student1 = ["Grace", 76, 56, 67]
student2 = ["Archer", 93, 89, 99]
student3 = ["Judy", 100, 80, 97]
average2 = (student2[0]+student2[1]+student2[2])/3
print("First student average score is "+str(average2))
```

Exercise 121

```
student1 = ["Grace", 76, 56, 67]
student2 = ["Archer", 93, 89, 99]
student3 = ["Judy", 100, 80, 97]
sum3 = student3[1]+student3[2]+student4[3]
print("Third student has a total of "+str(sum3))
```

Exercise 122

```
student1 = ["Grace", 76, 56, 67]
student2 = ["Archer", 93, 89, 99]
student3 = ["Judy", 100, 80, 97]
print(student3[0] + " has a science score of "+student3[2])
```

Answers

Exercise 108

```
Matt
```

Exercise 109

```
The second employee is Steve and his age is 45
```

Exercise 110

```
The two employees are Matt and Steve
```

Exercise 111

```
Matt is 34 years old and from Minneapolis and has a r
```

Exercise 112

```
Andy has a rating of 7.3
```

Exercise 113 (math1[1] or math6[1])

Exercise 114 (math1[1]+math2[1])

Exercise 115 (str(math4[0])+"'s Math score is "+str(math4[1])

Exercise 116 ((math3[1]+math4[1])/2)

Exercise 117 (math6[0]+math7[0])

Exercise 118

In line 5, student1[1] needs to be converted to a string before it is added to the rest of the print statement. The correct code is below:

```
1 student1 = ["Grace", 76, 56, 67]
2 student2 = ["Archer", 93, 89, 99]
3 student3 = ["Judy", 100, 80, 97]
4 print("First student name is "+student1[0])
5 print("First student math score is "+str(student1[1]))
```

Exercise 119

In line 5, average1[0] does not exist as average1 is not a list or array, it is a simple variable. It is replaced with average1 as shown in correct code below.

```
1 student1 = ["Grace", 76, 56, 67]
2 student2 = ["Archer", 93, 89, 99]
3 student3 = ["Judy", 100, 80, 97]
4 average1 = (student1[1]+student1[2]+student1[3])/3
5 print("First student average score is "+str(average1))
```

Exercise 120

In line 4, student2[0] is a string that contains name of student. It cannot be added with numbers unless numbers are converted to a string. In this case, we use student2[1] as it is the relevant number. This is shown in correct code below.

```
student1 = ["Grace", 76, 56, 67]
student2 = ["Archer", 93, 89, 99]
student3 = ["Judy", 100, 80, 97]
average2 = (student2[1]+student2[2]+student2[3])/3
print("Second student average score is "+str(average2))
```

Exercise 121

In line 4, student4[3] does not exist and produces an error. It is replaced with student3[3] as shown in correct code below.

```
1 student1 = ["Grace", 76, 56, 67]
2 student2 = ["Archer", 93, 89, 99]
3 student3 = ["Judy", 100, 80, 97]
4 sum3 = student3[1]+student3[2]+student3[3]
5 print("Third student has a total of "+str(sum3))
```

Exercise 122

In line 4, student3[2] needs to be converted to a string before it is added to the rest of the print statement. The correct code is below.

```
1 student1 = ["Grace", 76, 56, 67]
2 student2 = ["Archer", 93, 89, 99]
3 student3 = ["Judy", 100, 80, 97]
4 print(student3[0] + " has a science score of "+str(student3[2]))
```

Exercises to Practice

1. Create a list of history Create lists of names and favorite sports for 10 students.
2. Print out both the names of the students and their favorite sport. scores of 10 students. Print the score of the first student, last student, and the average of the scores of all the students.
3. You are conducting a survey to understand students' favorite subjects and preferences. Here's what you need to do:

   a. Create a list containing the names of 10 students.

   b. Create another list containing each student's favorite subject.

   c. Print out the names of the students along with their favorite subject.

   d. Determine and print out the most popular subject among the students.

Python Drawings using turtle

Can You Do Drawings in Python?

There are several libraries that allow you to create drawings animations in Python. Our favorite library for drawings is the turtle library due to its simplicity and diverse functionality. It is a great way for beginners to start animating in Python.

What is Turtle in Python

Turtle is a virtual canvas that allows users to create shapes and pictures on a virtual canvas in Python. It uses a virtual pen called turtle for drawing. It's a fun and interactive way for new programmers to enjoy Python coding. It's like a turtle is moving across the screen and is dragging a pen along the screen while it moves.

Turtle Operations

Below are some of the main operations for the Python turtle library.

Turtle Screen

All turtle operations occur on a separate screen outside the command prompt.

```
1 import turtle
2 s=turtle.getscreen()
3 s.exitonclick()
```

We use the turtle function getscreen() to open up a screen on which the turtle operations can occur. The screen is saved as a variable s which can be used in the program.

In line 3, we set it up to so the screen doesn't close until we click on the screen.

So, when you run the program, a screen should pop up, which closes once we click on the screen.

The arrow represents the turtle which can move on the screen.

Output Screen:

Turtle Creation

We can create a turtle using the Turtle() function below. In below program, we create a turtle and name it as a variable called tim. The turtle is like a pen, and the screen is the canvas.

```
import turtle
s=turtle.getscreen()
tim = turtle.Turtle()
s.exitonclick()
```

Moving the Turtle

A turtle can either move forward or backward. We do this using the forward() function or backward() function. Within the brackets we enter the number of pixels we want it to move. For example, forward(90) makes it move 90 pixels forward.

We can also rotate the turtle to change direction. We can rotate the turtle right or left using the right() or left() function. Within the brackets we enter the number of degrees we want it to rotate. For example, right(90) makes it rotate 90 degrees to the right.

In below code, turtle moves as shown in the output screen below:

```
import turtle
s=turtle.getscreen()
tim = turtle.Turtle()
tim.forward(50)
tim.right(90)
tim.backward(50)
tim.left(90)
s.exitonclick()
```

Output Screen:

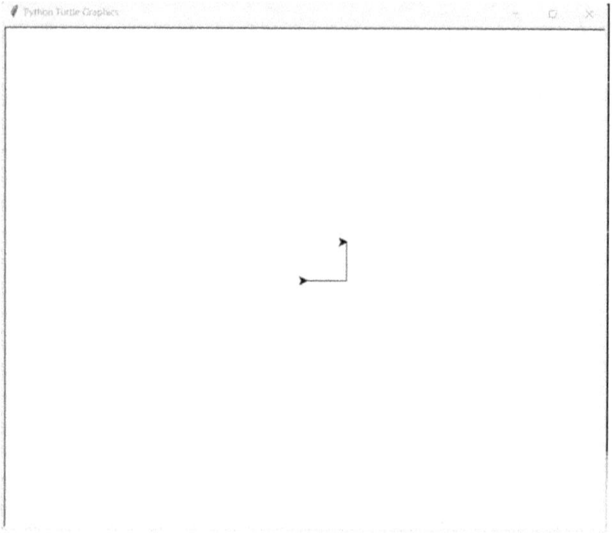

Turtle Coordinates

The turtle coordinates are a cartesian based co-ordinate system. At any time, the turtle's location can be described using a x and y co-ordinate system.

We can get a turtle to go to a particular location using goto() function and we can get it to go to (0,0) using home() function.

In below code, the turtle starts at home(0,0) and then goes to (100,100) in line 4. It goes back to home(0,0) in line 6 and then to (100,-100) in line 7. We can see the motion of the turtle in the output screen.

```
import turtle
s=turtle.getscreen()
tim = turtle.Turtle()
tim.goto(100,100)
tim.home()
tim.goto(100,-100)
s.exitonclick()
```

Output Screen:

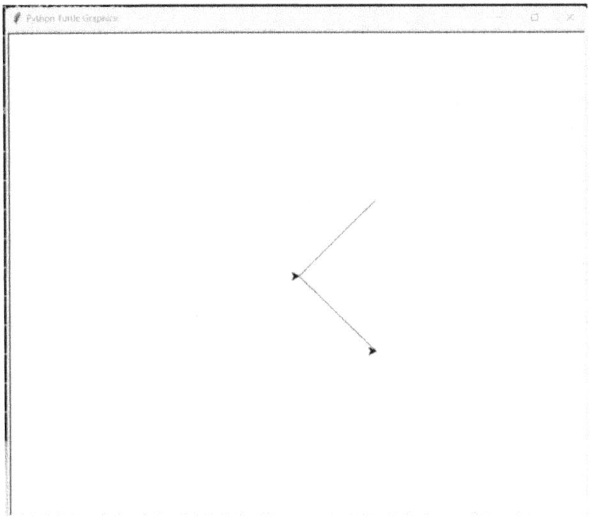

Turtle Size and Color

You can change the turtle size using shapesize() function and color using fillcolor() function.

The three parameter for shapesize are length, width and outline thickness.

In below code, the green turtle has a length of 10 pixels, width of 5 pixels and outline thickness of 1 pixel.

```
import turtle
s=turtle.getscreen()
tim = turtle.Turtle()
tim.shapesize(10,5,1)
tim.fillcolor("green")
s.exitonclick()
```

Output Screen:

Draw a Line

We can draw a line using the turtle forward or backward function for the length that we want.

In below code, we draw a line of size 200 pixels using forward(200) function below.

```
import turtle
s=turtle.getscreen()
tim = turtle.Turtle()
tim.forward(200)
s.exitonclick()
```

Output Screen:

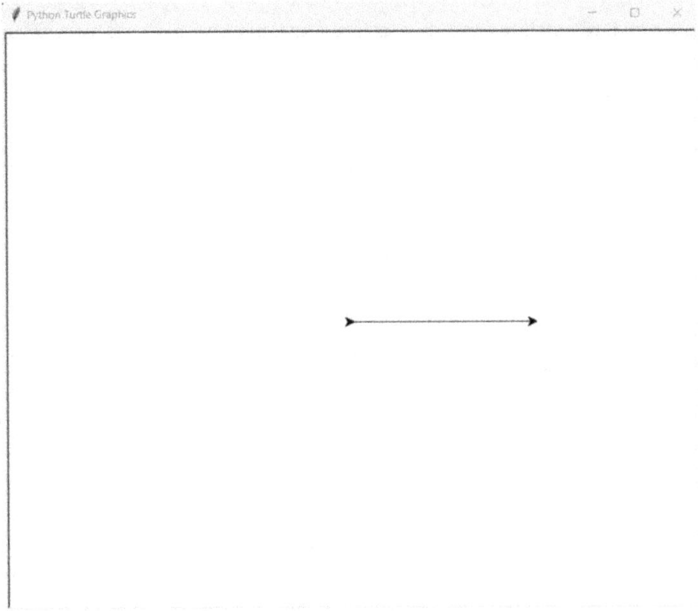

Draw a Circle

We can draw a circle using the circle() function for the radius that we want.

In below code, we draw a circle of radius 100 pixels using the circle(100) function below.

```
import turtle
s=turtle.getscreen()
tim = turtle.Turtle()
tim.circle(100)
s.exitonclick()

```

Output Screen:

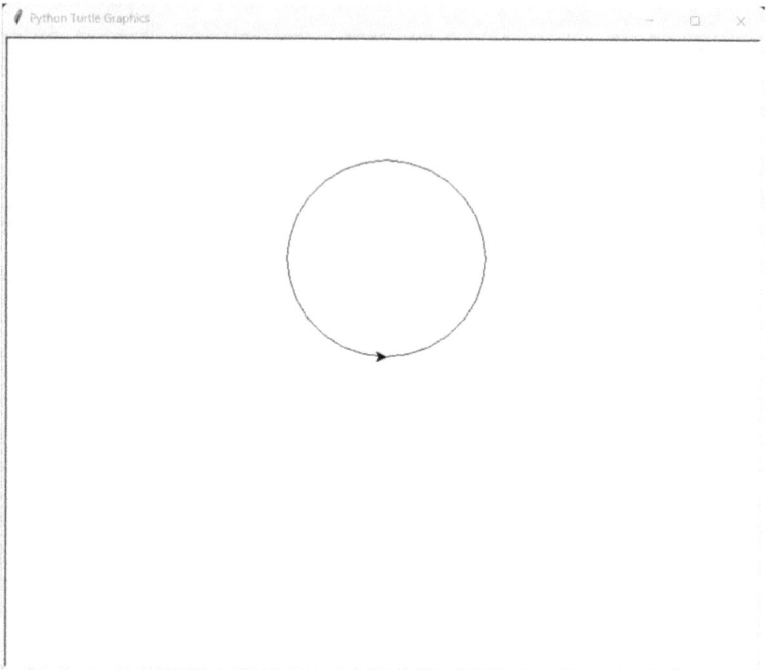

Draw a Rectangle

We can draw a rectangle by drawing four lines using the forward() and rotate() functions. Each rotation is by 90 degrees to the left, and the lengths of the forward function follow the lengths of the rectangle where opposite sides are of equal length.

In below code, we draw a rectangle of length 200 pixels and width 100 pixels with four forward() function and 3 left(90) rotations.

```python
import turtle
s=turtle.getscreen()
tim = turtle.Turtle()
tim.forward(200)
tim.left(90)
tim.forward(100)
tim.left(90)
tim.forward(200)
tim.left(90)
tim.forward(100)
s.exitonclick()
```

Output Screen:

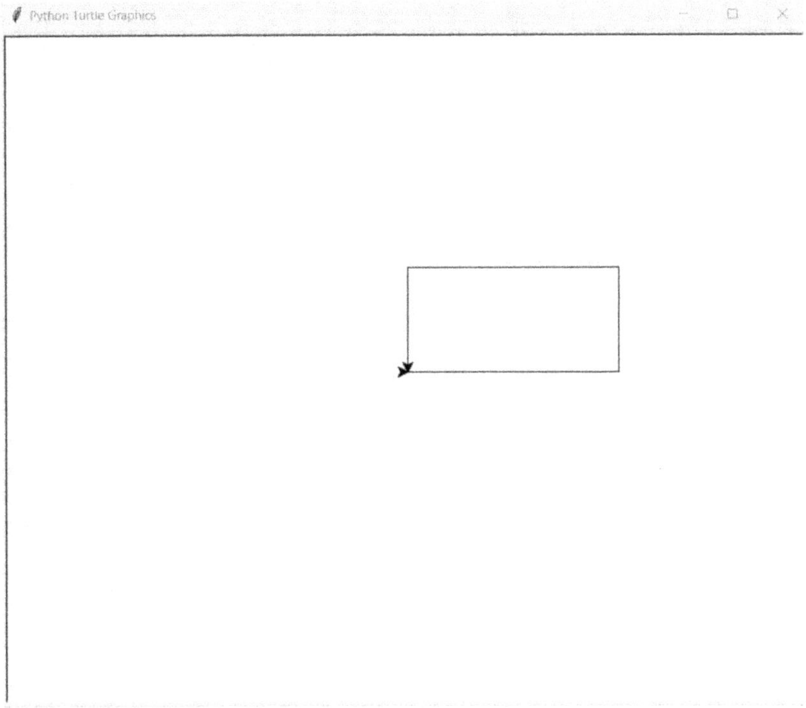

Predict Output

For the following exercises, read the code and the user input and predict the output. Draw your answer in a notebook and predict the output. Check your answer at the end of the chapter.

Exercise 123

```
import turtle
s=turtle.getscreen()
tim = turtle.Turtle()
tim.circle(50)
s.exitonclick()

```

Exercise 124

```
import turtle
s=turtle.getscreen()
tim = turtle.Turtle()
tim.circle(50)
tim.circle(100)
s.exitonclick()
```

Exercise 125

```
import turtle
s=turtle.getscreen()
tim = turtle.Turtle()
tim.forward(60)
tim.left(90)
tim.forward(30)
s.exitonclick()
```

Exercise 126

```
import turtle
s=turtle.getscreen()
tim = turtle.Turtle()
tim.forward(60)
tim.left(90)
tim.forward(30)
tim.right(90)
tim.forward(50)
s.exitonclick()
```

Exercise 127

```
import turtle
s=turtle.getscreen()
tim = turtle.Turtle()
tim.forward(60)
tim.left(90)
tim.forward(30)
tim.right(90)
tim.forward(50)
tim.circle(35)
s.exitonclick()
```

Exercise 128

```
import turtle
s=turtle.getscreen()
tim = turtle.Turtle()
tim.forward(200)
tim.left(120)
tim.forward(200)
tim.left(120)
tim.forward(200)
s.exitonclick()
```

Exercise 129

```
import turtle
s=turtle.getscreen()
tim = turtle.Turtle()
tim.circle(50)
tim.forward(100)
tim.left(90)
tim.forward(100)
tim.left(90)
tim.forward(100)
tim.left(90)
tim.forward(100)
tim.left(90)
s.exitonclick()
```

Exercise 130

```
import turtle
s=turtle.getscreen()
tim = turtle.Turtle()
tim.circle(50)
tim.forward(50)
tim.left(90)
tim.forward(100)
tim.left(90)
tim.forward(100)
tim.left(90)
tim.forward(100)
tim.left(90)
tim.forward(50)
s.exitonclick()
```

Exercise 131

```
import turtle
s=turtle.getscreen()
tim = turtle.Turtle()
tim.forward(200)
tim.left(90)
tim.forward(100)
tim.home()
tim.left(90)
tim.forward(100)
tim.right(90)
tim.forward(200)
s.exitonclick()
```

Exercise 132

```
import turtle
s=turtle.getscreen()
tim = turtle.Turtle()
tim.goto(200,0)
tim.goto(0,-300)
tim.home()
tim.goto(-100,-100)
s.exitonclick()
```

Complete the code (Obtain the Output).

In the next few exercises, figure out what is missing from the program to obtain the output on the screen. Answers are the end of the chapter.

Exercise 133

```
import turtle
s=turtle.getscreen()
tim = turtle.Turtle()
tim.forward(200)
tim.left(90)
tim.forward(100)
tim.left(90)
tim.forward(___)
tim.left(90)
tim.forward(100)
tim.left(90)
s.exitonclick()
```

Output Screen:

Exercise 134

```
import turtle
s=turtle.getscreen()
tim = turtle.Turtle(
tim.forward(100)
tim.left(90)
tim.forward(100)
_______________
tim.forward(100)
tim.left(90)
tim.forward(100)
tim.left(90)
s.exitonclick()
```

Output Screen:

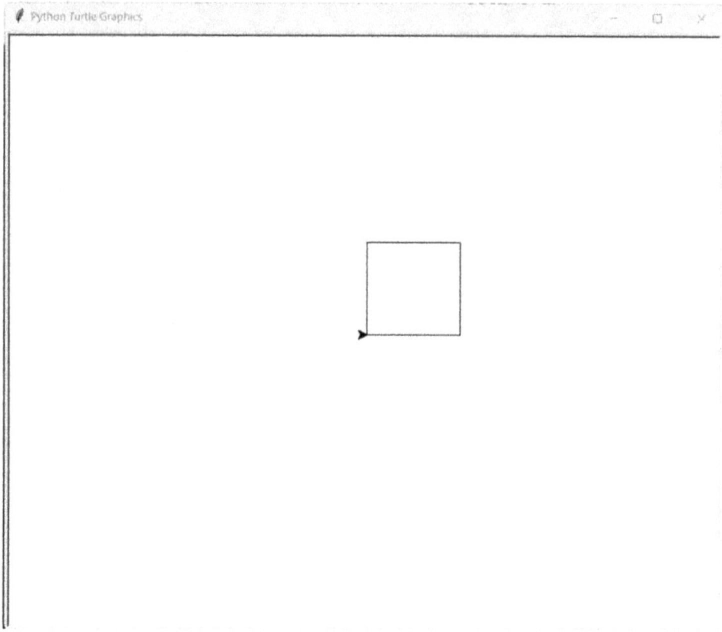

Exercise 135

```
import turtle
s=turtle.getscreen()
tim = turtle.Turtle()
tim.forward(100)
tim.left(___)
tim.forward(100)
tim.left(___)
tim.forward(100)
s.exitonclick()
```

Output Screen:

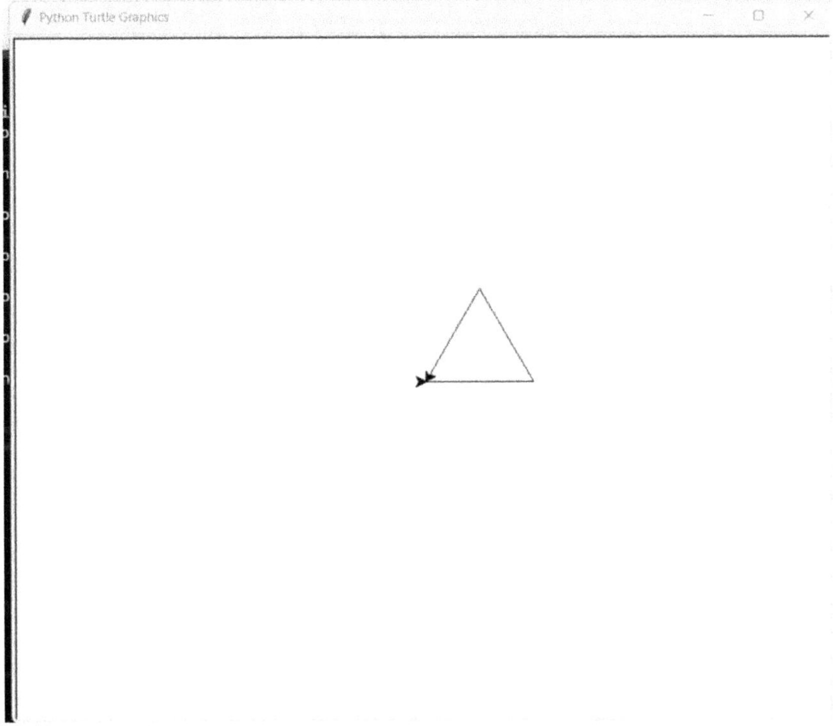

Exercise 136

```
import turtle
s=turtle.getscreen()
tim = turtle.Turtle()
tim.forward(___)
tim.left(120)
tim.forward(150)
tim.left(120)
tim.forward(150)
s.exitonclick()
```

Output Screen:

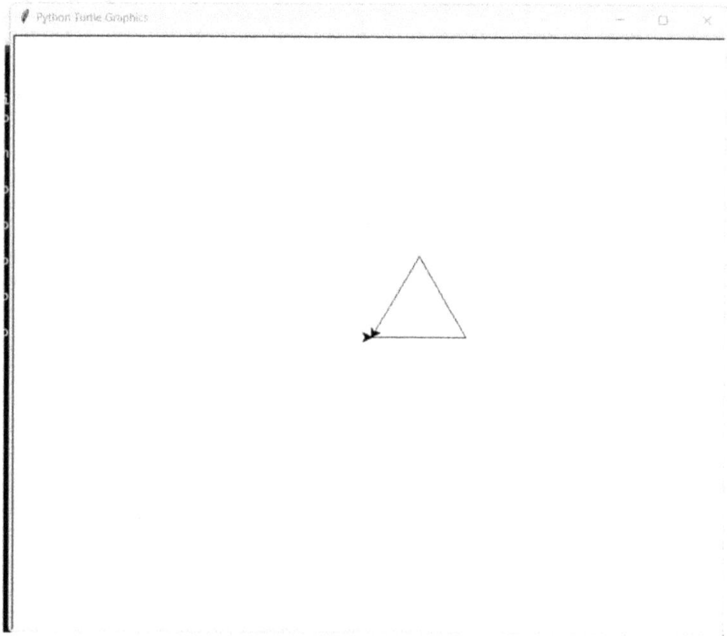

Exercise 137

```
import turtle
s=turtle.getscreen()
tim = turtle.Turtle()
tim.circle(__)
tim.forward(50)
tim.left(90)
tim.forward(100)
tim.left(90)
tim.forward(100)
tim.left(90)
tim.forward(100)
tim.left(90)
tim.forward(50)
s.exitonclick()
```

Output Screen:

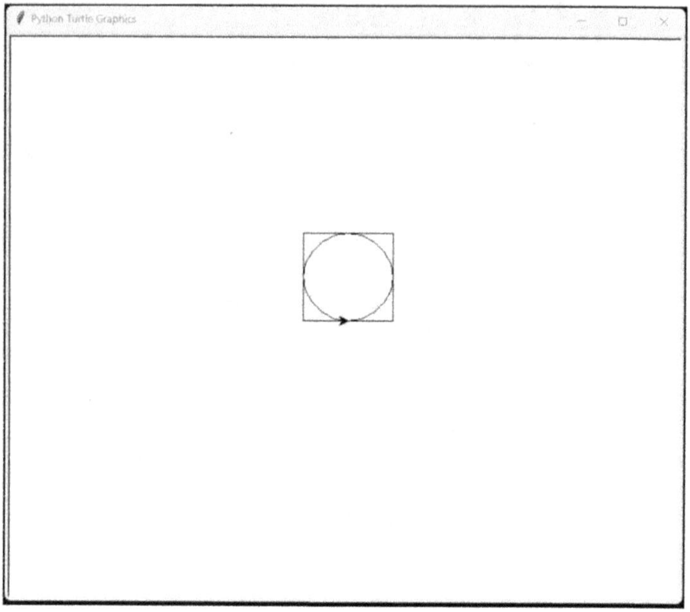

Exercise 138

```
import turtle
s=turtle.getscreen()
tim = turtle.Turtle()
tim.circle(50)
tim.forward(50)
tim.left(90)
tim.forward(___)
tim.left(90)
tim.forward(100)
tim.left(90)
tim.forward(100)
tim.left(90)
tim.forward(50)
s.exitonclick()
```

Output Screen:

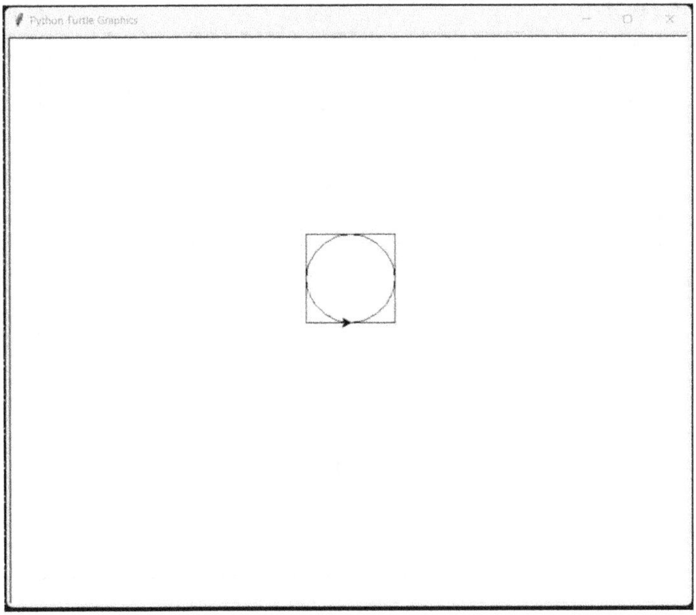

Exercise 139

```
import turtle
s=turtle.getscreen()
tim = turtle.Turtle()
tim.forward(200)
tim.left(90)
tim.forward(100)
____________
tim.left(90)
tim.forward(100)
tim.right(90)
tim.forward(200)
s.exitonclick()
```

Output Screen:

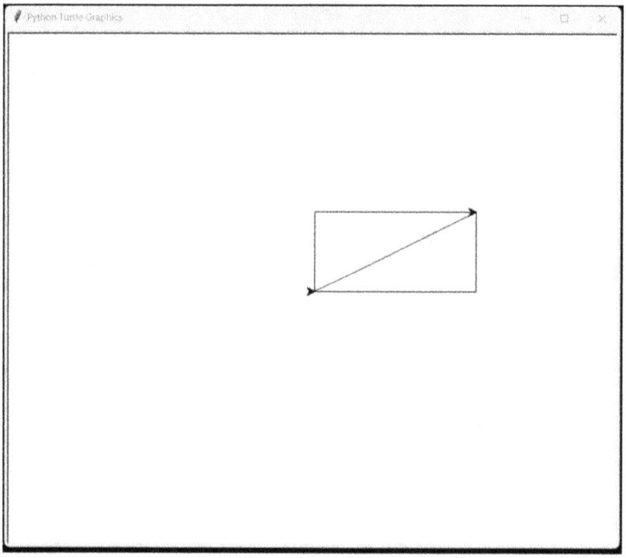

Exercise 140

```
import turtle
s=turtle.getscreen()
tim = turtle.Turtle()
tim.forward(___)
tim.left(90)
tim.forward(100)
tim.home()
tim.left(90)
tim.forward(100)
tim.right(90)
tim.forward(200)
s.exitonclick()
```

Output Screen:

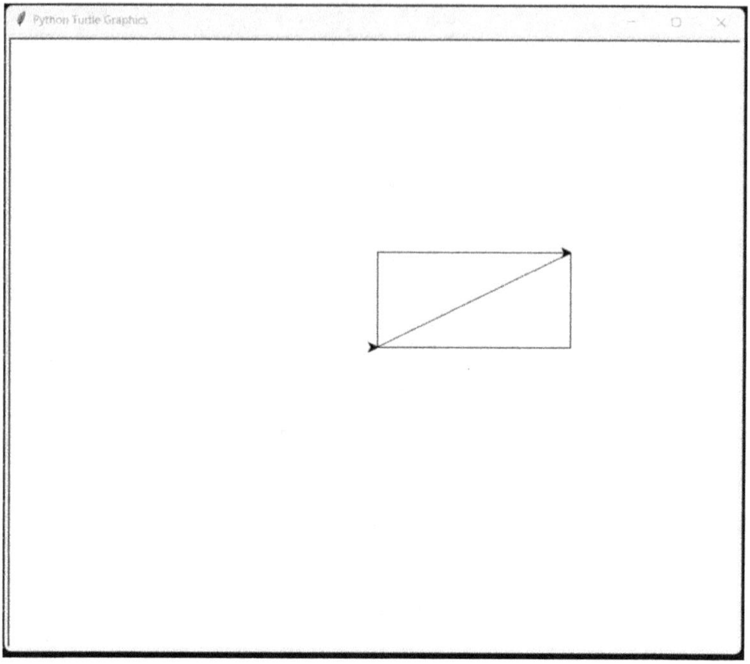

Exercise 141

```
import turtle
s=turtle.getscreen()
tim = turtle.Turtle()
tim.forward(200)
tim.left(90)
tim.forward(100)
tim.home()
tim.left(90)
tim.forward(___)
tim.right(90)
tim.forward(200)
s.exitonclick()
```

Output Screen:

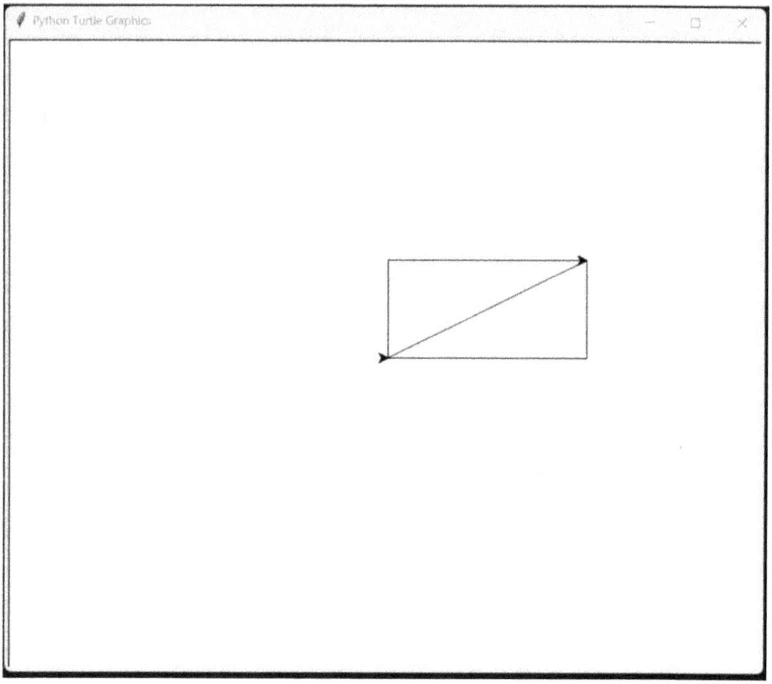

Find the Error in the Code

For the next few exercises, read the code and spot the mistake. Correct the mistake and check if your answer is correct at the end of the chapter.

Exercise 142

```
import turtle
tim = turtle.Turtle()
tim.goto(200,0)
tim.goto(0,-300)
tim.home()
tim.goto(-100,-100)
s.exitonclick()
```

Exercise 143

```
import turtle
s=turtle.getscreen()
tim.goto(200,0)
tim.goto(0,-300)
tim.home()
tim.goto(-100,-100)
s.exitonclick()
```

Exercise 144

```
s=turtle.getscreen()
tim = turtle.Turtle()
tim.forward(100)
tim.left(120)
tim.forward(150)
tim.left(120)
tim.forward(150)
s.exitonclick()
```

Exercise 145

```
import turtle
s=turtle.getscreen()
tim = turtle.Turtle()
tim.straight(100)
tim.left(120)
tim.straight(150)
tim.left(120)
tim.straight(150)
s.exitonclick()
```

Exercise 146

```
import turtle
s=turtle.getscreen()
tim = turtle.Turtle()
tim.forward(100)
tim.left(120)
tim.forward(150)
tim.left(120)
tim.forward(150)
screen.exitonclick()
```

Exercise 147

```
import turtle
s=turtle.getscreen()
tim = turtle.Turtle()
tim.round(50)
s.exitonclick()
```

Exercise 148

```
import turtle
tim = turtle.Turtle()
tim.forward(200)
tim.left(90)
tim.forward(100)
tim.home()
tim.left(90)
tim.forward(100)
tim.right(90)
tim.forward(200)
s.exitonclick()
```

Exercise 149

```
import turtle
s=turtle.getscreen()
tim = turtle.Turtle()
tim.forward(200)
tim.left(90)
tim.forward(100)
tim.Home()
tim.left(90)
tim.forward(100)
tim.right(90)
tim.forward(200)
s.exitonclick()
```

Exercise 150

```
import turtle
s=turtle.getscreen()
tim = turtle.Turtle()
tim.Goto(200,0)
tim.Goto(0,-300)
tim.home()
tim.Goto(-100,-100)
s.exitonclick()
```

Answers

Exercise 123

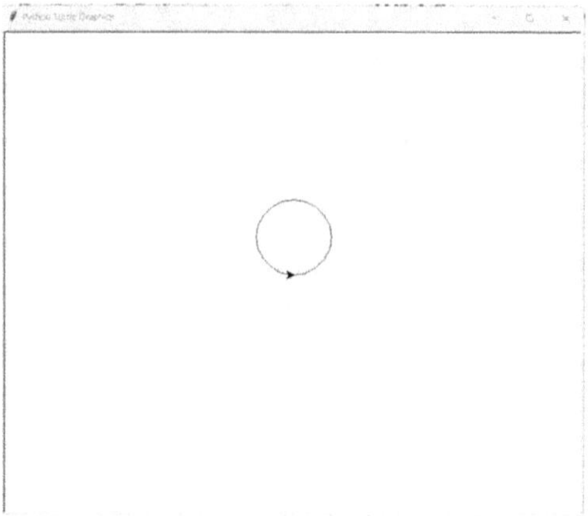

Exercise 124

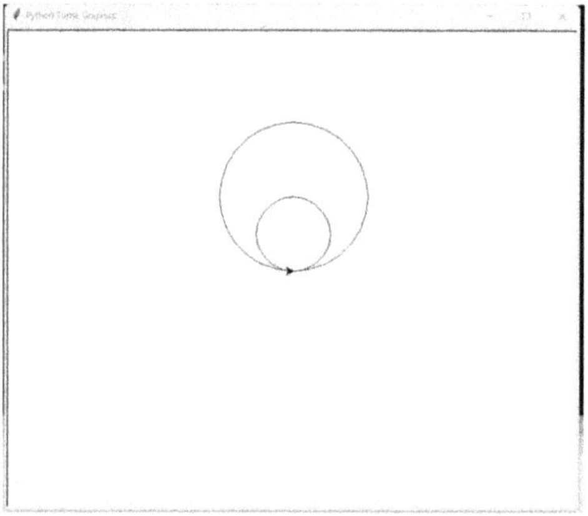

Exercise 125

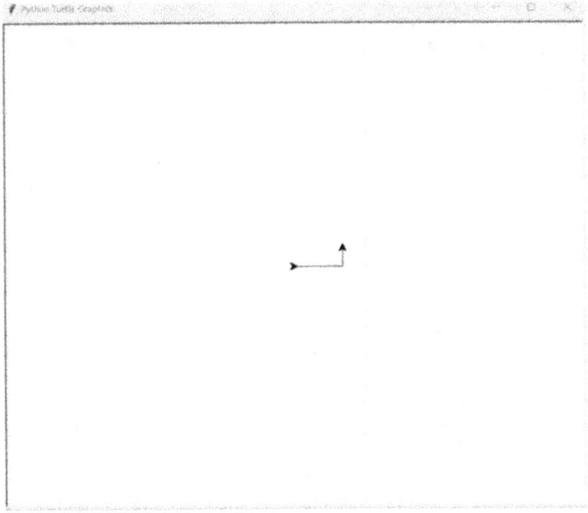

Exercise 126

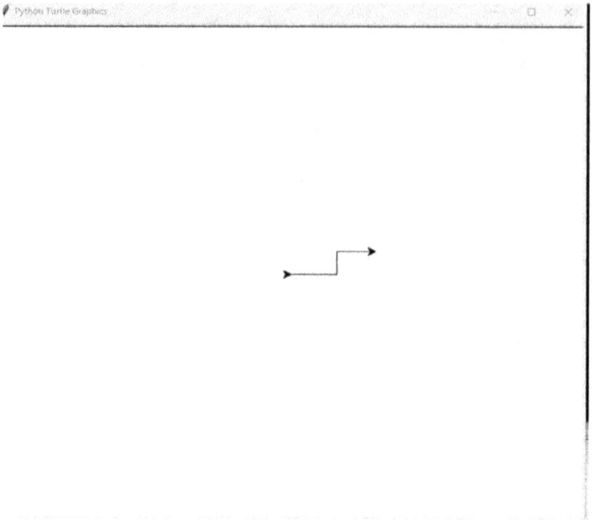

Exercise 127

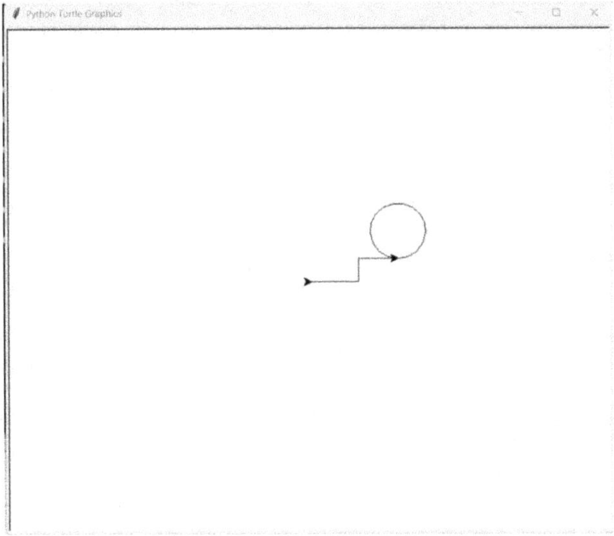

Exercise 128

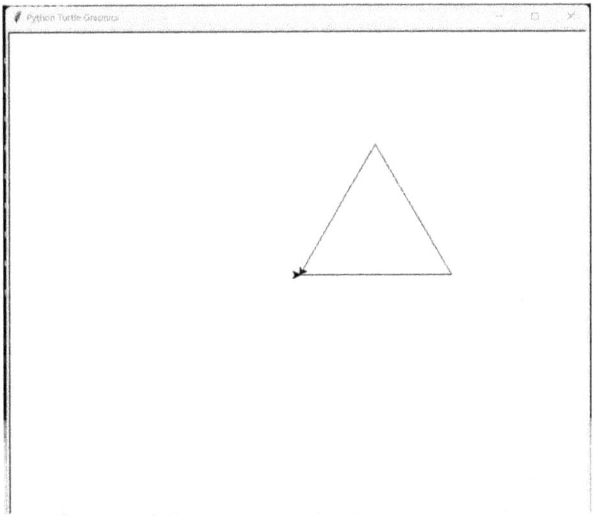

Exercise 129

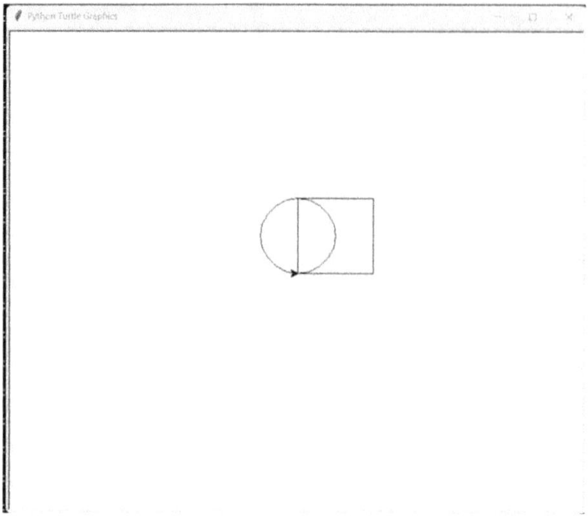

Exercise 130

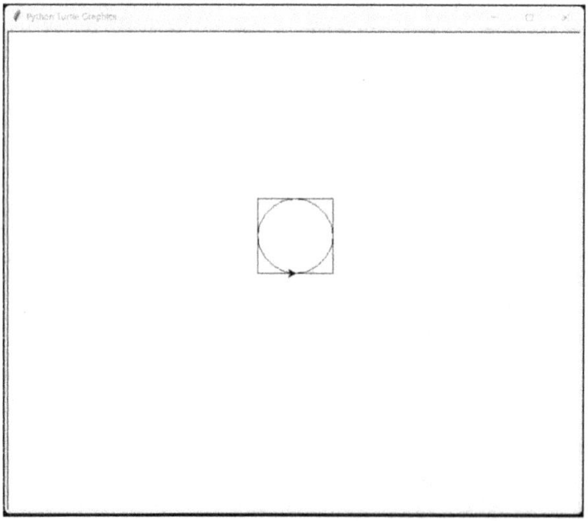

Exercise 131

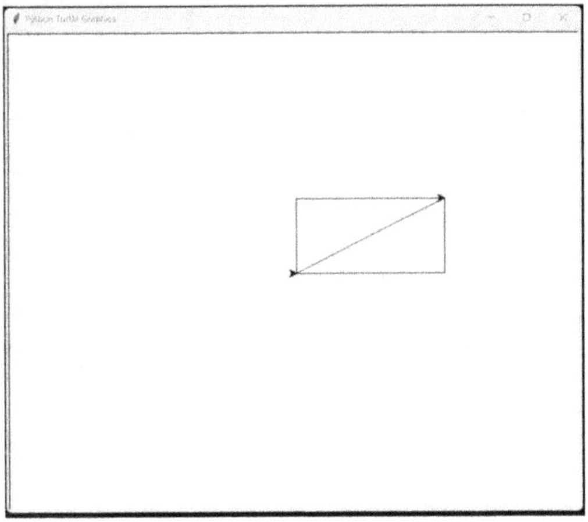

Exercise 132

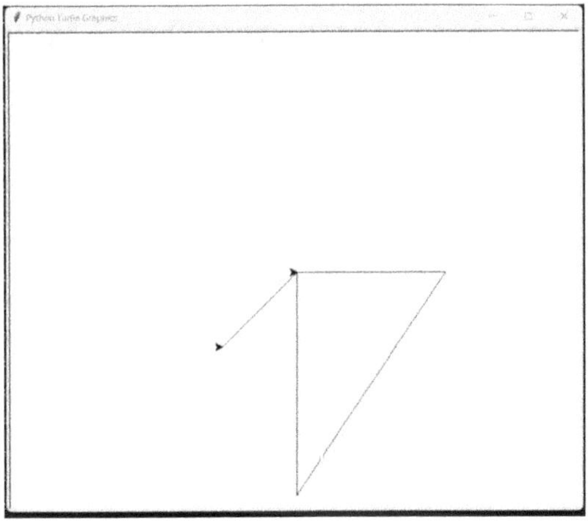

Exercise 133 (Answer:200)

Exercise 134 (Answer: tim.left(90))

Exercise 135 (Answer:120)

Exercise 136 (Answer: 150)

Exercise 137 (Answer: 50)

Exercise 138 (Answer: 100)

Exercise 139 (Answer: tim.home())

Exercise 140 (Answer: 200)

Exercise 141 (Answer: 100)

Exercise 142

The screen s is not initialized in the code. The correct code below shows the screen initialization in line 2.

```
1 import turtle
2 s=turtle.getscreen()
3 tim = turtle.Turtle()
4 tim.goto(200,0)
5 tim.goto(0,-300)
6 tim.home()
7 tim.goto(-100,-100)
8 s.exitonclick()
```

Exercise 143

The turtle variable tim is not initialized in the code. The correct code below shows the turtle tim created in line 3.

```python
import turtle
s=turtle.getscreen()
tim = turtle.Turtle()
tim.goto(200,0)
tim.goto(0,-300)
tim.home()
tim.goto(-100,-100)
s.exitonclick()
```

Exercise 144

The turtle library is not imported in the code. The correct code below shows the turtle library imported in line 1.

```
1 import turtle
2 s=turtle.getscreen()
3 tim = turtle.Turtle()
4 tim.forward(100)
5 tim.left(120)
6 tim.forward(150)
7 tim.left(120)
8 tim.forward(150)
9 s.exitonclick()
```

Exercise 145

In lines 4,6 and 8 the straight() function does not exist. We replace it with the forward() function in correct code below.

```
1 import turtle
2 s=turtle.getscreen()
3 tim = turtle.Turtle()
4 tim.forward(100)
5 tim.left(120)
6 tim.forward(150)
7 tim.left(120)
8 tim.forward(150)
9 s.exitonclick()
```

Exercise 146

In line 9, there is no object called 'screen'. The actual screen is the variable 's', and we use that in the correct code below.

```
1 import turtle
2 s=turtle.getscreen()
3 tim = turtle.Turtle()
4 tim.forward(100)
5 tim.left(120)
6 tim.forward(150)
7 tim.left(120)
8 tim.forward(150)
9 s.exitonclick()
```

Exercise 147

In line 4, there is no function called round(). It is replaced with the circle() function in correct code below.

```
1 import turtle
2 s=turtle.getscreen()
3 tim = turtle.Turtle()
4 tim.circle(50)
5 s.exitonclick()
```

Exercise 148

The screen s is not initialized in the code. The correct code below shows the screen initialization in line 2.

```
1  import turtle
2  s=turtle.getscreen()
3  tim = turtle.Turtle()
4  tim.forward(200)
5  tim.left(90)
6  tim.forward(100)
7  tim.home()
8  tim.left(90)
9  tim.forward(100)
10 tim.right(90)
11 tim.forward(200)
12 s.exitonclick()
```

Exercise 149

In line 7, the “Home()” function should be “home()”. Python turtle is case sensitive and we need to make sure that the current case is used as it is done in the code below.

```
1   import turtle
2   s=turtle.getscreen()
3   tim = turtle.Turtle()
4   tim.forward(200)
5   tim.left(90)
6   tim.forward(100)
7   tim.home()
8   tim.left(90)
9   tim.forward(100)
10  tim.right(90)
11  tim.forward(200)
12  s.exitonclick()
```

Exercise 150

In line 4,5 and 8, the “Goto()” function should be “goto()”. Python turtle is case sensitive and we need to make sure that the current case is used as it is done in the code below.

```
1   import turtle
2   s=turtle.getscreen()
3   tim = turtle.Turtle()
4   tim.goto(200,0)
5   tim.goto(0,-300)
6   tim.home()
7   tim.goto(-100,-100)
8   s.exitonclick()
```

Exercises to Practice

1. Draw a pentagon of size 100 using the Python turtle library.
2. Draw a hexagon of size 150 using the Python turtle library.
3. Draw a square of size 200 with a circle of size 10 in the middle.
4. Draw a series of 3 concentric circles, starting with a radius of 20 units and increasing by 20 units for each subsequent circle, using the Python turtle library.
5. Draw a star with five points, each side of length 100 units, using the Python turtle library.
6. Draw a spiral pattern consisting of 3 squares, with each side increasing by 10 units, using the Python turtle library.

Conclusion

Thank you for taking the time to read this book.

I hope you had lots of fun and found it useful. If you've been through the exercises, you now understand the basics of Python, and on the right path to program much more advanced applications in the future.

If you liked my book and you'd like to learn more, check out my Author page below. I have other books on Python that you can use to further your Python career.

https://www.amazon.com/Bob-Mather/e/B07HHQZC4Y

I'd also recommend looking at the other books in the section, especially the ones on how Artificial Intelligence will take over the world.

If you'd like any clarification regarding the topics; or any suggestions; please email me at: abiprod.pty.ltd@gmail.com

I also do one-one coaching online if you are interested in personalized help.

www.ingramcontent.com/pod-product-compliance
Lightning Source LLC
LaVergne TN
LVHW020349111126
852251LV00003B/10
* 9 7 8 1 9 2 2 4 6 2 7 9 4 *